T0337633

ISRAELIAN HEBREW IN THE BOOK OF KINGS

Gary A. Rendsburg

CDL Press
Bethesda, Maryland
2002

LIBRARY OF CONGRESS CATALOGING-IN-PUBLICATION DATA

Rendsburg, Gary.
　Israelian Hebrew in the book of Kings / Gary A. Rendsburg.
　　　p. cm. — (Occasional publications of the Department of Near Eastern
　　Studies and the Program of Jewish Studies, Cornell University ; no. 5)
　　Includes bibliographical references and index.
　　ISBN 1-883053-692
　　　1. Bible. O.T. Kings—Language, style.　2. Bible. O.T. Kings—Criticism,
　　interpretation, etc.　3. Hebrew language—Dialects.　I. Title.　II. Occasional
　　publications of the Department of Near Eastern Studies and the Program of
　　Jewish Studies, Cornell University ; v. 5.

　　BS1335.55 .R46 2002
　　492.4'7—dc21　　　　　　　　　　　　　　　　　　　　　2002019301

ISBN: 1883053-692

OCCASIONAL PUBLICATIONS OF THE
DEPARTMENT OF NEAR EASTERN STUDIES
AND THE
PROGRAM OF JEWISH STUDIES
CORNELL UNIVERSITY

NUMBER 5

Edited by

Ross Brann
and
David I. Owen

Editorial Committee

Ross Brann,
David I. Owen,
Gary A. Rendsburg

The publication of volume 5 of
The Occasional Publications of the Department of Near Eastern Studies and the Program of Jewish Studies, Cornell University
was made possible thanks to a generous subvention by
Marianne Willems-Hendrix, Amsterdam, The Netherlands
and
The Occasional Publication Fund of
the Department of Near Eastern Studies and the Program of Jewish Studies, Cornell University, Ithaca, New York.

TABLE OF CONTENTS

PREFACE

The first volume of the Occasional Publication series of the Department of
Near Eastern Studies and the Program of Jewish Studies at Cornell University
appeared in 1993, the year Gary Rendsburg began research on the current
volume. It is perhaps natural that his study on *Israelian Hebrew in the Book of
Kings* should follow in the same series as Isaac Rabinowitz's *A Witness Forever*.
Rabinowitz would have taken great delight in this critical study of the
Hebrew language in the book of Kings since he spent virtually all his career
in similar pursuits. It is also appropriate that this volume is dedicated to the
memory of Jonas Greenfield, who was a friend of Rabinowitz and an
occasional visitor to Cornell University. Rendsburg's study continues his
series of books and articles (see bibliography below) that examine the northern dialectal features in various sections of the Hebrew Bible.

I would like to thank Ms. Marianne Willems-Hendrix of Amsterdam, The
Netherlands, for the generous subsidy that made the prompt publication of
this volume possible. It was her late husband, Kees Willems, who made possible the Paul and Berthe Hendrix Professorship in memory of Marianne's
parents, who perished in the Shoah, that Gary Rendsburg now holds. Theirs
is a special commitment to Biblical and Judaic studies that has found a
welcome home in Cornell University's Department of Near Eastern Studies
and Program of Jewish Studies and for which we are most grateful.

As is obvious from the titles of volumes 1 to 4 and the forthcoming volume
6 of this series, the subject matter is eclectic and reflects the topical diversity
that the faculty of the Department of Near Eastern Studies and the Program
of Jewish Studies each represents. Future volumes will continue to reflect this
diversity.

David I. Owen
The Bernard and Jane Schapiro Professor of
Ancient Near Eastern and Judaic Studies
Director, Program of Jewish Studies
Cornell University
March 2002

FOREWORD

Basic research for this book began in 1993 during a sabbatical semester in Jerusalem. I am grateful to my many friends and colleagues in the Departments of Bible and Hebrew Language at the Hebrew University for their gracious hospitality. In addition, as anyone who has sat in the main reading room of the Hebrew University and National Library at Givat Ram, Jerusalem, can attest, there is no better setting for conducting one's research in the field of Biblical Studies. I am indebted to the librarians there for many courtesies extended to me.

On these shores, the most conducive place to carry out one's research is the Center for Advanced Judaic Studies of the University of Pennsylvania. It was my privilege to spend a year's sabbatical at the Center in 1997–98, and although my main activity there was scholarship in another direction (echoes of Egyptian literary and magical texts in Exodus 1–15), I was able to find time to write significant portions of the present work as well. My thanks to David Ruderman, the director of the Center, to his excellent and professional staff, and to my fellow scholars who helped make the year so stimulating and enriching.

Final work on this monograph was accomplished in 2000 at my home institution, Cornell University. In short, this book was written in starts and stops, with long intervals during which my attention was turned to other projects. Of course, those familiar with my scholarship know that the question of regional dialects in ancient Hebrew is never far from my mind. In any case, my hope is that the finished product reads smoothly, notwithstanding the seven years from commencement to completion, and that the presentation of the basic thesis is clear.

It is my pleasant duty to thank my former student Gregg A. Serene, who did a marvelous job at proofreading and indexing the volume. I am indebted to him for his efficient work and good cheer.

I am grateful to my colleagues David I. Owen and Ross Brann for accepting this volume into the series Occasional Publications of the Department of Near Eastern Studies and the Program of Jewish Studies, Cornell University.

The publication of this volume was underwritten by Mrs. Marianne Willems-Hendrix, whose support of Jewish Studies and Near Eastern Studies at Cornell University is never-ending. I am privileged to hold the Paul and Berthe Hendrix Memorial Professorship in Jewish Studies at Cornell University, which Marianne's late husband, Kees Willems, established in memory of her parents, who perished in Auschwitz. Thank you, Marianne, for your vision and your benefactions, for your friendship and cheerfulness, and for the trust that you place in me, my colleagues, and Cornell University.

The single scholar who was most supportive of my research into ancient Hebrew dialects was Jonas Greenfield ז״ל. I recall with great fondness our many discussions over the course of fifteen years: stretching back to 1980 when we first met at Tel Dor, at length during my two sabbaticals in Israel in 1987 and in 1993, and during Jonas's trips to upstate New York to visit friends in Binghamton and family in Syracuse. It is no coincidence that, the present author excepted, Jonas is the scholar most represented in the bibliography of this work. Everyone in the field knows what a loss to scholarship Jonas's untimely passing was. Those who knew him well also understand the great void in our personal lives. I dedicate this book to Jonas's memory, may it be for a blessing, as a small token of thanks for the years of interest, support, and friendship.

G. A. R.

Abbreviations

AB	Anchor Bible
ACEBT	*Amsterdamse Cahiers voor Exegese en Bijbelse Theologie*
AJBI	*Annual of the Japanese Biblical Institute*
AOS	American Oriental Series
ArOr	*Archiv Orientální*
ASTI	*Annual of the Swedish Theological Institute*
AuOr	*Aula Orientalis*
BASOR	*Bulletin of the American Schools of Oriental Research*
BDB	F. Brown, S. R. Driver, and C. A. Briggs, *A Hebrew and English Lexicon of the Old Testament*
BeO	*Bibbia e Oriente*
BETL	Bibliotheca Ephemeridum Theologicarum Lovaniensium
BH	Biblical Hebrew
BHS	*Biblia Hebraica Stuttgartensia*
BMAP	E. G. Kraeling, *The Brooklyn Museum Aramaic Papyri*
BO	*Bibliotheca Orientalis*
BSOAS	*Bulletin of the School of Oriental and African Studies*
BZAW	Beihefte zur Zeitschrift für die alttestamentliche Wissenschaft
DCH	D. J. A. Clines, ed., *The Dictionary of Classical Hebrew*
DLU	G. del Olmo Lete and J. Sanmartín, *Diccionario de la lengua ugarítica.*
DNWSI	J. Hoftijzer and K. Jongeling, *Dictionary of the North-West Semitic Inscriptions*
DSD	*Dead Sea Discoveries*
FzB	Forschung zur Bibel
GKC	E. Kautzsch, *Gesenius' Hebrew Grammar.* Trans. A. E. Cowley.
HALOT	M. E. J. Richardson, ed., *The Hebrew and Aramaic Lexicon of the Old Testament*
HDHL	Academy of the Hebrew Language, *The Historical Dictionary of the Hebrew Language*, Materials for the Dictionary, Series I, 200 B.C.E.–300 C.E.
HLHDP	Academy of the Hebrew Language, *Maʿagarim: The Hebrew Language Historical Dictionary Project*
HKAT	Handkommentar zum Alten Testament
HSM	Harvard Semitic Museum
HUCA	*Hebrew Union College Annual*
ICC	International Critical Commentary
IEJ	*Israel Exploration Journal*

IH	Israelian Hebrew
IOS	Israel Oriental Studies
JANES	Journal of the Ancient Near Eastern Society
JAOS	Journal of the American Oriental Society
JBL	Journal of Biblical Literature
JCS	Journal of Cuneiform Studies
JH	Judahite Hebrew
JHS	Journal of Hebrew Scriptures
JNES	Journal of Near Eastern Studies
JNSL	Journal of Northwest Semitic Languages
JQR	Jewish Quarterly Review
JRAS	Journal of the Royal Asiatic Society
JSS	Journal of Semitic Studies
JTS	Journal of Theological Studies
KAI	H. Donner and W. Röllig, Kanaanäische und aramäische Inschriften
KB	L. Koehler and W. Baumgartner, Lexicon in Veteris Testamenti libros
LBH	Late Biblical Hebrew
MH	Mishnaic Hebrew
MUSJ	Mélanges de l'Université Saint-Joseph
NJPSV	New Jewish Publication Society Version = Tanakh: The Holy Scriptures
OTA	Old Testament Abstracts
OTL	Old Testament Library
REJ	Revue des Études Juives
SBH	Standard Biblical Hebrew
SBLDS	Society of Biblical Literature Dissertation Series
SBLMS	Society of Biblical Literature Monograph Series
SVT	Supplements to Vetus Testamentum
UF	Ugarit-forschungen
UT	C. H. Gordon, Ugaritic Textbook
VT	Vetus Testamentum
WBC	Word Biblical Commentary
WO	Die Welt des Orients
ZAH	Zeitschrift für Althebräistik
ZAW	Zeitschrift für die alttestamentliche Wissenschaft

BOOKS CITED BY AUTHOR AND BRIEF TITLE

Burney, *Kings* — C. F. Burney, *Notes on the Hebrew Text of the Books of Kings.*

Cogan and Tadmor, *II Kings* — M. Cogan and H. Tadmor, *II Kings.*

Jastrow, *Dictionary* — M. Jastrow, *A Dictionary of the Targumim, the Talmud Babli and Yerushalmi, and the Midrashic Literature.*

Montgomery and Gehman, *Kings* — J. A. Montgomery and H. S. Gehman, *A Critical and Exegetical Commentary on the Book of Kings.*

Payne Smith, *Dictionary* — J. Payne Smith, *A Compendious Syriac Dictionary.*

Rendsburg, *Psalms* — G. A. Rendsburg, *Linguistic Evidence for the Northern Origin of Selected Psalms.*

Schniedewind and Sivan, "Elijah-Elisha Narratives" — W. Schniedewind and D. Sivan, "The Elijah-Elisha Narratives: A Test Case for the Northern Dialect of Hebrew," *JQR* 87 (1997) 303–37.

Segal, *Diqduq* — M. H. (M. Z.) Segal, *Diqduq Leshon ha-Mishna.*

Segal, *Grammar* — M. H. (M. Z.) Segal, *A Grammar of Mishnaic Hebrew.*

Sokoloff, *Dictionary* — *A Dictionary of Jewish Palestinian Aramaic of the Byzantine Period.*

A NOTE ON CITATIONS

Most of the research for this volume was conducted before the CD-ROM version of *HLHDP* was available. Accordingly, I have cited Mishnaic Hebrew material from the microfiche version, abbreviated as *HDHL*. Entries are cited by microfiche and plate numbers, e.g., *HDHL* 067/13715–17 refers to microfiche 067, plates 13715–17. The CD-ROM version is now available, so all this material can be checked there as well.

When I felt the need to direct the reader's attention to general information in dictionaries of Biblical Hebrew, I cited only BDB and KB. If a specific comment in one of the more recent dictionary projects was apposite, then I cited *HALOT* and/ or *DCH*.

INTRODUCTION

For about fifteen years, I have been engaged in ongoing research into the question of regional dialects in ancient Hebrew. Although scholars had theorized that regional Hebrew dialects existed,[1] in the main, very little data was put forward to defend this hypothesis. My research, presented in a series of articles and in one monograph,[2] has provided (or at least I hope that it has) the empirical evidence necessary to shift this approach from the realm of hypothesis to that of fact.

The picture that emerges is of two main geographical dialects in ancient Hebrew. One we call "Judahite Hebrew" (JH), that is, the dialect of Judah. Since so much of the Bible emanates from Judah in general or Jerusalem in particular (or is written by exiles from that community), JH is the dominant dialect in the Bible. It is, for all intents and purposes, what we may call Standard Biblical Hebrew (SBH).

The second dialect we call "Israelian Hebrew" (IH), that is, the dialect of those regions that formed the kingdom of Israel. In reality, this is most likely a dialect cluster, incorporating a variety of dialects such as Ephraimite Hebrew, Transjordanian Hebrew, and Galilean Hebrew. In general, we do not possess the quantity of data necessary to make such small distinctions, so we content ourselves with the umbrella term IH, recognizing it as the polar contrast to JH. Since only a minority of the Bible stems from northern Israel, this dialect is less represented in the corpus. Nevertheless, my research has shown that significant portions of the Bible are written in this dialect.

The most obvious place to look for IH is in the history of the northern kingdom of Israel recorded in the book of Kings,[3] especially given the well-

---

1. The clearest statements are by C. Rabin, "The Emergence of Classical Hebrew," in *The Age of the Monarchies: Culture and Society* (ed. A. Malamat; World History of the Jewish People; Jerusalem: Masada Press, 1979) 71–78, 293–95; and C. Rabin, *A Short History of the Hebrew Language* (Jerusalem: Jewish Agency, 1973) 25–33.

2. These publications will be cited below, as necessary.

3. I have decided to use the term "book of Kings" instead of "books of Kings," because the division into First and Second Kings is a later development. See,

nigh universal agreement that this material stems from northern Israel. This is so "obvious" that one colleague told me that I should have begun my project on regional dialects with the Israelian material in Kings and, only then, should I have moved in the direction of other northern compositions. My original thought, however, was to assume that scholars accepted the fact that large sections of Kings are written in IH, especially after the early study by C. F. Burney and the confirmation by M. Cogan and H. Tadmor (see below for details). Thus, I began my schedule of publications with studies on other Israelian texts (2 Sam 23:1–7 was the first composition presented).[4] In hindsight, perhaps I should have taken the route suggested by my colleague, in order to have the material in Kings serve as a template for the identification of IH texts elsewhere in the corpus. In any case, I herewith answer the call with a monograph presenting in detail the northern dialect of those portions of Kings that deal with the northern kings and the northern prophets Elijah and Elisha.

I have outlined the methodology involved in this research in my book on the northern Psalms.[5] The treatment there is heavily indebted to the work of Avi Hurvitz in his attempts to identify Late Biblical Hebrew (LBH) texts. Without repeating the details here, note that the basic key words, as they are for Hurvitz, are the following: "distribution," that is, the lexical or grammatical feature should be found exclusively, or almost exclusively, in northern texts; "extra-biblical sources," that is, the feature should have a cognate in a language used to the north of Israel, typically Ugaritic, Phoenician, or Aramaic (the Transjordanian dialects as well, but the corpus is much smaller);[6] and "opposition," that is, one should be able to contrast the IH usage with a JH usage. Ideally, all three of these criteria should be present to establish a particular feature as an IH usage. But due to the limited nature of the evidence, this is not always possible, so at times only one or two of these criteria can be invoked. Our assumption is: if we had the total picture of

---

for example, the famous *beraita* in B. Bava Batra 14b–15a referring to the work as *sēfer mĕlākîm* "the book of Kings."

4. G. A. Rendsburg, "The Northern Origin of 'The Last Words of David' (2 Sam 23,1–7)," *Biblica* 69 (1988) 113–21; and G. A. Rendsburg, "Additional Notes on 'The Last Words of David' (2 Sam 23,1–7)," *Biblica* 70 (1989) 403–8.

5. Rendsburg, *Psalms*, 15–16.

6. For the classification of the Northwest Semitic languages, I follow H. L. Ginsberg, "The Northwest Semitic Languages," in *Patriarchs* (ed. B. Mazar; World History of the Jewish People; New Brunswick: Rutgers University Press, 1970) 102–24, 293. Note, in particular, Ginsberg's position that Ugaritic and Phoenician together comprise a sub-group within Canaanite called "Phoenic."

ancient Hebrew and its surrounding dialects and languages, we would be able to prove the point to the extent that a linguist working in the field of dialect geography would like.[7]

Once we are able to isolate IH elements using the above methodology, the next step is to look for a "concentration" of such elements in specific texts. This naturally arises, as I have demonstrated in my previous publications. As noted above, this is an ongoing project, so some of the material that has been collected still awaits publication. In such cases, the reader is requested to consult my published work (as well as that of others, especially by my students[8]) on selected biblical texts for references to IH features in other biblical texts. Using this approach, my research points to a northern provenience for the following books and chapters of the Bible: the material in Kings to be discussed herein, the stories of the northern judges in the book of Judges (Deborah, Gideon, Jephthah, etc.), the northern prophets Hosea and Amos,[9] selected Psalms (the largest collections being the Asaph and Korah collections), Proverbs, Qohelet, Song of Songs, Deuteronomy 32, 2 Sam 23:1–7, Nehemiah 9, and the blessings to the northern tribes in Genesis 49 and Deuteronomy 33.

In addition, one must keep in mind that other compositions are presented in an Aramaizing dialect (whether they were written in the north or the south) for stylistic reasons. Here, one may point most of all to Job, with its Transjordanian setting, and the Balaam story, which both has a Transjordanian setting and centers on a prophet who hailed from Aram. Furthermore, when the prophets address the foreign nations, they typically incorporate linguistic features of those countries into their speeches, again for stylistic purposes. The former technique is called "style-switching"; the latter technique is called "addressee-switching."[10] Since IH often aligns with languages

---

7. Compare, for example, the dialect atlases that have been produced for French, German, Italian, etc., based on a complete survey of the living languages today.

8. In particular, S. B. Noegel, Y. J. Yoo, and Y. Chen. Their studies will be cited below, as necessary.

9. The northern home of Hosea is accepted by all. The northern home of Amos was posited first by David Qimhi in the late twelfth to early thirteenth centuries. For the rabbinic sources that refer to a northern Tekoa, see S. Klein, *Sefer ha-Yishuv* (2 vols; Jerusalem: Bialik, 1938–39) 1.157. For a recent monograph devoted to this view, see S. N. Rosenbaum, *Amos of Israel* (Macon, Ga.: Mercer University Press, 1990). On the linguistic evidence, see the important article by C. Rabin, "Leshonam shel ʿAmos ve-Hosheaʿ," in ʿ*Iyyunim be-Sefer Tre-ʿAsar* (ed. B. Z. Luria; Jerusalem: Kiryath Sepher, 1981) 117–36.

10. For the former, see S. A. Kaufman, "The Classification of the North West Semitic Dialects of the Biblical Period and Some Implications Thereof," in

such as Aramaic and Phoenician, these portions of the Bible frequently contain IH grammatical and lexical features or, at least, close parallels.

Three additional sources for IH need to be mentioned here. The first is Mishnaic Hebrew (MH) (the term Tannaitic Hebrew is preferable, but we shall adhere to the former term, since it is in more general use), which, in my view, is the northern dialect of Hebrew in the Roman period.[11] As such, it has many features in common with IH (notwithstanding the fact that the IH found in the Bible, like JH, is a literary language, whereas MH represents a colloquial dialect). Even where it does not connect directly with IH, MH by itself has many isoglosses—mainly of a lexical nature—with Ugaritic and Phoenician (as well as with Aramaic, as has been widely recognized).[12]

The second additional source that requires brief comment is the Benjaminite dialect. The best source for this dialect is the prophet Jeremiah, who hailed from Anathoth in Benjamin. In addition, elements of the Benjaminite dialect most likely occur in the stories of Saul and Jonathan recorded in 1 Samuel.[13] While Benjamin was part of the kingdom of Judah, this does not automatically mean that its dialect was the same as Judah's. Benjaminite Hebrew was probably a border dialect, at times closer to JH, other times closer to IH. Of special interest is the opening section of Psalm 80, one of the Asaph psalms:[14] after "Israel" and "Joseph" are presented in parallel in v. 2,

---

Proceedings of the Ninth World Congress of Jewish Studies: Panel Sessions: Hebrew and Aramaic Languages (Jerusalem: World Congress of Jewish Studies, 1988) 54–55. For additional material on "style-switching" and on the device of "addressee-switching," see G. A. Rendsburg, "Linguistic Variation and the 'Foreign Factor' in the Hebrew Bible," *IOS* 15 (1996) 177–90.

11. G. A. Rendsburg, "The Galilean Background of Mishnaic Hebrew," in *The Galilee in Late Antiquity* (ed. L. I. Levine; New York: Jewish Theological Seminary, 1992) 225–40.

12. I presented much of this material in a talk entitled "The Geographical and Historical Background of the Mishnaic Hebrew Lexicon," presented at the symposium on "Mishnaic Hebrew Grammar and Lexicon," organized by Moshe Bar-Asher at the Institute for Advanced Studies, Hebrew University, September 1996. I am happy to supply a copy of the handout to any interested reader upon request.

13. On these chapters, along with other material that touches upon our thesis, see A. Rofé, "Ephraimite Versus Deuteronomistic History," in *Storia e tradizioni di Israele: Scritti in onore di J. Alberto Soggin* (eds. D. Garrone and F. Israel; Brescia: Paideia, 1992) 221–35.

14. The northern provenance of Psalm 80 was posited by the following scholars: H. Gunkel, *Die Psalmen* (HKAT; Göttingen: Vandenhoeck & Ruprecht, 1926) 353; O. Eissfeldt, "Psalm 80," in *Geschichte und Altes Testament: Albrecht Alt zum 70. Geburtstag dargebracht* (Tübingen: J.C.B. Mohr, 1953) 65–78

the poet evokes "Ephraim, Benjamin, and Manasseh" in v. 3. And although one would not want to reconstruct either Israelite history or Hebrew dialect geography based on the stories in Genesis, it is noteworthy that Benjamin and Joseph are paired as the two Rachel tribes. Thus, although a thorough linguistic study still needs to be accomplished, evidence from these Benjaminite sources may be used—with all due caution—to enlarge the IH picture.

The third additional source is LBH, a stratum of the language in which one may encounter northern features. Cyrus Gordon proposed, even without full documentation, that this phenomenon is due to the reunion of Israelian and Judahite exiles in Mesopotamia in the sixth century BCE.[15] One must exercise caution and not rely on this explanation too frequently, lest it become a "crutch." Indeed, of the approximately ninety different grammatical and lexical features isolated in this study (see the Appendix for the list), fewer than a dozen of them involve LBH evidence. And even in those cases in which we apply the theory of the reunion of northerners and southerners during the Babylonian exile, often we are dealing with only one or two attestations of the particular feature in LBH sources (see, e.g., the discussions at 1 Kings 13 [2], 1 Kings 14 [2], 2 Kings 4 [2], 2 Kings 5 [1], 2 Kings 6 [9]).

Most of the words, phrases, and usages that form the database for this study are unique or unusual within the biblical corpus. However, uniqueness does not by itself mean that a particular word is northern; a unique word could be simply a rare word in the language. Thus, for example, the noun ʾāsûk "container" occurs only in 2 Kgs 4:2. But that is the extent of our evidence; we cannot posit a specific JH equivalent and we have no parallels in Northwest Semitic sources. This word might represent an IH lexical feature, but we cannot demonstrate the point. Accordingly, this item is not treated in our presentation below. However, since there are many such instances in the material concerning the northern kingdom in Kings, I append a few pages at the end of this study in which I briefly treat such unusual items. It is possible that future discoveries will allow us to identify some of these features as IH traits.

(reprinted in O. Eissfeldt, *Kleine Schriften* [6 vols.; Tübingen: J.C.B. Mohr, 1962–79] 3.221–32); O. Eissfeldt, "Psalm 80 und Psalm 89," *WO* 3 (1964–66) 27–31 (reprinted in Eissfeldt, *Kleine Schriften*, 4.132–36); and H. L. Ginsberg, *The Israelian Heritage of Judaism* (New York: Jewish Theological Seminary, 1982) 31–32.

15. C. H. Gordon, "North Israelite Influence on Postexilic Hebrew," *IEJ* 5 (1955) 85–88. This view was accepted by E. Y. Kutscher, *A History of the Hebrew Language* (Jerusalem: Magnes, 1982) 55. On the historical issues, see now J. W. Mazurel, *De Vraag naar de Verloren Broeder: Terugkeer en herstel in de boeken Jeremia en Ezechiël* (Ph.D. dissertation, Universiteit van Amsterdam, 1992); I have not seen this work, rather I rely on the abstract in *OTA* 16 (1993) 633.

In general, however, as we shall see, time and again unique words and usages in the northern segments of the book of Kings have cognates in Aramaic or Phoenician-Ugaritic, and/or they are more common in MH, and/or they stand in linguistic opposition to a standard BH word that undoubtedly is the JH equivalent. When these situations arise over and over, it becomes more and more clear that uniqueness is not uniqueness or rarity *per se*, but further evidence of the IH dialect in which this material was composed.

I hasten to note that I am not the first to utilize this approach to these unusual features in Kings. As intimated above, already C. F. Burney compiled a long list of such features,[16] introduced by the following laconic statement: "Certain peculiarities of diction probably belong to the dialect of North Palestine."[17] More recently, M. Cogan and H. Tadmor confirmed this conclusion, though they limited their comment in the following way: "Furthermore, evidence for a residue of the north-Israelite dialect of Hebrew embedded in the Elisha cycle, which was earlier collected and commented upon by Burney (208–9), has been confirmed."[18]

Ian Young also addressed this issue,[19] agreeing that many of the features in these chapters are northern. He concluded that these items do not appear at random, but "in controlled environments, within a standard framework," namely, in direct quotations specifically used by the author "as a means of characterization via 'peculiar' speech."[20] We shall return to this issue in our conclusion.

During the final stages of my research, I was able to consult the detailed study of William Schniedewind and Daniel Sivan devoted to the Elijah and Elisha narratives.[21] They took a more minimalist approach to identifying IH features in these stories, dividing the isolated items into four groups: "problematic terms," "unique linguistic features," those that reflect "Aramaic influence," and "northernisms." According to Schniedewind and Sivan, only the last group of items (17 in number) represents IH. Moreover, they reached the conclusion, in some ways similar to Young's, that "there is little evidence for significant differences in the literary dialects of Samaria and

---

16. Burney, *Kings*, 208–9.
17. *Ibid.*, 208.
18. Cogan and Tadmor, *II Kings*, 9.
19. I. Young, "The 'Northernisms' of the Israelite Narratives in Kings," *ZAH* 8 (1995) 63–70.
20. *Ibid.*, 70.
21. Schniedewind and Sivan, "Elijah-Elisha Narratives."

Jerusalem," but that "the main differences were in the spoken dialects of Northern and Southern kingdoms."[22]

I do not deny altogether the approach(es) taken by Young and by Schniedewind and Sivan. Even before reading their articles, I had noted that a particular usage might be employed for stylistic reasons, specifically to portray the Aramean setting of certain stories (e.g., 2 Kings 5 concerning Naaman and 2 Kings 6 describing the Aramean attack on Israel). But in the main, as I hope to show in this study, these scholars have understated the case. There are many more IH features in the northern sections of Kings than Young and Schniedewind and Sivan have isolated.

The corpus for this study is the following material from Kings (with Judahite material noted in parentheses):

1 Kgs

12:25–35	
13:1–34	
14:1–20	(JH 14:21–31)
15:25–34	(JH 15:1–24)
16:1–34	
17:1–24	
18:1–46	
19:1–21	
20:1–43	
21:1–29	
22:1–40, 52–54	(JH 22:41–51)

2 Kgs

1:1–18	
2:1–25	
3:1–27	
4:1–44	
5:1–27	
6:1–33	
7:1–20	
8:1–15, 28–29	(JH 8:16–27)
9:1–28, 30–37	(JH 9:29)
10:1–35	
———	(JH 11:1–20)

---

22. *Ibid.*, 337.

———	(JH 12:1–22)
13:1–25	
14:11–16, 23–29	(JH 14:1–10, 17–22)
15:8–31	(JH 15:1–7, 32–38)
———	(JH 16:1–19)
17:1–41	

A few comments are necessary here regarding this list. First, in identifying the northern material, I have included even those sections that contain formulae and editorial comments. The former, to be sure, originated in the north, as demonstrated conclusively by S. R. Bin-Nun.[23] The latter generally are seen as Judahite additions, the work of the overall compiler of the book of Kings. And yet occasionally, as we shall see, even in the editorializing material IH features are to be found. The largest chunk of editorial material is, of course, 2 Kings 17, which at first glance appears to present the view from Judah. But this chapter also evinces IH elements. Accordingly, I have been driven by the linguistic evidence—by far the most objective criterion for making such judgments—to view these portions of Kings as Israelian in origin.[24]

The mere mention of an Israelian king does not automatically indicate an Israelian source. Obviously, on occasion the northern kings appear within the context of the history of Judah. A good example is 1 Kgs 15:16–17, which mentions Baasha. Clearly this is a Judahite source, since both the preceding and following material focuses on Asa king of Judah. Moreover, in v. 16 the label *melek yiśrāʾēl* "king of Israel" for Baasha, in contrast to the simple introduction of Asa without a corresponding label, points to this conclusion (though, admittedly, both kings gain labels in v. 17, and clearly there is no absolute consistency regarding this point in Kings).

Occasionally, the seams between Israelian and Judahite sources are not clear. I have decided each case individually based on the evidence, though another scholar easily could arrive at the opposite decision. A good example is 2 Kgs 8:25–29, which is treated as a single unit by the Masora (in both the Aleppo Codex and the Leningrad Codex). The first three verses of this pericope introduce Ahaziah king of Judah and clearly are Judahite, with all the customary formulae. But the last two verses return the reader to the career

---

23. S. R. Bin-Nun, "Formulas from Royal Records of Israel and of Judah," *VT* 18 (1968) 414–32. My thanks to Hayim Tadmor for bringing this article to my attention.

24. Of course, even if one is not convinced of this evidence for the editorializing material, and therefore wishes to continue to view these portions as Judahite additions, this has only a minor effect on the thesis of this book as a whole.

of J(eh)oram king of Israel and are Israelian in origin. Note how the king of Israel requires no label. He is simply either *yôrām*, *yôrām hammelek*, or *yôrām ben ʾaḥʾāb*, whereas the king of Judah is *ʾăḥazyāhû ben yĕhôrām melek yĕhûdāʰ* (v. 29).

Another example is 2 Kgs 9:29, which appears to introduce a single verse of Judahite origin into the otherwise Israelian material of this chapter. In this case, the Masora as represented in the Leningrad Codex marks the verse as a single unit, with *petuḥa* preceding and *setuma* following (though the Aleppo Codex has only the former).

One of the most difficult cases to judge is 2 Kings 14. The chapter begins in a Judahite manner, introducing Amaziah as the new king of Judah. But this section ends in vv. 15–16 in an Israelian manner, with the death notice of Jehoash king of Israel. Where in the intervening verses is the seam between Judahite and Israelian sources? The clue is provided in v. 11, with the expression *bêt šemeš ʾăšer lîhûdāʰ* "Beth-Shemesh, which is to Judah," a phrase that indicates an Israelian viewpoint. Accordingly, I conclude that vv. 1–10 are from Judah and that vv. 11–16 are from Israel (even though the Masora recognizes no break here).

Finally, 1 Kgs 22:1–40 has been included in the above list as Israelian material. Most scholars have inclined toward this view, but the picture is not altogether clear. See further the Conclusion of this work.

One final point: the decisions discussed in the preceding paragraphs are important, not so much for the immediate issue of isolating IH features (they tend to surface "automatically"), but rather for the purposes of the statistical analysis to be presented in the Conclusion.

The IH grammatical and lexical items are presented in the order in which they appear in the book of Kings, detailed in a chapter-by-chapter treatment. Taken collectively, these elements provide the "concentration" described above that enables us to conclude that the history of the northern kingdom of Israel incorporated into the canonical book of Kings was composed in the northern dialect of ancient Hebrew.[25]

---

25. The methodology employed in this monograph is, as noted above, the same as that employed in my earlier work devoted to northern poems in the book of Psalms. Reviewers of my *Psalms* book typically accepted the general hypothesis of the presence of IH compositions in the Bible, though many questioned the methodology that I employed and/or various specific findings. I only can repeat what I have stated on several occasions, including above, namely, that we are working with limited data. My supposition (and that of the majority of scholars, I believe) is: if we had a complete picture of ancient Hebrew, we would be able to demonstrate the differences between JH and IH beyond doubt. We are left with two options, it seems. One option is to accept

the existence of the two dialects in a largely hypothetical manner, but to wait until we have epigraphic data from the northern kingdom with which to work (I refer to material much more sizable than the Samaria Ostraca, for example). The other is to proceed given the admittedly limited nature of the evidence at our disposal. No doubt archaeological work will continue to reveal inscriptions from the northern kingdom, but the odds of any truly sizable corpus ever being discovered are extremely slim. Accordingly, I have selected the second route, to progress as best as we can, using the biblical corpus and the cognate information available. For an example of a review that endorses my approach wholeheartedly, I direct the reader to J. C. L. Gibson's comments in *BSOAS* 55 (1992) 543–44.

I KINGS 12

[1]

The word *miqṣôt* "from among, some of" in v. 31 is used in the Bible only in northern contexts. It is repeated in 1 Kgs 13:33 and 2 Kgs 17:32 with reference to the same event, Jeroboam's having appointed priests from among the whole people, not just from the tribe of Levi. It occurs earlier in Judg 18:2 in the story of the Danite migration northward.

Under Aramaic influence, the word occurs as *miqṣāt* in Dan 1:2 (also 1:5, 1:15, 1:18, but with a different connotation; in these passages the word means "at the end of") and Neh 7:69. It is attested epigraphically at Elephantine in the form *mn qṣt* in Cowley 29:3, 35:4, where it also means "from among, some of."[1] In addition, *min qĕṣāt* occurs in Dan 2:42 with the meaning "some of, part of."

The distribution of *miqṣôt* in the Bible and the presence of an Aramaic cognate allow us to conclude that this usage was a trait of IH.

[2]

The root *bdʾ* "invent, devise (often with a pejorative sense)" occurs in v. 33 in the discussion of Jeroboam I's invention of a new holiday on the 15th day of the eighth month of the year, corresponding to the Judahite festival of Sukkot, on the 15th day of the seventh month of the year. The root is attested elsewhere in the Bible only in Neh 6:8. It occurs more commonly in MH[2] and in Aramaic (in both languages usually as the root *bdy* as a result of the merger of III ʾ and IIIy roots). Its earliest Aramaic attestation is Ahiqar 30,[3] and it appears more consistently in Middle Aramaic.[4]

---

1. A. E. Cowley, *Aramaic Papyri of the 5th Century B.C.* (Oxford: Clarendon Press, 1923) 107, 131.

2. *HDHL*, 027/5298.

3. Cowley, *Aramaic Papyri*, 221. The text is not perfectly clear, but the reading seems ensured and the meaning fits the context. See *DNWSI*, 1.144.

4. Jastrow, *Dictionary*, 1.139; and Sokoloff, *Dictionary*, 85.

The use of *bdʾ* in a biblical text relating the history of the northern kingdom, in MH, and in Aramaic points to the conclusion that this verb was a feature of IH.[5] The other biblical occurrence, Neh 6:8, most likely is the result of Aramaic influence on LBH; in fact the form *bôdāʾm* "(you) devise them" reflects the merger of IIIʾ and IIIy verbs characteristic of Aramaic.[6]

Finally, we should note the view of M. Wagner that the root *bdʾ* in the Bible is, in general, an Aramaism.[7] To uphold this view, he needed to label the occurrence in 1 Kgs 12:33 "unbestb.(=unbestimmbar)," and then to consider the occurrence in Neh 6:8 to be the result of Aramaic influence. I already have stated the same for the latter attestation, so I have no qualms with this particular claim. Quite obviously, however, there is no need to question the use of *bdʾ* in 1 Kgs 12:33. Instead, this usage stands as important evidence for admitting this root into the lexicon of IH.

---

5. E. Ullendorff, "Ugaritic Marginalia II," *JSS* 7 (1962) 347, proposed that *bdʾ* is the root of the Ugaritic form *ybd*, which in two different texts is followed by the word *wyšr* "and he sings" (see *UT*, 370). But since one would not expect consonantal ʾ to drop in Ugaritic, this proposal is very unlikely. Instead, the root of *ybd* is apparently *bdd*, which yields the Hebrew nominal form *baddîm* "idle talk" (it occurs once in Phoenician as well, in Eshmunazar [KAI 14] 6). The base meaning of the verb refers to speech of some sort, which in Hebrew and Phoenician yields the sense of "idle talk" (as a noun) and which in Ugaritic yields the sense of "sing" (as a verb). In general, see E. Lipiński, "Banquet en l'honneur de Baal: CTA 3 (V AB), A, 4-22," *UF* 2 (1970) 86.

6. In G. A. Rendsburg, *Diglossia in Ancient Hebrew* (AOS 72; New Haven: American Oriental Society, 1990) 85–94, I concluded that, in general, the merger of IIIʾ and IIIy verbs in BH is a trait of colloquial Hebrew, without Aramaic influence necessarily at work. On the other hand, I now am willing to admit that an occasional example, such as the one in Neh 6:8, is due to Aramaic interference.

7. M. Wagner, *Die lexikalischen und grammatikalischen Aramaismen im alttestamentlichen Hebräisch* (BZAW 96; Berlin: Alfred Töpelmann, 1966) 32.

I KINGS 13

[1]

In v. 7 the root *s ͨd* is used in a unique way in the Bible. In the words of Montgomery and Gehman, "the verb is used absolutely as in LHeb [=MH],"[1] or as BDB noted, with "obj. om." [=object omitted].[2] These terse comments require expansion in order for us to understand fully the uniqueness of the usage in v. 7.

The root *s ͨd* means "support, sustain" in a general sense in the Bible.[3] In four passages (Gen 18:5, Judg 19:5, 19:8, Ps 104:15) it is used with *lēb* "heart" as the object in connection with food (compare the English usage "sustenance" = "food"). Only in 1 Kgs 13:7 is it used to mean "eat, dine" without a required object: Jeroboam speaks to the man of God and says *bô ͗āʰ ͗ittî habbayĕtāʰ ûsĕ ͨādāʰ* "come home with me and dine" (see also the prophet's response in v. 8, which indicates clearly that the king's words were an invitation to eat).

Montgomery and Gehman were not perfectly accurate in their reference to MH, but they certainly were correct to point the reader's attention to postbiblical usage. They erred because the verb *s ͨd* "eat, dine" does not occur in MH. On the other hand, the noun *sĕ ͨûdāʰ* "meal, feast," derived from the root *s ͨd*, is exceedingly common in Tannaitic texts.[4]

The root *s ͨd* does occur in Aramaic, however, in exactly the same fashion in which it occurs in 1 Kgs 13:7, that is, with the meaning "eat, dine," and without the need for a direct object.[5] In addition, the root may occur in Punic, specifically in Poenulus 947, in the form *sed*, though admittedly one must agree with M. Sznycer's assessment "trois lettres difficilement explicables."[6]

---

1. Montgomery and Gehman, *Kings*, 264.
2. BDB, 703.
3. BDB, 703; and KB, 662.
4. *HDHL*, 067/13715–17.
5. Sokoloff, *Dictionary*, 384–85.
6. M. Sznycer, *Les passages puniques en transcription latine dans le "Poenulus" de Plaute* (Paris: C. Klincksieck, 1967) 127.

In summary, we have one instance in a northern biblical text where s^cd = "eat, dine." Cognate material from MH, Aramaic, and perhaps Phoenician point to the conclusion that this unique biblical usage is to be identified as an element of IH.

[2]

Another northern feature in v. 7 is the noun *mattāt* "gift" (the standard JH form is *mattānāʰ*). The form *mattāt* occurs in two other northern compositions: Qoh 3:13, 5:18, Prov 25:14. In addition, it is used twice by Ezekiel (46:5, 46:11), a fact that may be explained by the theory that the prophet's language was influenced by the reunion of northern and southern exiles in Mesopotamia.

Support for the identification of *mattāt* as an IH trait is forthcoming from Phoenician. The word *mtt* occurs in line 2 of the Ur box inscription. M. Dahood utilized this fact to argue for the northern origin (actually, he argued for a Phoenician origin) of the book of Qohelet.[7] His use of this datum was correct, and I utilize it here in a similar fashion to support the conclusion that the presence of *mattāt* in 1 Kgs 13:7 results from the northern provenance of the material.

[3]

In v. 11 we encounter the use of *ʾeḥād* as the indefinite article. Burney already identified this usage as a northern feature,[8] and his position was seconded by Montgomery and Gehman.[9] The issue calls for a more detailed investigation.

All standard grammars of BH note this usage, but agree that at times it is difficult to determine whether, in fact, *ʾeḥād* (and its feminine counterpart *ʾaḥat*) is the indefinite article to be translated simply as "a(n)," whether it corresponds to something like the English "a certain," or whether it equals the numeral "one." Accordingly, it is difficult to compile a list of examples of *ʾeḥād/ʾaḥat* = indefinite article to which all students of BH can adhere. So, with the ready admission that there is a certain subjectivity to the following list, I here present my list of biblical passages in which the phenomenon under discussion may be found: Exod 16:33, Judg 9:53, 13:2, 1 Sam 1:1, 6:7, 7:9,

---

7. M. Dahood, "Canaanite-Phoenician Influence in Qoheleth," *Biblica* 33 (1952) 46.

8. Burney, *Kings*, 209.

9. Montgomery and Gehman, *Kings*, 264. See now also Schniedewind and Sivan, "Elijah-Elisha Narratives," 327.

7:12, 2 Sam 18:10, 1 Kgs 13:11, 19:4, 19:5, 20:13, 22:9, 2 Kgs 4:1, 7:8, 8:6, 12:10, Ezek 8:7, 8:8, 17:7, 33:2, Zech 5:7.[10]

Thirteen of these twenty-one passages have northern settings. Judg 9:53 is in the Abimelech story, set in Shechem and Thebez. The four examples from 1 Samuel are in the stories of Samuel and of the ark, both set in the territory of Ephraim. 1 Kgs 13:11 concerns Jeroboam and the prophet of Bethel; 1 Kgs 19:4 and 19:5 are in the story of Elijah; 1 Kgs 20:13 appears in the story of Ahab; 1 Kgs 22:9 occurs in the story of the unnamed king of Israel; 2 Kgs 4:1, 7:8, and 8:6 occur in the story of Elisha.

Of the remaining passages, it would be unfair to label Judg 13:2 as northern, but since it concerns Samson's parents of the tribe of Dan (before it emigrated northward), at least one could state that it is non-Judahite. Also, 2 Sam 18:10 is part of the history of David's reign, clearly a Judahite source. On the other hand, the scene is the woods of Ephraim (see v. 6) and it is not inconceivable that the author utilized the words *ʾîš ʾeḥād* "a man" in a purposeful manner to reflect the story's northern setting. Furthermore, the four examples from Ezekiel and the one instance from Zechariah could be explained by the theory of northern influence on exilic and post-exilic writers as a result of the reunion of northern and southern exiles in Mesopotamia. Thus, we may wish to count not thirteen of the twenty-two passages as non-Judahite, but twenty of the twenty-one, an even greater proportion.

The only passages that clearly are Judahite in every respect are Exod 16:33, for I find no signs of northern language in the Torah except in certain sections for specific reasons, and 2 Kgs 12:10, which describes the prophet Jehoiada in the reign of Jehoash king of Judah.

Regardless of which arithmetical calculation one utilizes, the proportional distribution of *ʾeḥād/ʾaḥat* = indefinite article in the Bible demonstrates clearly that this usage was a feature of IH.

Extra-biblical support for this conclusion comes from the domains of MH and Aramaic. In the former, the employment of *ʾeḥād/ʾaḥat* as the indefinite article is widespread.[11] In the latter, there are five examples of the use of the

---

10. I have culled my list from the following sources: E. König, *Historisch-comparative Syntax der hebräischen Sprache* (3 vols.; Leipzig: J. C. Hinrichs, 1881–97) 3.279; Burney, *Kings*, 209; B. K. Waltke and M. O'Connor, *An Introduction to Biblical Hebrew Syntax* (Winona Lake, Ind.: Eisenbrauns, 1990) 251; and P. Joüon and T. Muraoka, *A Grammar of Biblical Hebrew*, 2 vols. (Rome: Pontifical Biblical Institute, 1991) 2.513.

11. Burney, *Kings*, 181, noted that the usage is "common in Rabbinic Hebrew" —anyone familiar with Tannaitic texts can confirm this. Oddly, the usage is not mentioned in Segal, *Grammar*, and it is barely mentioned in the more complete Hebrew version, Segal, *Diqduq*, 56.

numeral "one" for the indefinite article in the rather restricted corpus of Biblical Aramaic (Dan 2:31, 4:16, 6:18, Ezra 4:8, 6:2);[12] eventually this usage becomes standard in Aramaic.[13]

[4]

In v. 29 we read as follows: *wayyiśśāʾ hannābîʾ ʾet niblat ʾîš hāʾĕlôhîm wayya-nîḥēhû ʾel haḥămôr* "the prophet picked up the corpse of the man of God and placed it on the donkey." This sentence is predicated of the anonymous prophet of Bethel, a character who appears within the life story of Jeroboam I of Israel. The grammatical issue in this verse is the use of the preposition *ʾel*, normally "to," with the force of *ʿal*, normally "on." Clearly, the latter is expected in this context (and, thus, I have translated the Hebrew with the English preposition "on"), but it is the former that appears.

This usage is far from unique in the Bible. In fact, there are many instances in which an unexpected *ʾel* occurs for an expected *ʿal*. The corollary is also true: there are many (in fact more) instances in which an unexpected *ʿal* occurs for an expected *ʾel*. Typically this phenomenon is called by the reference works "the confusion of *ʾel* and *ʿal*." No one should be perfectly happy with this term, because, quite obviously, one must exercise extreme caution when treating the preposition. It is the single part of speech that is most idiomatic in a particular language and sense does not always translate preposition-to-preposition between languages.

Consider, for example, that in English one can say "I am going on the plane," "I am going onto the plane," "I am going in the plane," and "I am going into the plane." Does each of these English sentences present a different sense or do they all convey the same idea, without differentiation? The question is not as simple as it seems, even for a native speaker. And, of course, a foreign speaker would have even more difficulty with this issue. To use another example, although NO SMOKING IN ELEVATOR seems to be the preferred sign, I have seen NO SMOKING ON ELEVATOR (the latter presumably contains an ellipsis of sort, viz., NO SMOKING [WHILE YOU ARE] ON ELEVATOR.

The best way to approach this problem is through a systematic study. In another context, also concerning prepositions (specifically the issue of *b*, *l*, and *m*[*n*]), Ziony Zevit wrote: "What is desired is an inner Hebrew study...

---

12.   BDB, 1079; S. Segert, *Altaramäische Grammatik* (Leipzig: VEB Verlag, 1975) 336; and K. Beyer, *Die aramäischen Texte vom Toten Meer* (Göttingen: Vandenhoeck & Ruprecht, 1984) 572.

13.   T. Noeldeke, *Grammatik der neusyrischen Sprache* (Leipzig: T. O. Weigel, 1868) 265–66.

All verbs which are coordinated with at least two proclitic prepositions should be isolated and their systematic and syntactic contexts described, catalogued, and compared.... Once collected, the data should be analyzed with an eye to the synchronic and diachronic distribution of the phenomena insofar as this is possible."[14] To my knowledge, the kind of study described by Zevit has not been carried out for *ʾel* and *ʿal*,[15] but there have been attempts to study the matter closely. Not surprisingly, each scholar who has tackled the issue arrived at a different list of examples of unexpected *ʾel* for expected *ʿal*, and vice versa. No matter how objective one remains in such an undertaking, in the end there will always be a certain amount of subjectivity and, thus, the lists compiled by different scholars do not correlate perfectly. I admit, moreover, to having not conducted the desired study either. Instead, I rely on the findings of previous scholars who have tackled the problem and I state very frankly that the issue deserves further detailed investigation.

With all due caution, then, we proceed with our discussion (and notwithstanding my comments above, I, too, shall use the term "confusion [or interchange] of *ʾel* and *ʿal*"). An excellent starting point for our treatment is an aside to BDB. In their entry on *ʾel*, the authors wrote: "There is a tendency in Hebrew, esp. manifest in S K Je Ez, to use *ʾel* in the sense of *ʿal*; sometimes *ʾel* being used exceptionally in a phrase or construction which regularly, and in acc. with analogy, has *ʿal*; sometimes, the two preps. interchanging, apparently without discrimination, in the same or parallel sentences."[16] In their entry on *ʿal*, they wrote the following: "and in gen. *ʿal* in such cases seems to be used merely as a syn.—perh. as a slightly more graphic syn.—of *ʾel* (cf. p. 41); in the later language, also, it may be due partly to the infl. of Aram., which does not use *ʾel*."[17] I do not understand BDB's comment about "a slightly more graphic syn[onym]," but the remainder of their exposition is excellent. The point about Aramaic is to be noted; we shall return to this factor below.

Now to the data, for which I shall utilize the findings of three different scholars. We begin with Avraham Even-Shoshan, who took a minimalist approach. In his concordance he listed only sixteen examples of *ʾel* with the force of *ʿal*, and only twenty-eight examples of *ʿal* with the force of *ʾel*.[18] Of

---

14. Z. Zevit, "The So-Called Interchangeability of the Prepositions *b*, *l*, and *m(n)* in Northwest Semitic," *JANES* 7 (1975) 103–11, in particular p. 111.

15. Nor for that matter are *b*, *l*, and *m(n)*; see Rendsburg, *Psalms*, 21–23.

16. BDB, 41.

17. *Ibid.*, 757.

18. A. Even-Shoshan, *Qonqordanṣya Ḥadasha le-Torah Neviʾim u-Khtuvim* (Jerusalem: Kiryath Sepher, 1989) 64, 866, 868, 870.

the sixteen examples of unexpected *ʾel* for expected *ʿal*, three appear in the Elisha cycle (2 Kgs 7:7, 8:3 [2×]) and two occur in Jeremiah (27:4, 40:16). There is little here to support our thesis, although always one must keep in mind that Israelian texts form only a minority of the biblical corpus. On the other hand, of the twenty-eight examples of unexpected *ʿal* for expected *ʾel*, sixteen occur in northern settings: 1 Sam 1:10, 1:13, 2:11 (all in the story of Elkanah and Hannah of Ephraim); 1 Kgs 17:21, 17:22, 20:43 (all concerning Elijah and Ahab); 2 Kgs 18:27 (2× [one of which is duplicated in Isa 36:12]) (in the mouth of Rabshakeh);[19] and Jer 1:7, 21:9, 23:16, 23:35, 25:1, 36:12, 37:14. This is a significant distribution, pointing in the direction of the conclusion to be presented more forcefully below, that the interchange of *ʾel* and *ʿal* is a feature of IH.

BDB presented many more cases of *ʾel* with the sense of *ʿal*. According to BDB, there are at least forty-three cases of the former (I say "at least" because BDB noted "etc." after listing six cases in the book of Ezekiel). Of these, thirty-one examples—a very large proportion (72.1% if we utilize forty-three as the total sum of examples)—are in northern contexts. They are Judg 6:39 (the story of Gideon); 1 Sam 13:13, 14:12, 14:34, 16:13, 16:16, 16:23, 17:3, 18:10, 19:16, 2 Sam 2:9 (3×) (all in accounts of Samuel, Saul, Jonathan, or Ishbosheth); 1 Kgs 13:29 (the verse that served as the springboard of this discussion; see above) (in the reign of Jeroboam I); 1 Kgs 18:46 (an episode about Elijah); 2 Kgs 8:3, 8:5, 9:3, 9:6 (all in the Elisha cycle); Jer 19:15, 25:2, 26:15, 27:19, 28:8, 33:14, 34:7, 35:15, 36:31, 37:13, 37:14; and one from a northern psalm (79:6).[20] If we add to this list BDB's six additional attestations from Ezekiel (2:6, 7:18, 18:6, 18:11, 18:15, 21:12), which presumably are due to Aramaic influence (see below), there remains only a handful of examples in BDB's list in pure Judahite contexts (specifically Josh 5:14, 1 Sam 25:17, 25:25, 27:10, 2 Sam 6:3, 20:3).

Above, I quoted BDB to the effect that "sometimes, the two preps. interchang[e], apparently without discrimination, in the same or parallel sentences." A few examples of this phenomenon may be pointed out now. In Judg 6:39 Gideon asks God, *yĕhî nāʾ ḥōreb ʾel haggizzāh lĕbaddāh wĕ ʿal kol hāʾāreṣ yihyeh ṭāl* "May there be dryness on the fleece only, and on all the ground may there be dew," using the preposition *ʾel* with the sense of "on" in one of the

---

19. On Rabshakeh as an Aramean or an Israelian, see H. Tadmor, "Rabšāqē," *ʾEnṣiqlopedya Miqrāʾit* 7 (1976) 323–25, especially col. 324; and C. Cohen, "Neo-Assyrian Elements in the First Speech of the Biblical Rab-šaqê," *IOS* 9 (1979) 32–48.

20. Psalm 79 is in the Asaph collection; see Rendsburg, *Psalms*, 73–81. However, I did not include this example in my treatment of the Asaph poems.

phrases and the preposition *ʿal* in one of the phrases. Two verses earlier, in v. 37, he desired of God that *ṭāl yihyeʰ ʿal haggizzāʰ lĕbaddāh wĕʿal kol hāʾāreṣ ḥōreb* "dew will be on the fleece only, and on all the earth (will be) dryness," using the preposition *ʿal* as expected in both phrases. Why switch in v. 39 to the unexpected *ʾel*? As Robert Ratner described in detail, biblical style typically steers away from verbatim repetition by using an alternative grammatical form.[21] This is such an example. However, the biblical narration cannot invent a grammatical form *ex nihilo*; it must utilize an existing form in the language. Such has been accomplished here. In this case, specifically, the alternative form presented is a regional dialectal variation in keeping with Gideon's Mannasite origin.

This explanation holds also for *ʿălû ʿālēnû* in 1 Sam 14:10, followed by the parallel *ʿălû ʾēlēnû* in v. 12; and the threefold use of *ʾel* in 2 Sam 2:9 followed the threefold use of *ʿal* in the same verse. In such instances we are dealing with the fact that the House of Saul of Benjamin utilized a dialect in which the two prepositions were interchanged frequently, thus the author who recorded these events introduced the variation as a stylistic device in the narrative.

Finally, to quote an example from poetry, note that in Ps 79:6, the root *špk* "pour (out)" governs first the preposition *ʾel* and then the expected form *ʿal*. Again, the alternation is possible because the northern dialect in which this poem was composed was characterized by the interchange of the two elements.

We now examine BDB's list of 141 corollary examples of unexpected *ʿal* for expected *ʾel*—an exceedingly large number. That list is too long to allow for a separate discussion of each example; accordingly I present a summary of my findings. Of the 141 cases listed by BDB, I estimate that 50 occur in pure Judahite texts (5 in the Torah, 4 in Joshua, 7 in 2 Samuel, 6 in 1 Kings, 7 in 2 Kings, 11 in Isaiah, 3 in Micah, 7 in Psalms); 54 in Israelian texts (2 in Judges 20, 6 in 1 Samuel, 4 in 1 Kings, 28 in Jeremiah, 1 in Hosea, 1 in Amos, 1 in Psalm 48, 4 in Proverbs, 5 in Job, 1 in Song of Songs, 1 in Qohelet); and 37 in cases where Aramaic influence is strong (4 in Isaiah 55–66, 3 in Ezekiel, 2 in Malachi, 1 in Haggai, 1 in Esther, 7 in Ezra-Nehemiah, 19 in Chronicles). The percentages are 35.5% in Judahite texts, 38.3% in Israelian texts, and 26.2% in late texts in which Aramaic influence is likely. On the one hand, these figures could be interpreted to reflect an even distribution throughout the Bible. However, when one again keeps in mind that Israelian texts repre-

---

21. R. Ratner, "Morphological Variation in Biblical Hebrew Rhetoric," in *Let Your Colleagues Praise You: Studies in Memory of Stanley Gevirtz*, 2 vols. (eds. R. J. Ratner, L. M. Barth, M. L. Gevirtz, and B. Zuckerman) = *Maarav* 7–8 (1991/ 92) 2.143–59.

sent only a small portion of the biblical corpus, these figures take on a new meaning. Clearly, there is a greater tendency for Israelian texts (note that Jeremiah—with 28 examples according to BDB—is here so defined) to use unexpected ʿal for expected ʾel than there is for Judahite texts.

More than a century ago, H. G. Mitchell wrote an exhaustive article classifying all attestations of the preposition ʾel in the Bible (as such, his article comes closest to answering the call above à la Zevit).[22] His study, as one would expect, treated only cases of ʾel in which ʿal is expected (and not the reverse), so the statistics are only in one direction. Furthermore, Mitchell took a maximalist approach; he isolated 125 examples of ʾel with the force of ʿal—by far the most any scholar has suggested. Of these, sixty occur in Israelian contexts (once more I refrain from listing them here; Mitchell's own list can be consulted), again with a concentration in 1 Samuel and Jeremiah. Of the remainder, fully 44 examples appear in Ezekiel and 4 others in exilic or post-exilic prophets (Joel 4:3, Jon 1:4, Hag 2:15, Zech 5:8), for which we reiterate that Aramaic influence is most likely the proper explanation. Thus, there are only 17 instances in Mitchell's long list that can be considered truly Judahite without Aramaic interference (e.g., Lev 14:51, Num 4:19, Deut 33:28, 2 Sam 13:33, 18:24).

I repeat our caveat: no matter how objectively we approach the issue, we must make subjective judgments as to whether ʾel or ʿal is the expected preposition. Thus, the compiled lists differ considerably. Nevertheless, the findings of all three (Even-Shoshan, BDB, and Mitchell) agree that the confusion of ʾel and ʿal is more likely to occur in IH than in JH. In addition, there is a trend for ʿal to replace ʾel in post-exilic works (see BDB's list in particular), no doubt due to the absence of ʾel in Aramaic, whose influence over Hebrew increased during this period. Either various IH subdialects did not utilize ʾel either and thus the confusion was more common in northern Israel, and/or the loom of Aramaic was so great that, in this usage, its influence spread to IH.[23]

In sum, I present a list of those instances in our corpus that reflect the interchange between the prepositions ʾel and ʿal: 1 Kgs 13:29, 17:21, 17:22, 18:46, 20:43, 2 Kgs 7:7, 8:3 (2×), 9:3, 9:6 (3×).

[5]

On miqṣôt "from among" in v. 33, see our above discussion, at 1 Kings 12 [1].

---

22. H. G. Mitchell, "The Preposition ʾel," JBL 8 (1888) 43–120.

23. For additional references, see S. R. Driver, Notes on the Hebrew Text of the Books of Samuel (Oxford: Clarendon Press, 1890) 12, 101, 311; and A. Sperber, A Historical Grammar of Biblical Hebrew (Leiden: E. J. Brill, 1966) 288, 631–33.

1 KINGS 14

[1]

In v. 2 the unique form *hištannî̄t* "disguise yourself" (f. sg. imperative) occurs. This is the only Hitpaᶜel of the root *šny* in the Bible. In Aramaic-Syriac-Mandaic, however, the corresponding ʾItpaᶜal or ʾEtpeᶜel forms are common, with a range of connotations centered around the basic meaning "be changed."[1] In the specific case of Syriac, the T-stem of *šny* also can bear the meaning "disguise oneself"; as Burney noted, the Peshitta uses this form not only here in our verse, but elsewhere (e.g., 1 Kgs 22:30) to translate the more common Hebrew form *hithappēś* "disguise oneself."[2]

[2]

In v. 2 the 2 f. sg. independent pronoun appears as *ʾty* in the Ketiv, with the Qeri presenting SBH *ʾatt*. The Ketiv points to the vocalization *ʾattî*, which is closer to the proto-Semitic form than *ʾatt*. This form occurs elsewhere in the Bible: Judg 17:2, 2 Kgs 4:16, 4:23, 8:1, Jer 4:30, Ezek 36:13—always as Ketiv. This distribution points to a northern home for *ʾattî*.[3]

Judg 17:2 is spoken by Micah of Ephraim to his mother; 1 Kgs 14:2 is spoken by Jeroboam I to his wife; 2 Kgs 4:16, 8:1 are spoken by Elisha; and in 2 Kgs 4:23 the husband of the Shunammite woman addresses his wife.

There is nothing particularly northern about the settings of Jer 4:30 and Ezek 36:13. However, as previously noted, Jeremiah's Hebrew shares many IH features and it is probable that his native Anathoth dialect was closer to IH than to JH. In this particular case we also suggest that Jer 4:30 continues the words of the messenger who had arrived from the north (Dan and Ephraim, in particular) in v. 15, earlier in the chapter. As also noted earlier, northern features in Ezekiel may be explained by the theory that IH influ-

1. Sokoloff, *Dictionary*, 560; Jastrow, *Dictionary*, 1606; Payne Smith, *Dictionary*, 586–87; and E. S. Drower and R. Macuch, *A Mandaic Dictionary* (Oxford: Clarendon Press, 1963) 471.

2. Burney, *Kings*, 187.

3. See already Burney, *Kings*, 208.

enced exilic and post-exilic writers after the reunion of Israelian and Judahite exiles in Mesopotamia in the early sixth century BCE. In this particular case we note that Ezek 36:13 occurs in one of the prophet's addresses to the "mountains of Israel." It is not clear exactly what is meant by this term (does it incorporate Judah?), but it is noteworthy that Ezekiel never links Jerusalem or Zion to the expression "mountains of Israel."[4] Perhaps the general mountainous region of the country is intended, which quantitatively would incorporate more of the north than the south. If so, then the prophet might purposefully have chosen *ʾattî* as the 2 f. sg. independent pronoun in this pericope, not the standard form *ʾatt*. Alternatively, one could explain the Ezekiel usage as an Aramaism (see below for a brief summary of the Aramaic evidence).

Whatever the rationale for the presence of *ʾattî* "you" (f. sg.) in these last two passages, we conclude that this form was an element of IH. Cognate support for this opinion comes from two realms: Samaritan Hebrew and Aramaic. In the former, the 2 f. sg. independent pronoun is spelled *ʾty* and is pronounced *ættî*.[5] In the latter, *ʾty* is widespread in many dialects;[6] in the case of Samaritan Aramaic the preserved pronunciation is again *ættî*.[7]

In summary, the internal biblical data and the cognate evidence indicate that the form *ʾty* was the 2 f. sg. independent pronoun utilized in IH.[8]

[3]

In v. 14 we encounter the unusual syntax *zeʰ hayyôm* "this day." This construction appears elsewhere in the Bible: Josh 9:12–13(3×) *zeʰ laḥmēnû* "this bread of ours," *ʾēlleʰ nôʾdôt hayyayin* "these wineskins of ours," *ʾēlleʰ śalmôtēnû* "these clothes of ours"; 2 Kgs 6:33 *zôʾt hārāʿāʰ* "this evil"; Isa 23:13 *zeʰ hāʿām* "this people"; and Song 7:8 *zôʾt qômātēk* "this stature of yours." All these passages occur in northern settings (see below for details).

---

4. See L. Boadt, "Rhetorical Strategies in Ezekiel's Oracles of Judgment," in *Ezekiel and His Book* (BETL 74; ed. J. Lust; Leuven: Leuven University Press, 1986) 190–93.

5. Z. Ben-Hayyim, "ʿIvrit Nusaḥ Shomron (Sof)," *Leshonenu* 12 (5703/4 [1942/44]) 115; and R. Macuch, *Grammatik des samaritanischen Hebräisch* (Berlin: Walter de Gruyter, 1969) 240.

6. F. Schulthess, *Lexicon Syropalaestinum* (Berlin: Georg Reimer, 1903) 14; E. Y. Kutscher, *Studies in Galilean Aramaic* (Ramat-Gan: Bar Ilan University Press, 1974) 31; and Sokoloff, *Dictionary*, 79–80. The form *ʾt* occurs in Galilean Aramaic as well, perhaps under Hebrew influence.

7. R. Macuch, *Grammatik des samaritanischen Aramäisch* (Berlin: Walter de Gruyter, 1982) 131.

8. See now Schniedewind and Sivan, "Elijah-Elisha Narratives," 333.

Some scholars have attempted to explain these phrases as "this is the day," "this is our bread," and so forth. This approach argues that the demonstrative pronoun in these cases is used not attributively as a modifier, but substantively as the subject of the sentence. Certainly there are such instances in the Bible, e.g., Ps 104:25 $ze^h hayy\bar{a}m$ "this is the sea" (NJPSV "there is the sea").

In addition, in expressions such as Exod 32:1 $ze^h m\hat{o}\check{s}e^h$ "this Moses," the demonstrative pronoun does not bear its usual deictic or anaphoric function; instead a distancing function is present, i.e., "the speakers take their distance from Moses."[9]

In contrast to examples such as Ps 104:25 and Exod 32:1, in the aforelisted seven passages (1 Kgs 14:14, etc.) the contexts argue that the paradigm $ze^h hayy\hat{o}m$ is the semantic equivalent of $hayy\hat{o}m hazze^h$, with no difference in meaning. Accordingly, I conclude that the above seven cases represent a different syntactic construction only.

This usage is well known from both Arabic and Aramaic,[10] the latter being particularly germane for the present enterprise. In Aramaic this construction is relatively frequent (for examples in Biblical Aramaic, see Ezra 5:4, Dan 4:15); in some dialects (e.g., Syriac and Mandaic) it is the norm.[11] It is once or twice attested also in Phoenician.[12] Furthermore, this usage occurs with some frequency in MH (e.g., M. Ketubbot 4:6, M. Nazir 3:2, 7:2).[13]

With this cognate evidence in hand, it remains for us to demonstrate that the above passages occur in northern contexts. The two passages from Kings occur respectively in the history of Jeroboam I and in the Elisha cycle. Song 7:8 occurs in a book whose northern provenance is clear.

The three occurrences in Josh 9:12–13 are an excellent example of style-switching. As the story makes clear, the Gibeonites arrived in Gibeon from afar. The story does not tell us of their exact origins, but internal evidence suggests they originated in the northern part of Canaan. The text refers to the people of Gibeon as Hivites (Josh 9:7), and from elsewhere in the Bible we

---

9. J. Joosten, "The Syntax of *zeh Mošeh* (Ex 32,1.23)," *ZAW* 103 (1991) 412–15, in particular p. 413.

10. See Z. Harris, *Development of the Canaanite Dialects* (New Haven: American Oriental Society, 1939) 69.

11. See W. H. Rossell, *A Handbook of Aramaic Magical Texts* (Ringwood Borough, N.J.: Shelton College, 1953) 27; Sokoloff, *Dictionary*, 153; and R. Macuch, *Handbook of Classical and Modern Mandaic* (Berlin: Walter de Gruyter, 1965) 406–9.

12. S. Segert, *A Grammar of Phoenician and Punic* (Munich: C. H. Beck, 1976) 170–71.

13. Segal, *Diqduq*, 51.

learn that the Hivites lived "at the base of Hermon" (Josh 11:3) and in "Mount Lebanon from the mountain of Baal Hermon unto Lebo Hamath" (Judg 3:3). Although the exact origin of the Hivites of Gibeon still eludes us, the evidence suggests a home to the north. Thus, the author of this pericope attempted to paint the foreign atmosphere of these folk by thrice placing in their mouth the syntactic construction here under discussion.

Finally, Isa 23:13 is an example of addressee-switching. This passage occurs in the prophet's address to Tyre. In addition, it makes mention of the Chaldeans and Assyrians. The former in the Bible are related to the Arameans (cf. Gen 22:21–22), later to become a designation for the Aramaic-speaking Neo-Babylonians; the latter also spoke Aramaic in Isaiah's time.

In summary, the evidence indicates that the *ze^h hayyôm* construction was a northern syntagma, attested to in Aramaic, Phoenician, MH, and seven places in the Bible with northern settings.[14]

[4]

In v. 14 we encounter the form *me^h* before the word *gam*.[15] According to the norms of Hebrew grammar, *me^h* occurs before words beginning with *'ā, ḥā,* or *hā*.[16] However, not infrequently, it stands before non-laryngeal consonants: Exod 22:26, 33:16, Judg 16:5(2×), 16:6(2×), 16:10, 16:13, 16:15, 1 Sam 1:8(3×), 4:6, 4:14, 6:2, 15:14, 29:4, 1 Kgs 14:14, 22:16, 2 Kgs 1:7, 4:13, 4:14, Isa 1:5, 2:22, Jer 8:9, 16:10, Hag 1:9, Mal 1:6, 1:7, 3:7, 3:8, Ps 4:3, 10:13, 119:9, Prov 4:19, 31:2, Job 7:21. This list includes attestations of *lāme^h*, *kamme^h*, and *bamme^h*.

An investigation of these passages reveals that a disproportionate number occurs in non-Judahite contexts. In the seven instances in Judges 16 and in

---

14. For further details, see G. A. Rendsburg, "Shimush Bilti Ragil shel Kinnuy ha-Remez ba-Miqra': 'Edut Nosefet le-'Ivrit Ṣefonit bi-Tqufat ha-Miqra'," *Shnaton* 12 (2000) 83–88.

15. According to my analysis of this passage, the form *me^h* here is not the standard interrogative pronoun, but stands with the *waw* before it as the emphasizing particle *wm-* in Biblical Hebrew, cognate to Eblaite *ù-ma* (see G. A. Rendsburg, "Eblaite *ù-ma* and Hebrew *wm-*," in C. H. Gordon, G. A. Rendsburg, and N. H. Winter, eds., *Eblaitica: Essays on the Ebla Archives and Eblaite Language*, vol. 1 [Winona Lake, Ind.: Eisenbrauns, 1987] 34–41). However, this has no effect on the discussion at hand, for regardless of whether *me^h* here is an interrogative or an emphatic, its presence before *gam* still violates the standard rules of Hebrew phonology. Schniedewind and Sivan ("Elijah-Elisha Narratives," 316) included this feature in their list of problematic items.

16. H. Bauer and P. Leander, *Historische Grammatik der hebräischen Sprache des Alten Testamentes* (Halle: Max Niemeyer, 1922) 266.

1 Sam 4:6, 6:2, 29:4 it is the Philistines who are speaking; in 1 Sam 1:8(3×)
it is Elkanah of Ephraim; in 1 Sam 4:14 it is Eli priest of Shiloh; in 1 Sam 15:14
it is Samuel of Ephraim; in our passage 1 Kgs 14:14 it is Ahijah of Shiloh; in
1 Kgs 22:16 it is the Israelian king Ahab; in 2 Kgs 1:7 it is his son Ahaziah; in
2 Kgs 4:13, 4:14 it is the northern prophet Elisha; Ps 10:13 is a northern poem;
Prov 4:19 occurs in a section replete with northernisms; in Prov 31:2 we have
the words of Lemuel king of Massa; and, of course, Job 7:21 places us once
again outside Judah. Thus 24 of the 36 attestations (=67%) of me^h before a
non-laryngeal consonant are in non-Judahite contexts. Further, if we include
the two passages in Jeremiah—considering his Benjaminite dialect as non-
Judahite—and if we also include the five post-exilic examples from Haggai
and Malachi—for reasons described—then 29 of the 36 attestations, or 81%,
can be explained according to the thesis of this monograph.[17] Given the fact
that the majority of biblical literature stems from Judah, specifically Jerusalem,
statistically these figures are even more striking. They indicate that the Masora
has preserved a feature with an isogloss stretching from Philistia in the south-
west,[18] through the area of northern Israel, to Massa in the northeast.[19]

---

17. These figures correct slightly the figures presented in Rendsburg, *Psalms*, 25–
    26, where I neglected to include 1 Kgs 14:14 in the list. See also G. A. Rends-
    burg, "Morphological Evidence for Regional Dialects in Ancient Hebrew,"
    in *Linguistics and Biblical Hebrew* (ed. W. R. Bodine; Winona Lake, Ind.: Eisen-
    brauns, 1992) 71.

18. Ginsberg, "The Northwest Semitic Languages," 110–11, already postulated
    including Philistine in his Phoenic group.

19. On the location of Massa, see I. Eph'al, *The Ancient Arabs* (Jerusalem: Magnes,
    1982) 218–19.

1 KINGS 15

[1]

Various commentators have noted that the expression *bêt yiśśākār* "house of Issachar" in v. 27 is "unique" in the Bible.[1]

The phrase *bêt* X(= the name of an Israelite tribe) does occur elsewhere in the Bible, but in these instances the phrase can be readily explained (for the sole exception, see below). For example, the expression *bêt yôsēp* "house of Joseph" in Josh 17:17, 2 Sam 19:21, 1 Kgs 11:28, and elsewhere, is a special designation, since this "house" is comprised of two tribes (note esp. Josh 17:17). Other instances of the *bêt* X formula occur in royal contexts. Thus, *bêt yĕhûdāh* "house of Judah" is common (e.g., 2 Sam 2:7), but always refers to the royal house, because David stemmed from this tribe. Similarly, *bêt binyāmîn* "house of Benjamin" occurs once (2 Sam 3:19), but, again, the reference is to the royal house, because Saul stemmed from this tribe.

Neither of these explanations fits the context of 1 Kgs 15:27. Here, *bêt yiśśākār* "house of Issachar" simply designates a single tribe. Issachar is not like Joseph, the "house" comprised of two tribes; nor can it be considered royal in any way (notwithstanding the mention of Baasha at this point in the narrative).

The only other biblical passage that evinces this usage is also in a northern setting, at the beginning of the story of Jephthah. In Judg 10:9 *bêt ʾeprayim* "house of Ephraim" refers simply to a tribe, yet with *bêt* occurring as *nomen regens* (note the lack of *bêt* in the adjoining tribal names *yĕhûdāh* and *binyāmîn*).

The closest parallels to the *bêt yiśśākār* (and *bêt ʾeprayim*) usage occur in Aramaic phraseology, in which the form *bêt* X is quite regularly used to designate relatively minor geographical areas or small kingdoms. Examples are forthcoming from Aramaic inscriptions themselves, from Assyrian and Babylonian references to Aramean entities, and from biblical references to Aramean kingdoms.

---

1. Montgomery and Gehman, *Kings*, 281; and J. Gray, *I & II Kings* (OTL; London: SCM Press, 1970) 357 n. b.

Examples from Aramaic texts include references in the Sefire inscriptions to the minor kingdoms of *byt ṣll* (*KAI* 222:B:3, 223:B:10) and *byt gš* (*KAI* 222:B:11, 223:B:10) and the references in the Ashur ostracon to the minor kingdoms *byt ʾwkn* (*KAI* 233:4,5,9,13,15), *byt ʿdn* (*KAI* 233:14,15), and *byt dblʾ* (*KAI* 233:21).

In Assyrian and Babylonian documents, Arameans states repeatedly are referred to as *Bit-X*, e.g., *Bit-Adini* (note, above, *byt ʿdn*), *Bit-Amukkani* (note, above, *byt ʾwkn*), *Bit-Bahyani*, *Bit-Dakkuri*, *Bit-Garbaia*, *Bit-Halupe*, *Bit Saʾalla*, *Bit-Sillani*, *Bit-Sin*, *Bit-Yahiri*, *Bit-Yakini*, and *Bit-Zamani*.[2]

Interestingly, the two instances in the Bible in which the phrase *bêt* X denotes a kingdom both refer to Aramean entities: *bêt ʿeden* in Amos 1:5 and *bêt rĕḥôb* in Judg 18:28 and 2 Sam 10:6.[3] Also note *ʾābēl bêt maʿăkāʰ* in 2 Sam 20:14–15, 1 Kgs 15:20, and 2 Kgs 15:29, which, from the context, is obviously an Israelite site, but which, at one time, must have belonged to the Aramean entity called simply *maʿăkāʰ* in 2 Sam 10:6. Similarly, when Amos reproaches Israel's neighbors, it is not coincidental that only in his words to Damascus does Amos elect to use the *bêt* X formula—in the aforementioned *bêt ʿeden* (1:5).[4]

In light of this evidence, the phrase *bêt yiśśākār* "house of Issachar" probably emanates from a scribal school with close ties to Aramaic practice. Such a school most naturally would be located in the northern regions of Israel, in territory close to or bordering on Aramean lands.[5]

---

2. See briefly J. A. Brinkman, "Babylonia in the Shadow of Assyria (747–626 B.C.)," *Cambridge Ancient History*, 3rd edition, III/2 (1991) 9. On the most important of these groups, see A. Malamat, "The Arameans," in *Peoples of Old Testament Times* (ed. D. J. Wiseman; Oxford: Clarendon Press, 1973) 138.

3. I have excluded from the discussion the numerous Israelite cities designated with this construction, such as *bêt leḥem* and *bêt šemeš*.

4. The same can be said of the phrase *bêt ḥăzāʾēl* (1:4). Naturally, this term refers to a specific king and his dynasty and does not represent a specific toponym. Still, it may be significant that only with reference to Aram does the prophet utilize the *bêt* X formula in this way.

5. See my more detailed discussion in G. A. Rendsburg, "On the Writing *bytdwd* in the Aramaic Stele Inscription from Dan," *IEJ* 45 (1995) 22–25.

I KINGS 16

[1]

The noun *ʾarmôn* "palace, citadel, royal building" occurs in v. 18 and in 2 Kgs 15:25. 1 Kgs 16:18 concerns the seven-day reign of Zimri, with specific reference to the citadel at Tirzah. 2 Kgs 15:25 concerns the short reign of Pekahiah and his murder by Pekah in the citadel at Samaria. The fact that only in these two cases in the book of Kings is the word *ʾarmôn* used suggests that it was a northern lexeme. The distribution of this word elsewhere in the Bible seems to confirm this supposition.

Brown-Driver-Briggs already noted that the word *ʾarmôn* is "esp. common in Am & Jer."[1] Indeed, it occurs eleven times in Amos (1:4, 1:7, 1:10, 1:12, 1:14, 2:2, 2:5, 3:9, 3:10, 3:11, 6:8), a book of one of the Bible's two northern prophets.[2] Jeremiah utilizes *ʾarmôn* five times (6:5, 9:20, 17:27, 30:18, 49:27)—perhaps once more we must consider a Benjaminite dialect with more links to IH than to JH. Hos 8:14 is in a book of northern prophecy; Prov 18:19 appears in a northern collection; and Ps 48:4, 48:14 are in a poem of northern provenance.[3]

The attestations of *ʾarmôn* in Judahite context are: Isa 23:13, 25:2, 32:14, 34:13, Mic 5:4, Ps 122:7, Lam 2:5, 2:7, and 2 Chr 36:19.

Is it significant that in Isa 23:13 the prophet utilizes the word *ʾarmôn* in his oracle against Tyre? This word is unknown to us from Phoenician (see below), so no clear answer can be forthcoming. However, if *ʾarmôn* was an IH feature, then we may hypothesize that it was used in Phoenician as well.

Including Jeremiah's dialect in my calculations, 22 of the 31 attestations of *ʾarmôn* occur in a context in which northern language is present. And if we include Isa 23:13, then the total is 23 of the 31 attestations. This ratio,

---

1. BDB, 74.

2. On the famous crux *haharmônāʰ* in Amos 4:3, see S. M. Paul, *Amos* (Hermenia; Minneapolis, Minn.: Fortress Press, 1991) 135–36.

3. Psalm 48 belongs to the Korah collection; see Rendsburg, *Psalms*, 51–60. At the time that I wrote my work on Psalms, I had decided not to include *ʾarmôn* in my list of IH features.

especially when one keeps in mind that only a minority of the Bible is northern in origin, suggests a northern home for this word.

We do lack cognate evidence—except for Hebrew, the word *ʾarmôn* is unattested.[4] Thus, we must be cautious. However, at the very least, it is striking that in the book of Kings only in the annals of the northern kings is the word utilized. It is never used in Samuel, Kings, or Chronicles to refer to structures in Jerusalem (though, admittedly, the prophets use the word with reference to Jerusalem). I conclude, therefore, that *ʾarmôn* was an element of IH, with the hope that evidence one day will come to light to add support to this conclusion.

---

4. Also the etymology of the word is debatable. For a well-known suggestion, see E. A. Speiser, "The Etymology of *ʾarmôn*," *JQR* 14 (1923/24) 329. For further insight, see S. M. Paul, "Cuneiform Light on Jer 9, 20," *Biblica* 49 (1968) 373–76.

[1]

In v. 11, the prophet Elijah, when addressing the woman of Zarepath, uses the form *liqḥî* for the f. sg. imperative. The homeland of the speaker and the setting of the story immediately suggest that the form is a regional variation of the standard form *qěḥî*. Biblical evidence and cognate data support this supposition. Elijah was from Gilead in Transjordan, an area whose local dialect shared many features with Aramaic. In addition, the story occurs to the north of Israel, in Phoenician territory, for, as v. 9 makes clear, Zarepath "belonged to Sidon."

Although this is the only attestation of *liqḥî* in the Bible, its m. sg. counterpart *lěqaḥ* occurs three times: Exod 29:1, Ezek 37:16, and Prov 20:16.

I have no linguistic explanation for Exod 29:1; clearly, there is no concentration of northern features in the Tabernacle account or in other sections of the Torah dealing with priestly matters.[1] Prov 20:16, on the other hand, occurs in a book with many IH features.

In Ezek 37:16 we are treated to a most effective use of the form *lěqaḥ*:

qaḥ lěkā ʿēṣ ʾeḥād ûkětōb ʿālāw lîhûdāʰ wělibnê yiśrāʾēl ḥăbērāw
ûlěqaḥ ʿēṣ ʾeḥād ûkětōb ʿālāw lěyôsēp ʿēṣ ʾeprayim wěkol bêt yiśrāʾēl ḥăbērāw

Take one piece of wood and write on it:
"FOR JUDAH AND FOR THE CHILDREN OF ISRAEL THEIR FRIENDS"
and take one piece of wood and write on it:
"FOR JOSEPH THE WOOD OF EPHRAIM AND FOR THE WHOLE
HOUSE OF ISRAEL THEIR FRIENDS."

The instructions are repeated in virtually the same manner, but, in keeping with biblical style, there is minor variation.[2] Moreover, ancient Hebrew

---

1. On a literary level, however, note the alliteration that is produced by *lěqaḥ* and the preceding words *lěqaddēš* "to sanctify" and *lěkahēn* "to minister." This example will be treated with greater detail in my forthcoming study on alliteration as a rhetorical device in BH.

2. Again, see Ratner, "Morphological Variation in Biblical Hebrew Rhetoric."

rhetoric invites the reader to note the variation and to grasp its importance.[3] In the instructions to Ezekiel on what to write on the wood for Judah, the standard, or JH, form *qaḥ* is used, but in the instructions on what to write on the wood for Joseph/Ephraim, the non-standard, or IH, form *lĕqaḥ* is used.[4] This is a very clever stylistic and rhetorical usage,[5] one that undoubtedly would have been recognized by Ezekiel's audience.

Thus, of the four instances in the Bible in which the *lamed* is retained in the imperative of *lqḥ*, three are in northern contexts. The supposition of S. J. DeVries that "perhaps [1 Kgs 17:11] preserves an authentic North-Israelite form" is correct. The Aramaic evidence supports this conclusion. We do not possess any examples of the imperative of *lqḥ* in Old Aramaic, but since the imperative and the *yqtl* form are intimately related in Semitic morphology, we may use attestations of the latter as a guide. The evidence is split. Some cases of the *yqtl* of *lqḥ* indicate assimilation of the *lamed* to the following *qof*, but the majority of cases retain the *lamed*.[7] We should follow the opinion of S. Segert: "So zeigt es dich, dass im Altaramäischen das Verbum *lqḥ* nicht assimiliert wurde."[8] If such is the case, it is highly probable that the imperative forms of *lqḥ* in Old Aramaic also retained the *lamed*, positive proof notwithstanding.

3. See J. Licht, *Storytelling in the Bible* (Jerusalem: Magnes, 1978) 51–95; and M. Sternberg, *The Poetics of Biblical Narrative* (Bloomington: Indiana University Press, 1985) 365–440. Their topic was large sweeps of biblical narrative with repetition, but the same approach holds for snippets of biblical literature, with minor variation.

4. See further G. A. Rendsburg, "Linguistic Variation and the 'Foreign' Factor in the Hebrew Bible," *IOS* 15 (1996) 177–90.

5. In addition, note that the use of the form *lĕqaḥ* in v. 16, with all three root consonants present, serves to heighten the connection with the participle *lôqēaḥ* in v. 21. See also F. Hossfeld, *Untersuchungen zu Komposition und Theologie des Ezechielbuches* (Würzburg: Echter, 1977) 312; and D. Baltzer, "Literarkritische und literarhistorische Anmerkungen zur Heilsprophetie im Ezechiel-Buch," in *Ezekiel and His Book* (BETL 74; ed. J. Lust; Leuven: Leuven University Press, 1986) 178.

6. S. J. DeVries, *1 Kings* (WBC; Waco, Tex.: Word Books, 1985) 213. By contrast, Schniedewind and Sivan ("Elijah-Elisha Narratives," 322) considered this usage to be only a unique linguistic feature without northern overtones.

7. A sampling of the attested forms is presented in *DNWSI*, 1.582. Even in the same set of closely related texts, e.g., the Sefire inscriptions, there is no consistency; see J. A. Fitzmyer, *The Aramaic Inscriptions of Sefire* (Rome: Pontifical Biblical Institute, 1967) 67.

8. S. Segert, "Noch zu den assimilierenden Verba im Hebräischen," *ArOr* 24 (1956) 133.

In summary, the retention of the *lamed* in the imperative forms of the verb *lqḥ* "take" was a feature of IH and, most likely, Aramaic too, thereby creating another isogloss linking these two speech communities.[9]

[2]

The noun *kad* "jar" occurs three times in this chapter (vv. 12, 14, 16). James Davila was the first to identify this word as an IH feature;[10] Schniedewind and Sivan concurred.[11] This conclusion was based upon (1) the word's distribution in the Bible; (2) its contrast with SBH (and thus JH) *ṣinṣenet*; and (3) its common usage in both MH and Aramaic.

The noun *kad* "jar" occurs eighteen times in the Bible.[12] The word occurs once more in the Elijah stories (1 Kgs 18:34); four times in the Gideon narratives (Judg 7:16[2×], 7:19, 7:20); and in Qoh 12:6. The greatest concentration of attestations is in Genesis 24, where *kad* appears a remarkable nine times (vv. 14, 15, 16, 17, 18, 20, 43, 45, 46). In Genesis 24 we may explain the repeated use of *kad* as part of the author's attempt to portray the Aramean scenery in the story.[13] An additional attestation of the word is in an inscription from Tel

---

9. The form *qāḥām* in Hos 11:3 also deserves comment. Probably we should interpret it as the 3 m. sg. *qtl* form (with pronominal suffix as direct object) of the verb *lqḥ*, and conclude that it, too, was a northern trait. I have no proof to support this supposition, except to say that its presence in Hosea points in this direction. At first glance, it seems contradictory that I have just argued that the *retention* of the *lamed* in the imperative and the *yqtl* form is a characteristic shared by IH and Aramaic, and now I am suggesting that the *dropping* of the *lamed* in the *qtl* is an IH feature. Keep in mind, however, that (1) the verb *lqḥ* is *sui generis* in Hebrew morphology and, therefore, the unexpected should not be surprising; and (2) Hosea's (sub)dialect and the (sub)dialect that lies behind 1 Kgs 17:11, Ezek 37:16, and Prov 20:16 may be different species, that is to say, within the umbrella of IH one subdialect may have dropped the *lamed* in all forms, including the *qtl*, whereas another may have retained the *lamed* in all forms, including the imperative. On *qāḥ* in Ezek 17:5, see now M. Greenberg, *Ezekiel 1–20* (AB 22; New York: Doubleday, 1983) 310–11, with the attractive suggestion that the word derives not from the root *lqḥ*, but is instead the name of a particular plant, with cognates in Syriac and Akkadian.

10. J. R. Davila, "Qoheleth and Northern Hebrew," in *Sopher Mahir: Northwest Semitic Studies Presented to Stanislav Segert* (ed. E. M. Cook) = *Maarav* 5–6 (1990) 86. Davila cited a brief remark by M. J. Dahood ("Canaanite-Phoenician Influence in Qoheleth," *Biblica* 33 [1952] 216) to this effect, though the latter did not produce much evidence.

11. Schniedewind and Sivan, "Elijah-Elisha Narratives," 327–28.

12. Schniedewind and Sivan ("Elijah-Elisha Narratives," 327) incorrectly stated "21 times," although they presented 18 verses.

13. A. Rofé ("La composizione di Gen. 24," *BeO* 23 [1981] 161–65) identified

el-ʿOreme (on the Sea of Galilee) dated to the eighth century: *kd hšʿr* "jar of the gate."[14]

The equivalent JH term most likely is *ṣinṣenet* "jar," which is attested only once, in Exod 16:33. This is slender evidence, of course, but this section of the Bible is undoubtedly Judahite in origin.

The word *kad* continues in MH, occurring 53 times.[15] It is attested also in Ugaritic (once in the poetic corpus [*UT* ʿnt:I:16] and frequently in the administrative texts);[16] in Phoenician, although both attestations are in difficult contexts;[17] and in Aramaic.[18]

[3]

In the Ketiv of v. 14 we encounter the unusual infinitive construct of the root *ntn* "give" as *ttn* (the Qeri reads the standard form *tēt*). The only parallel to this form occurs in 1 Kgs 6:19, where the infinitive construct with prefixed *lamed* appears as *lětittēn*. The latter form occurs within the description of the building of the Temple, where we suspect the hand of Phoenician scribes at work.[19] There is no direct evidence from Phoenician, in particular, or from elsewhere in Northwest Semitic, in general, to bolster our conclusion. But the presence of these two forms in these two sections of Kings is sufficient reason to include (*lě*)*tittēn* in our list of IH grammatical features. The contrasting JH form is SBH (*lā*)*tēt*.

Support for our conclusion is forthcoming from MH.[20] In this dialect of Hebrew, the form appears as *lîtēn* (with prefixed *lamed*), with the infinitive construct built on the analogy of the *yqtl* form of the verb.[21] The BH forms cited above are "half-way" to the MH form. And so M. H. Segal claimed that

---

other so-called "Aramaisms" in Genesis 24 (see the list on pp. 162–63) and utilized them to bolster his position that the chapter was authored in the Persian period. But these features are not Aramaisms of the type known from LBH; instead, they are to be seen as the Aramaic color of a story set in Aram.

14. See I. Ephʿal and J. Naveh, "The Jar of the Gate," *BASOR* 289 (1993) 59–65.

15. *HDHL*, 050/10146–47.

16. *UT*, 417; and *DLU*, 1.210.

17. *DNWSI*, 1.487–88.

18. *DNWSI*, 1.487–88; Jastrow, *Dictionary*, 1.612; and Sokoloff, *Dictionary*, 250.

19. See Rendsburg, *Psalms*, 29–30. In other words, not only did Phoenician architects and craftsmen build the Temple, but also their scribes recorded the activities of the realm.

20. See previously Rendsburg, *Diglossia in Ancient Hebrew*, 102, n. 21.

21. This is a widespread feature of MH; see G. A. Rendsburg, "*Laqṭîl* Infinitives: Yiphʿil or Hiphʿil?" *Orientalia* 51 (1982) 231–38.

the former are *formae mixta* of literary (i.e., BH) *lātet* and colloquial (i.e., MH) *líttēn*.[22] In light of the Galilean background of MH, we have provisional support for concluding that the forms in 1 Kgs 6:19, 17:14K were characteristic of IH.

[4]

Verse 20 contains one of only two instances in the Bible of the Hitpolel form of *gwr* "dwell." The form is the m. sg. participle *mitgôrēr: hāʾalmānāʰ ʾăšer ʾănî mitgôrēr ʿimmāh* "the widow with whom I am residing (as a stranger)," spoken by Elijah. The second occurrence is in Hos 7:14: *ʿal dāgān wĕtîrôš yitgôrārû* "over new grain and new wine they debauch," which uses the extended meaning of the root *gwr* "reside (as a stranger)" > "debauch, prostitute oneself" (as recognized in NJPSV [with note]).[23] Hosea, of course, is a northern prophet.

Cognate usage for the base meaning "reside (as a stranger)" in the T-stem is forthcoming from Aramaic. The Targumim utilize this verb frequently.[24] Onqelos, Neofiti, and Pseudo-Yonatan consistently render the Hebrew Qal form *gwr* "dwell, reside" with the Itpaʿal form of the byform root *gyr*, thus, e.g., the prefix-conjugation form *ytgyyrwn* in all three Targumim at Lev 17:8 (rendering Hebrew *yāgûr*), and participle *mtgyyryn* in Neofiti and Pseudo-Yonatan (Onqelos uses the prefix-conjugation here) at Lev 17:10 (rendering Hebrew *gār*). The meaning of the Hitpolel in Hos 7:14 is also paralleled in Aramaic, although in this instance Aramaic utilizes the simple Peʿal form.[25]

The distribution of the Hitpolel of *gwr* in the Bible, limited to 1 Kgs 17:20 and Hos 7:14, and the presence of the related T-stem in Aramaic meaning "reside (as a stranger)" combine to demonstrate the northernness of this lexeme.[26]

---

22. Segal, *Grammar*, 78; and Segal, *Diqduq*, 141.

23. There is no need for textual emendation here to *yitgôdĕdû* "they cut themselves," as proposed by many scholars, e.g., H. W. Wolff, *Hosea* (Hermenia; Philadelphia: Fortress Press, 1974) 108; and F. I. Andersen and D. N. Freedman, *Hosea* (AB 24; Garden City, N.Y.: Doubleday, 1980) 475.

24. Jastrow, *Dictionary*, 1.226; Sokoloff, *Dictionary*, 127–28; and E. G. Clarke, *Targum Pseudo-Jonathan of the Pentateuch: Text and Concordance* (Hoboken, N.J.: Ktav, 1984) 139.

25. Jastrow, *Dictionary*, 1.226; and Sokoloff, *Dictionary*, 124.

26. Schniedewind and Sivan ("Elijah-Elisha Narratives," 320) recognized the uniqueness of the usage, but did not consider it to be an IH feature.

[5]

The word *wayyitmôdēd* "he stretched himself," predicated of Elijah in v. 21, is unique on two accounts. It marks the only Hitpolel form of the root *mdd* in the Bible and also indicates the meaning "stretch," derived from the base meaning "measure." Although the only parallel to this usage in all of Northwest Semitic is rather late, it may be germane. Several midrashic texts of the Amoraic period use the Pi ʿel form of *mdd* as the verb for "stretch" where the more common Hebrew verb *mth* might be expected.[27] Although Hebrew was no longer a living language by the Amoraic period, presumably this usage reflects a continuation of the Tannaitic Hebrew of the Galilee in the Mishna and related texts.

Accordingly, the cognate usage is neither as exact (Pi ʿel, not Hitpolel) nor as direct (Amoraic attestation is late) as one would like. Moreover, uniqueness is of itself not an indication of northernness. Nevertheless, in the present instance I am inclined to include this lexeme in our list of IH features.

[6]

In vv. 21 and 22 the expression ʿal qirbô "to his midst" occurs. Most scholars agree that this is an example of the confusion between the prepositions ʾel and ʿal.[28] See our discussion above, at 1 Kings 13 [4].

---

27. Jastrow, *Dictionary*, 732.

28. Indeed, some Hebrew manuscripts read ʾel in these verses; see *BHS, ad loc.*

I KINGS 18

[1]

In v. 29, the preposition ʿad lĕ- "until" occurs. Elsewhere in the Bible this preposition is restricted to Ezra and Chronicles, where it is recognized as a sign of late BH, most likely due to Aramaic influence.[1] Its presence in Aramaic is documented from Ahiqar onward (Ahiqar 52: ʿ[d] lywmn ʾḥrnn "until later days.") So the presence of ʿad lĕ- "until" in 1 Kgs 18:29 may seem surprising.

Apparently this is a northern feature, yet another linguistic element shared by IH and Aramaic. The history of this usage within Hebrew may be traced as follows. In pre-exilic times this preposition was restricted to IH, as attested to by its sole occurrence, in 1 Kgs 18:29. In post-exilic times, under Aramaic influence, the preposition penetrated JH as well and, thus, it appears with greater regularity in Ezra and Chronicles.[2]

Related to the use of ʿad lĕ- "until" in 1 Kgs 18:29 is the use of ʿad-ʾălêhem in 2 Kgs 9:20 (see our discussion below, at 2 Kings 9 [8]).

[2]

On the noun kad "jar," attested in v. 34, see our discussion above, at 1 Kings 17 [2].

[3]

The root ghr "bend, crouch" is predicated of Elijah in v. 42. It occurs again in the Bible only in 2 Kgs 4:34–35, where it is predicated of Elisha.[3] This

---

1. See S. R. Driver, *An Introduction to the Literature of the Old Testament* (Oxford: Clarendon Press, 1920) 538; Burney, *Kings*, 225; and Montgomery and Gehman, *Kings*, 311 (though these scholars did not state explicitly that Aramaic influence is at work).

2. However, the usage is virtually unknown in post-biblical Hebrew. Of the thousands of instances of the preposition ʿad, only a handful include the ʿad lĕ-construction, e.g., T. Nazir 1:4: min hāʾāreṣ ʿad lārāqîaʿ "from the earth until the firmament." See *HDHL*, 068/13897–967.

3. BDB, 155; and KB, 173. See also the literary comparison in Burney, *Kings*, 215.

distribution in stories geographically set in the north points to this verb being a characteristic of IH.

Exact cognates of this verb are lacking in the Semitic languages. Note, however, closely related roots in various Aramaic dialects. In Ahiqar 13 and in Syriac and Mandaic we encounter the form *gḥn*;[4] in Galilean Aramaic and in Babylonian Aramaic the form is *gḥn*;[5] and in Samaritan Aramaic the root is *gʿn*.[6] All these roots mean the same as Hebrew *gḥr* "bend, crouch."[7]

Most likely the original form of this verb is *gḥn*, which was weakened to *gʿn* and further softened to *gḥn* in various Aramaic dialects. The attested Hebrew variant *gḥr* in 1 Kgs 18:42 and 2 Kgs 4:34–35 shows the softest of these pronunciations, along with the interchange of *nun* and *reš*. This interchange is well attested in Semitic languages, including between Hebrew and Aramaic. I am not referring to the well-known examples, Hebrew *bēn* = Aramaic *bar* "son" and Hebrew *šnayim* = Aramaic *trēn* "two," which are to be explained otherwise,[8] but to examples such as Hebrew *ʾalmānāʰ* = Aramaic *ʾarmělāʰ* (the Hebrew and Aramaic forms also exhibit metathesis, not uncommon when *lamed* is present; the former has the consonantal string *l-m-n*, the latter has *r-m-l*). Although the weakening of the pharyngeals and the laryngeals occurs late in Aramaic and post-Biblical Hebrew, it is not unreasonable to posit its existence in the Hebrew of the Biblical Period.

Accordingly, we may add *gḥr* "bend, crouch" to the list of IH lexemes attested in these stories concerning the northern kings and northern prophets.[9] The distribution of this verb in the Bible, though limited to three attestations, points to that conclusion. The cognates in Aramaic, albeit not pure cognates, bolster this position. Finally, note that the JH equivalent is the verb *rbṣ* (perhaps also *škb* in some of its usages).

---

4. Cowley, *Aramaic Papyri*, 281; *DNWSI*, 215; Payne Smith, *Dictionary*, 62; and Drower and Macuch, *Mandaic Dictionary*, 81.

5. Jastrow, *Dictionary*, 1.233; and Sokoloff, *Dictionary*, 126.

6. Z. Ben-Hayyim, *ʿIvrit ve-ʾAramit Nusaḥ Shomron* (5 vols.; Jerusalem: Bialik, 1957) 2.557, where *gʿn* is listed as the Samaritan Aramaic rendering of Hebrew *npl* "fall, descend."

7. The Hebrew and Aramaic roots are correlated by C. Brockelmann, *Lexicon Syriacum* (Halle: Max Niemeyer, 1928) 106.

8. See D. Testen, "The Significance of Aramaic *r* < *⋆n*," *JNES* 44 (1985) 143–46.

9. Thus also Schniedewind and Sivan, "Elijah-Elisha Narratives," 330.

[4]

In v. 46 the preposition *ʾel* occurs instead of the expected *ʿal* in the expression *wĕyad YHWH hāyĕtā^h ʾel ʾēliyyāhû* "and the hand of YHWH was upon Elijah." See the detailed treatment above, at 1 Kings 13 [4].

[5]

In v. 46 the *hapax legomenon šns* "gird" occurs in the expression *wayĕšannēs motnāw* "he girded his loins" predicated of Elijah. A pure cognate to this verb occurs only in Ugaritic, where it is attested once in the corpus (*UT* ʿnt:II:12: *ʿtkt rišt lbmt šnst kpt bḥbšh* "she ties heads to her waist, she attaches hands at her belt").[10] The standard dictionaries of Ugaritic relate *šns* in this passage to Hebrew *šns*.[11] Note that the context is military; Anat is on the rampage. It would be stretching matters too far to state that Elijah also is on a military rampage. But we can aver that the expression "he girded his loins"— elsewhere with the verbs *ḥgr* and *ʾzr* (these two verbs would be the JH equivalents)—typically appears in military settings. Thus the contexts are similar and there should be no opposition to correlating the single attestations of the verb *šns* in the two corpora. The evidence is limited, but it points to the conclusion that Hebrew *šns* was a lexical trait of the northern dialect.[12]

A possible "non-pure" cognate to *šns* is the Aramaic verb *šnṣ* "tighten, bind," along with the MH and Aramaic noun *šeneṣ* "strap, lace, thong."[13] The correspondence between *s* and *ṣ* is irregular, but not unparalleled. An exact parallel is BH *ṣlp* "be crooked" = MH *ṣlp* "cross."[14] Other examples of this interchange are Hebrew *qsm* = Syriac *qṣm* "practice divination"; the Hebrew roots *ʿls* and *ʿlṣ* "exult"; and, perhaps, the unusual form *sāpûn* in Deut 33:21, if, in fact, it is a byform of *ṣāpûn* "hidden." Note that in all but one of these

10.   For parsing and a like translation, see D. G. Pardee, "The Preposition in Ugaritic," *UF* 7 (1975) 371.

11.   *UT*, 493 (with a qualifying question mark); and G. R. Driver, *Canaanite Myths and Legends* (Edinburgh: T & T Clark, 1956) 148. For a recent translation, using "fastens," see M. S. Smith, "The Baal Cycle," in *Ugaritic Narrative Poetry* (ed. S. B. Parker; Atlanta: Scholars Press, 1997) 107.

12.   Thus also Schniedewind and Sivan, "Elijah-Elisha Narratives," 331.

13.   Thus BDB, 1042; and *HALOT*, 4.1607. For the MH and Aramaic evidence, see Jastrow, *Dictionary*, 2.1607; Sokoloff, *Dictionary*, 560–61; and *HDHL*, 089/18205. This cognate material is lacking from KB, 999, which mentions only a derivation (with a question mark) from Egyptian *sndw.t* "apron." In light of the Northwest Semitic evidence, this proposal should be discarded.

14.   On this item, see H. Tawil, "Hebrew *slp*, Mishnaic Hebrew *ṣlp*: Akkadian *ṣalāpu/ṣullupu*: A Lexicographical Note II," *Beth Mikra* 41 (1996) 276–92.

roots there is present a *nun* or *lamed*, which may have affected the articulation of the sibilant (and the one remaining root has a *mem*).

The Ugaritic evidence, the probable MH and Aramaic evidence, and the fact that *šns* occurs in the Bible only in 1 Kgs 18:46 combine to allow us to conclude that *šns* "gird" was a feature of IH.[15]

---

15. Burney already sensed this, for he included *šns* in his list of *hapax legomena* "which take the place of ordinary words and thus may be dialectal" (Burney, *Kings*, 209). Had Burney had at his disposal the evidence from Ugaritic, almost assuredly he would have written the above statement without qualification.

I KINGS 19

[1]

Burney made the perceptive observation that *bĕʾēr šebaʿ ʾăšer lîhûdāʰ* "Beersheba, which is to Judah" in v. 3 points to a northern source for this chapter.[1] For a second such instance, see 2 Kgs 14:11, on which see below at 2 Kings 14 [1].

[2]

The use of the numeral "one" for the indefinite article in *rōtem ʾeḥāt* and *rōtem ʾeḥād*, both "a broom bush," in vv. 4–5, is a feature of IH. See our discussion above at 1 Kings 13 [3]. Apart from the typical biblical stylistic device of variation in grammatical form, I am unable to explain the difference in gender in these phrases.

[3]

The noun *ʾăkîlāʰ* "eating" in v. 8 is a *nomen actionis* of the *qĕtîlāʰ* formation, a relatively rare usage in BH. However, when it does occurs in BH, *qĕtîlāʰ* appears disproportionately in northern contexts.[2] Note the following examples: Judg 5:16 (*šĕrîqôt* "pipings" in the Song of Deborah); 1 Sam 13:21 (*pĕṣîrāʰ* "payment"(?) or "sharpening"(?) [both definitions fit the context] within the history of Saul); Job 41:10 (*ʿăṭîsôtāw* "his sneezes"); Qoh 12:12 (*yĕgîʿat* [in construct state] "tiring"); and 2 Chr 30:17 (*šĕḥîṭat* [in construct state] "slaughtering"). The last example is especially interesting, since this chapter, which has no parallel in the book of Kings, is concerned specifically with the remnant of Israelians residing in the north during the reign of Hezekiah of Judah.

  The above list, to which should be added our example *ʾăkîlāʰ* "eating" from 1 Kgs 19:8, in the Elijah cycle, points to a northern home for the *qĕtîlāʰ* formation. Burney already suspected that *ʾăkîlāʰ* was a northern lexeme, as he

---

1. Burney, *Kings*, 207.

2. I have treated this issue in Rendsburg, "The Galilean Background of Mishnaic Hebrew," 229.

included it in his list of rare words "which take the place of ordinary words and thus may be dialectal." In this particular case, he contrasted ᵓăkîlā^h with the more common words ᵓōkel, ᵓoklā^h, and maᵓăkāl, all meaning "food."[3]

In addition, note that the qĕtîlā^h formation is very common in MH. Our conclusion was anticipated by Segal: "The fact that in earlier BH it occurs only in the Song of Deborah and in the story of Elijah may, perhaps, tend to show that it was originally a Northern dialectal form."[4]

---

3. Burney, *Kings*, 209.

4. Segal, *Grammar*, 103. However, such a statement is lacking in the later Hebrew edition; see Segal; *Diqduq*, 73–74. I would add 1 Sam 13:21 pĕṣîrā^h to the short list of examples that Segal considered to be representative of "earlier BH." By contrast, Schniedewind and Sivan ("Elijah-Elisha Narratives," 314) concluded that ᵓăkîlā^h "eating" was not a northern lexical trait.

I KINGS 20

[1]

Biblical Hebrew has three words equivalent to "prevent, withhold." The most common root *ḥdl* is attested 59 times and is well distributed throughout the corpus. The root *ḥśk* is attested 27 times, and also appears throughout the Bible. The third root is *mnʿ*, occurring 29 times, but attested mainly in northern contexts and in style-switching situations.[1] Among the former is 1 Kgs 20:7, in the mouth of Ahab. The relevant other attestations of the root are: Prov 1:15, 3:27, 11:26, 23:13, 30:7; Job 20:13, 22:7, 31:16, 38:15; in the northern composition preserved in Nehemiah 9 (v. 20); in the Asaph poem Ps 84:12; in the northern prophet Amos 4:7; and in the northern text Qoh 2:10. In addition, *mnʿ* occurs six times in the book of the Benjaminite prophet Jeremiah (2:25, 3:3, 5:25, 31:16, 42:4, 48:10).

We may ascribe the two examples in the Balaam narrative to style-switching concerns. Num 22:16 is in the mouth of the messengers of Balak king of Moab, and Num 24:11 occurs in the mouth of Balak himself. The usage in Gen 30:2 occurs in the portion of the Jacob story set in Aram. Ezekiel uses the root *mnʿ* in 31:15, in a text addressed to the Pharaoh of Egypt, and in a verse that mentions specifically Lebanon.

We are left with only a handful of instances not explained by our theory: 1 Sam 25:26, 25:34, 2 Sam 13:13, Ps 21:3, Joel 1:13.[2] Even among these examples, however, a few points may be noted. Psalm 21 lacks a sufficient concentration of IH features and, therefore, it is not included in the corpus of Israelian poems that I have identified in my monograph; nevertheless, note the presence of the negative particle *bal* immediately before the root *mnʿ* in v. 3. Joel 1:13 might be explained as an Aramaism.

---

1. For much of this discussion, I am indebted to Y. Chen, *Israelian Hebrew in the Book of Proverbs* (Ph.D. dissertation, Cornell University, 2000) 28–29.

2. The root *mnʿ* occurs six times in Ben Sira; see *Sefer Ben Sira* (Jerusalem: Academy of the Hebrew Language, 1973) 202. I would ascribe this relatively common use of *mnʿ* to the influence of Proverbs over the language of Ben Sira; see further Chen, *Israelian Hebrew in the Book of Proverbs*, with numerous illustrations.

The Aramaic evidence demonstrates that the root *mn*ᶜ is the common verb for "prevent, withhold."[3] It is attested throughout Aramaic dialects: in Samalian (*KAI* 214:24), in the Ahiqar text (line 136), and in Galilean Aramaic,[4] Babylonian Aramaic,[5] and Mandaic.[6] Most significant is the use of the root *mn*ᶜ in the Targumim to render the Hebrew roots *ḥdl* and *ḥśk*.

For renderings of *ḥdl*, see Targum Neofiti to Exod 23:5, Targum Onqelos to Exod 9:29, Deut 23:23, Targum Pseudo-Yonatan to Exod 9:34, Targum Yonatan to Judg 15:7, etc. For renderings of *ḥśk*, see the Fragment Targum to Gen 39:9, Targum Neofiti to Gen 22:12, Targum Onqelos to Gen 22:12, Targum Pseudo-Yonatan to Gen 22:16, etc. In addition, the Targumim utilize *mn*ᶜ to translate other Hebrew verbs, as in Targum Neofiti to Exod 5:8, Lev 27:18, Num 9:7, etc., Targum Onqelos to Deut 13:1, etc., rendering *gr*ᶜ "diminish"; Targum Neofiti to Gen 16:2 rendering *ᶜṣr* "stop"; Targum Neofiti to Num 11:28 rendering *kl*ʾ "imprison"; and so on.

Finally, it should be noted that of the three Hebrew verbs noted at the outset, *mn*ᶜ is by far the most common in MH. It is attested in the corpus of Tannaitic texts 35 times in the Qal (M. Shevi ᶜit 2:9[2×], M. Yoma 1:4, etc.) and 39 times in the Niph ᶜal (M. Shevi ᶜit 10:3, M. Bikkurim 3:7, etc.).[7] By contrast, the root *ḥdl* occurs only three times (and two of these are in Mekhilta Kaspa 20, where the discussion is the use of the root *ḥdl* in Exod 23:5); and the root *ḥśk* [written *ḥsk* (with *samekh*) in the better manuscripts] occurs only eight times (e.g., M. Demai 7:3[2×], M. Avot 4:7).[8]

In summary, the root *mn*ᶜ appears mainly in northern settings; the cognate is widely attested in Aramaic; and we can establish an opposition between IH *mn*ᶜ and JH *ḥdl* and *ḥśk* (though the latter two also were known in the north, as they are amply attested in all strata of BH)

---

3. The root *ḥsk* (< *ḥśk*) also occurs, especially in Syriac (see n. 6 below), but as far as I can determine, it is not as widespread as *mn*ᶜ.

4. Sokoloff, *Dictionary*, 318–19. As further evidence, note that *mn*ᶜ is attested nine times in the Targum Sheni to Esther, all in the very expansive passages 4:13, 6:10–11, and thus not rendering a specific Hebrew verb. For the affiliation of the language of this Targum with Galilean Aramaic, and for the exact citations, see B. Grossfeld, *The Targum Sheni to the Book of Esther* (New York: Sepher-Hermon Press, 1994) x, 611.

5. Jastrow, *Dictionary*, 2.802.

6. Drower and Macuch, *Mandaic Dictionary*, 274. The verb *mn*ᶜ occurs also in Syriac (see Payne Smith, *Dictionary*, 282), but with a different meaning: "arrive, come, bring, lead." In Syriac, the root *ḥsk* is the primary verb meaning "prevent, withhold" (*ibid.*, 151).

7. HDHL, 062/12729–063/12731.

8. *Ibid.*, 041/8169–70 and 044/8854.

[2]

The verb *śpq* "be sufficient" occurs in v. 10. The other attestations of this verb, Isa 2:6 and Job 27:23, represent another root, properly *spq* "clap hands, shake hands"[9] (the spelling with *sin* in these two instances is hyper-correction[10]). Thus, 1 Kgs 20:10 is the sole attestation of the verb *śpq* "be suffi-cient" in the Bible. A related noun *śēpeq* "plenty" occurs in Job 20:22. The form *śāpeq* (in pause) appears in Job 36:18, but it is not clear how this noun is to be interpreted.

The verb *śpq*, spelled *spq* consistently due to the merger of *samekh* and *sin* in post-biblical times, is exceedingly common in MH and in Aramaic, with a range of meanings, such as "supply, suffice, be sufficient, have enough."[11] This fact led Burney to include *śpq* "be sufficient" in his list of northern elements "which betray the influence of Aram."[12] I agree, although the manner of Aramaic influence is open to debate.

The presence of *śpq* in 1 Kgs 20:10 could be explained as another feature of IH in the stories of the northern kingdom, indicating once more that IH and Aramaic shared many lexical items that did not extend as far south as Judah. However, it is important to note that the word appears in the mouth of Ben Hadad, king of Aram, and, thus, its presence in the story may be an intentional rhetorical device employed by the author to color the language of Arameans with Aramaic traits. This is certainly the explanation for the appearance of noun(s) derived from the root *śpq* in Job (20:22 certainly, 36:18 possibly), a book replete with style-switching. Accordingly, caution is ad-vised before stating without qualification that *śpq* was part of the IH lexicon. On the one hand, the very frequent usage of this verb in MH points to that conclusion; on the other hand, the biblical evidence suggests that style-switching may be operative in the few cases where the root appears in the corpus. Regardless, the issue clearly deserves treatment in the present study, and thus I have included it.[13]

---

9. BDB, 974; and KB, 928.

10. On this phenomenon, see J. Blau, *On Pseudo-Corrections in Some Semitic Lan-guages* (Jerusalem: Israel Academy of Sciences and Humanities, 1970).

11. Jastrow, *Dictionary*, 2.1015–16; Sokoloff, *Dictionary*, 386; *HDHL*, 067/13729–49 (including noun forms, several hundred cases of *sāpēq* and a handful of examples of *sēpeq*).

12. Burney, *Kings*, 209.

13. For Schniedewind and Sivan ("Elijah-Elisha Narratives," 325), this verb was merely a sign of Aramaic influence for stylistic purposes.

[3]

On the use of "one" for the indefinite article in *nābî' 'eḥād* "a prophet" in v. 13, see our discussion above, at 1 Kings 13 [3].

[4]

The word *mĕdînā^h* "district" appears four times in the expression *śārê ham-mĕdînôt* "district governors" in vv. 14, 15, 17, 19. Elsewhere in the Bible, *mĕdînā^h* appears in Ezek 19:8, Lam 1:1 (both from the early Exilic Period), and then several dozen times in books of the Persian Period (Esther [29×], Ezra, Nehemiah, Qohelet, Daniel). The word is extremely common in MH, occurring 256 times in Tannaitic texts,[14] and the cognate form is standard in Aramaic.[15]

This distribution suggests that in pre-exilic times *mĕdînā^h* was limited to IH, thus creating an isogloss with Aramaic—although the word is not attested in Old Aramaic, its existence may be assumed on the basis of its wide distribution in later Aramaic dialects, beginning with Official Aramaic.[16] This IH-Aramaic link explains the limitation of *mĕdînā^h* in pre-exilic literature to a single chapter dealing with the history of the northern kingdom.[17] In exilic and post-exilic times, as Aramaic influence over all varieties of Hebrew increased, the word became standard in BH.[18]

[5]

Twice in v. 25 inflected forms of the *nota accusativi* (henceforth '*ôt*-forms) appear where the syntax typically would require inflected forms of the preposition '*et* (henceforth '*itt*-forms). For some of the following examples, such as the first, I have rendered the passages in as literal a way as possible.

> 1 Kgs 20:25: *timne^h lĕkā ḥayil kaḥayil hannôpēl mē'ôtāk*
> "Assemble for yourself an army like the army that fell from you."

---

14. *HDHL*, 034/6700–5; see also Jastrow, *Dictionary*, 2.734.

15. Jastrow, *Dictionary*, 2.734; and Sokoloff, *Dictionary*, 291–92. See also E. Y. Kutscher, "Dating the Language of the Genesis Apocryphon," *JBL* 76 (1957) 291–92.

16. *DNWSI*, 2.597.

17. See already Burney, *Kings*, 209, where *mĕdînā^h* is listed as one of the words in Kings "which betray the influence of Aram." Schniedewind and Sivan ("Elijah-Elisha Narratives," 324) also considered this word to be a sign of Aramaic influence for stylistic purposes.

18. Wagner, *Aramaismen*, 72, listed it as an Aramaism.

1 Kgs 20:25: *wěnillāḥamā^h ʾōtām bammîsôr*
"And let us fight them in the plain."

The "harshness" of the former example is sensed immediately when one realizes that the standard Hebrew form is *mēʾittāk* "from you." The second example is unusual, because the verb *lḥm* typically governs the prepositions *b-* "against" or *ʾet* "with" and does not carry the *nota accusativi*.[19]

This problem in Hebrew grammar had been noted by earlier grammarians, but with no attempt to explain the phenomenon. Typical are the comments of Gesenius-Kautzsch-Cowley: "also in the later books, especially in Kings, and always in Jer. and Ezek. incorrectly,"[20] and Bauer-Leander: "wohl falsche Tradition."[21]

In his insightful analysis,[22] Shelomo Morag isolated 61 occurrences of the use of *ʾōt-* forms for expected *ʾitt-* forms in the Bible, of which 21 are in Ezekiel (2:1, 2:6, 3:22, 3:24, 3:27, 7:27, 10:17, 14:3, 16:8, 16:59, 16:60, 17:17, 20:17, 22:14, 23:23, 23:25, 23:29, 37:26, 38:9, 39:24, 44:5) and 17 in Jeremiah (1:16, 2:35, 4:12, 5:5, 10:5, 12:1, 16:8, 18:10, 19:10, 20:11, 21:2, 30:11, 32:40, 32:41, 33:9, 35:2, 46:28). In his study, Morag placed greatest emphasis on the concentration of forms in Jeremiah and Ezekiel. I repeat Morag's conclusion here (with total acceptance), and then I shall build upon his work to explain the examples from Kings.

Morag's approach holds that the replacement of *ʾitt-*forms by *ʾōt-*forms results "from the interference of foreign languages in the morphological system of Hebrew: Babylonian in the case of Ezekiel, Aramaic in that of Jeremiah."[23] Babylonian lacks an accusative particle, but does possess "a precise counterpart—and an etymological parallel—to the Hebrew preposition *ʾet* 'with,' which is *itti*."[24] Although one might expect the reverse to occur in Ezekiel, i.e., *ʾitt-*forms replacing *ʾōt-*forms, "at a certain stage of the formation of the Hebrew morphology of the bi-lingual speaker under the influence of Babylonian, hypercorrection played its role.... It is quite common for speakers to change their own speech features in the light of the 'correct' usage; as a result of this tendency, the speaker of Hebrew in

19. BDB, 535.

20. GKC, 300.

21. Bauer and Leander, *Historische Grammatik der hebräischen Sprache des Alten Testamentes*, 642.

22. S. Morag, "On the Historical Validity of the Vocalization of Biblical Hebrew," *JAOS* 94 (1974) 307–15, especially pp. 313–15.

23. Morag, "Historical Validity," 314.

24. *Ibid.*

the community of exiles occasionally employed" ʾôt-forms in place of ʾitt-forms.[25]

In the case of Jeremiah, Morag relied on Aramaic influence to explain the phenomenon. "Aramaic possesses an etymological equivalent and a syntactic counterpart for the accusative particle of Hebrew but not for the preposition ʾet; for Hebrew ʾet 'with' it uses ʿim."[26] Accordingly, the expected result occurred, the book of Jeremiah contains the repeated use of ʾôt-forms, i.e., inflections of the *nota accusativi*, for expected ʾitt-forms. In general, Morag's explanations for the concentration of instances in Ezekiel and in Jeremiah are convincing.

Morag further noted that the employment of ʾôt-forms in place of ʾitt-forms occurs repeatedly in Kings as well. In addition to the two verses cited above, the relevant passages are as follows:

1 Kgs 22:7:   haʾên pōʰ nābîʾ laYHWH ʿōd wěnidrěšāʰ mēʾôtô
               "Is there not another prophet of YHWH here that we may inquire
                   through him?"

1 Kgs 22:8:   ʿôd ʾîš ʾeḥād lidrōš ʾet YHWH mēʾôtô
               "There is another man through whom we may inquire of YHWH."

1 Kgs 22:24:   ʾê zeʰ ʿābar rûaḥ YHWH mēʾittî lědabbēr ʾōtāk
               "How did the spirit of YHWH pass from me to speak with you?"

These three passages appear in the parallel section of 2 Chr 18:6, 18:7, 18:23 (in the last verse, the word *hadderek* appears between ʾê zeʰ and ʿābar).

2 Kgs 1:15:   rēd ʾôtô ʾal tîrāʾ mippānāw
               "Go down with him; do not be afraid of him."

2 Kgs 1:15:   wayyāqom wayyēred ʾôtô ʾel hammelek
               "He arose and went down with him to the king."

2 Kgs 3:11:   haʾên pōʰ nābîʾ laYHWH ʿōd wěnidrěšāʰ ʾet YHWH mēʾôtô
               "Is there not another prophet of YHWH here that we may inquire
                   of YHWH through him?"

2 Kgs 3:12:   yēš ʾôtô děbar YHWH
               "The word of YHWH is with him."

2 Kgs 3:26:   wayyiqqaḥ ʾôtô šebaʿ mēʾôt ʾîš
               "He took with him seven hundred men."

2 Kgs 6:16:   kî rabbîm ʾăšer ʾittānû mēʾăšer ʾôtām
               "For those who are with us are more than those who are with them."

2 Kgs 8:8:   wědāraštā ʾet YHWH mēʾôtô
               "Inquire of YHWH through him."

---

25. *Ibid.*
26. *Ibid.*, 315.

Morag tentatively explained the replacement of ʾitt-forms by ʾôt-forms in these passages in a manner similar to his explanation of the phenomenon in Jeremiah; he wrote that Aramaic influence was the cause "possibly also in those passages in Kings which were composed not much earlier than Jeremiah."[27] However, a closer look at the setting of these passages from Kings reveals that all occur within the annals of the northern kings or within the stories of the northern prophets.[28] 1 Kgs 20:25 is part of the account of the war between Ahab of Israel and Ben-Hadad of Aram; moreover, the two attestations occur in the advice of the Aramean courtiers addressing their king (on this point, see also below). The three cases in 1 Kings 22 (=2 Chronicles 18) are in a northern source (see further the Conclusion), even though one is pronounced by Jehoshaphat of Judah; the other two are spoken by the unnamed king of Israel and by Zedekiah, prophet of Samaria. 2 Kgs 1:15 is within the Elijah cycle (the prophet is addressed by the angel of the Lord). 2 Kings 3 is part of the Elisha cycle within the setting of the annals of Jehoram of Israel, again even though two of the examples are in the mouth of Jehoshaphat of Judah. In 2 Kgs 6:16 Elisha is speaking, and in 2 Kgs 8:8 again Ben Hadad is speaking (again, see further below), this time with reference to Elisha.

Clearly, the use of ʾôt-forms for expected ʾitt-forms is a feature of IH. It is not coincidental that the twelve instances from Kings (three of which are repeated in Chronicles) occur uniformly in northern settings. There are instances of ʾitt-forms in these chapters (see 2 Kgs 6:16 above, for example), but generally the northern dialect of Hebrew, in which the annals of the Israelian kings and the stories of Elijah and Elisha were composed, made sparing use of such forms and usually employed ʾôt-forms in their stead. IH clearly did not utilize the preposition ʾet and its inflected forms with any regularity. It did not advance to the extreme of Aramaic, which utilized only ʿim for "with," but it is definitely closer to Aramaic in this regard than to JH. As such, we have isolated yet another IH feature that creates an isogloss between IH and Aramaic.

---

27. *Ibid.*

28. See already Burney, *Kings,* 237–38; and Montgomery and Gehman, *Kings,* 328. The former, however, added that the feature "can scarcely be counted dialectal, depending as it does upon vocalization and *scriptio plena,* and standing also beside the more ordinary form" (p. 238). But in light of recent research into the historical validity of the Masora (cf. especially the work of Shelomo Morag), the main objection raised by Burney is removed.

In addition, note that in three of the examples, 1 Kgs 20:25(2×) and 2 Kgs 8:8, Arameans are speaking. Thus, we also may have present additional examples of style-switching.

Of the remaining examples of this usage in the Bible, only Isa 54:15 and 59:21 are germane to our overall discussion; these two attestations from Second Isaiah can be explained by the same means used to analyze the examples in Ezekiel. The other examples in the Bible are all isolated cases (Num 26:3, Josh 10:25, 14:12, 2 Sam 24:23) for which no explanation is readily apparent—save for the possibility that the Joshua passages derive from an Ephraimite source. However, in general, there is no concentration of IH features in the book and in the second passage undoubtedly we are dealing with a southern source that presents Caleb at center stage.

[6]

In v. 27, in preparation for battle, the Israelites are assembled and counted, being likened to *šĕnê ḥăśîpê ʿizzîm* "two small flocks of goats," in comparison to the Arameans, "who filled the land." This phrase represents a unique usage in the Bible.[29] The root of *ḥăśîpê* is *ḥśp*, derived from proto-Semitic *ḫśp*, attested in Ugaritic, Phoenician, and Arabic. The Hebrew word is spelled with a *sin*, another case of hypercorrection;[30] probably the presence of another, more common Hebrew verb *ḥśp* "strip" affected the spelling of *ḥăśîpê*.

The meaning and root of the word are illuminated by Arabic, in which the verb *ḫsf* has a wide range of connotations (all or mostly negative), "sink, sink down, disappear, etc.," with derived nouns meaning "baseness, inferiority, etc."[31] This fits the context of 1 Kgs 20:27 nicely. The Arabic verb also sheds light on the Ugaritic usage of *ḫsp*, which appears in *UT* 1 Aqht 31 with the meaning "be deficient, emaciated" (note the parallel verbs *ḫrb* "be destroyed" and *ǵly* "droop."[32] Although Phoenician does not distinguish between *ḥ* and *ḫ* in its orthography, it seems most likely that *tḥtsp ḥṭr mšpṭh* in the Ahiram inscription, line 2, is to be interpreted as "may the scepter of his rule [=his power] be diminished," with the verb *tḥtsp* being derived from our root.[33]

---

29. See the dictionaries: BDB, 362; and KB, 339. BDB noted that the versions generally understood the phrase as "two little flocks," thus pointing the way for the correctness of our interpretation.

30. Again, see Blau, *On Pseudo-Corrections in Some Semitic Languages.*

31. H. Wehr and J. M. Cowan, *A Dictionary of Modern Written Arabic* (Wiesbaden: Otto Harrassowitz, 1979) 277.

32. *UT*, 403; Driver, *Canaanite Myths and Legends*, 139; and *DLU*, 1.200.

33. Thus the interpretation of J. C. L. Gibson, *Textbook of Syrian Semitic Inscriptions*,

A unique word occurs in the stories of the northern kings. It has cognates in Phoenician and Ugaritic. This conjunction points to the conclusion that the root *ḥsp* "be deficient, emaciated" is a lexical trait of IH.[34]

[7]

According to the standard dictionaries of BH, the verb *nḥš* in v. 33 is used in a unique way in the Bible.[35] In most of its occurrences in the corpus this verb has a pejorative meaning related to magic, a practice forbidden in ancient Israel. Thus, Lev 19:26 and Deut 18:10 are legal contexts that prohibit magic; 2 Kgs 17:17 refers to such practices among the sins of the northern kingdom; and 2 Kgs 21:6 and 2 Chr 33:6 relate such practices to the reign of the sinful Manasseh. Although in Gen 44:5 and 44:15 the hero Joseph divines (*nḥš*) through a goblet without a negative word, in this case clearly the author's attempt was to provide additional coloration to a story set in Egypt, a country well known for the magical praxes of its priest-magicians.

Only in two places is the verb *nḥš* used in a non-pejorative sense, Gen 30:27 and 1 Kgs 20:33, both in Aramean contexts. In the former, Laban uses the verb in addressing Jacob; the setting is Harran in Aram Naharaim and the speaker, himself, is an Aramean.[36] In 1 Kgs 20:33 the story relates the deliberations of the king of Aram and his courtiers. In both cases the verb *nḥš* is used matter-of-factly by the Aramean characters to refer to their normal course in decision-making.

---

3 vols. (Oxford: Clarendon Press, 1971–82) 3.16, with reference to both Arabic *ḥsf* and Ugaritic *ḥsp*.

34. Arabic also attests to this root, and, in fact, its presence in Arabic allowed scholars to understand its meaning in Hebrew, Ugaritic, and Phoenician. But since Arabic falls outside the Northwest Semitic group, its role in this case and in all other cases in this study is secondary for establishing a particular usage as northern instead of southern.

    Schniedewind and Sivan ("Elijah-Elisha Narratives," 324) opined that *ḥāśip* is employed to enhance the Aramaic coloring of the chapter. They stated that the word means "lamb, small flock," but at the same time they cited a putative Aramaic root, *ḥśp* "sort," supposedly utilized by G. R. Driver ("Studies in the Vocabulary of the Old Testament. II," *JTS* 32 [1931] 255) to elucidate the passage. But a check of this reference shows no such comment by Driver.

35. BDB, 638; and KB, 609–10.

36. On Aramaic usages in the story of Jacob and Laban, see J. C. Greenfield, "Aramaic Studies and the Bible," in *Congress Volume Vienna 1980* (SVT 32; ed. J. Emerton; Leiden: E. J. Brill, 1981) 110–30, especially pp. 129–30; and Rendsburg, "Linguistic Variation and the 'Foreign' Factor in the Hebrew Bible," 182–83.

In addition, note that the nominal form *naḥaš* "magic, divination" is used by the Aramean prophet Balaam in Num 23:23 and 24:1. Here, again, such practices are distanced from the people of Israel, and presumably the author placed this noun in Balaam's mouth for specific purposes.

In all these cases we are dealing with the phenomenon of style-switching. Arameans are speaking and, thus, their language is colored by certain Aramaic lexical items that would be recognizable to an educated Israelite reader. To support this position, note the relatively frequent use of the verb *nḥš* in Aramaic texts.[37]

In summary, the non-pejorative use of the root *nḥš* in BH can be ascribed to style-switching. Although there is no direct evidence for its having been an IH trait *per se*, I have included this lexical feature in this study.

[8]

Not only are the semantics and connotation of the root *nḥš* unusual in v. 33, the form that the verb takes is also unexpected. The form *yĕnaḥăšû* is a prefix conjugation form with preterite meaning. Scholars are in general agreement that this is an archaic usage, harking back to an earlier stratum of the language. It appears relatively often in biblical poetry and in prophetic discourse, but is rare in narrative prose.[38] The only examples known to me are: Gen 37:7, Judg 2:1, 1 Kgs 20:33 (our passage), 21:6, 2 Kgs 8:29, 9:15.[39] It is striking that the four examples from Kings all occur in Israelian contexts.

This observation is supported by the following cognate information. One example of this usage occurs in Phoenician: *KAI* 24:9–10 (Kilamuwa) *lpn hmlkm hlpnym ytlnn mškbm* "in the sight of the former kings, the settlers(?) complained."[40] Several instances occur also in the Aramaic Tel Dan inscrip-

---

37. This point was noted already by Montgomery and Gehman, *Kings*, 329, though without further elaboration or connection to the theory advanced here. For *nḥš* in an Aramaic text from Hatra, used as a noun meaning "augury, omen," see *DNWSI*, 2.726.

38. See T. D. Andersen, "The Evolution of the Hebrew Verbal System," *ZAH* 13 (2000) 51–52.

39. Prefix conjugation forms of the root *bwʾ* also occur in the passages listed below, but note that all are governed by the interrogative *mēʾayin* "from where?" Accordingly, this represents a specific idiom in Hebrew and, therefore, these forms are not relevant to our present study. For the evidence, see Josh 9:8, Judg 17:9, 19:17, 2 Kgs 20:14 = Isa 39:3, Jon 1:8, Job 1:7 (see also 2 Sam 1:3, Job 2:2 with the interrogative *ʾê mizzeh* "from where?"). The only counter-example is Gen 42:7 (see also Gen 16:8). I plan to deal with this usage in a future article.

40. See Segert, *A Grammar of Phoenician and Punic*, 194.

tion. The clear cases of preterite *yqtl* are line 2: *ʾby ysq* "my father went up" and line 3: *yhk* "he went." Other *yqtl* verbs, though preceded by *w-*, most likely function in this way as well.[41] Mesha Stele lines 5–6 affords still another instance of the prefix conjugation with preterite meaning (see our discussion below, at 1 Kings 21 [2]).

Possibly the presence of this usage in Gen 37:7 and Judg 2:1 can be explained as follows. In Gen 37:7 the young and excited Joseph is relating his first dream to his brothers (as a sign of his excitement, note the threefold use of *hinnē^h* in this verse); the use of *tĕsubbenā^h* with past reference would be an example of confused language as a deliberate literary device.[42] In Judg 2:1 the angel is speaking and, perhaps, the author intentionally placed in his mouth an archaic usage.[43] These last two examples aside, the four attestations in northern passages in the book of Kings represent an IH usage, especially given the cognate evidence presented above. For more details on the three other passages, see our discussion at 1 Kings 21 [2], 2 Kings 8 [6], and 2 Kings 9 [4].

[9]

Also in v. 33, the *hapax legomenon ḥlṭ* "decide" occurs; however, this verb is found often in Aramaic.[44] Again we assume that the author is attempting to portray the foreignness of the Aramaic speakers.[45] Unlike *nḥš* in this verse, the verb *ḥlṭ* is used widely in MH.[46] By contrast, *ḥlṭ* is unattested in Qumran Hebrew.

The evidence from post-biblical Hebrew and the use of style-switching in this passage (see above, [7]) suggest that the root *ḥlṭ* is a feature of northern Hebrew, a trait of IH in biblical times.

---

41. See T. Muraoka and M. Rogland, "The *Waw* Consecutive in Old Aramaic? A Rejoinder to Victor Sasson," *VT* 48 (1998) 99–104.

42. On this technique, see G. A. Rendsburg, "Confused Language as a Deliberate Literary Device in Biblical Hebrew Narrative," *Journal of Hebrew Scriptures*, vol. 2 (1998/99), at http://www.arts.ualberta.ca/JHS/.

43. I owe this suggestion to T. David Andersen, e-mail to the author dated November 24, 2000.

44. Jastrow, *Dictionary*, 1.467; and Sokoloff, *Dictionary*, 202. The root *ḥlṭ* occurs also in the Uruk cuneiform inscription, but there it appears to mean "mix," not "decide"; see *DNWSI*, 1.374 (and the references cited there).

45. Thus also Schniedewind and Sivan, "Elijah–Elisha Narratives," 325.

46. *HDHL*, 042/8509–13.

[10]

A unique vocalization occurs in v. 40, the m. sg. participle of the root ʿśh "do, make," a IIIy verb, occurs as ʿôśēʰ (with ṣere) instead of the expected form ʿôśeʰ (with segol). That is, the vocalization is equivalent to the m. sg. participle of strong verbs. This form is also the construct form of IIIy verbs, which must underlie Burney's strong language in labeling this usage "an impossibly harsh construction,"[47] with a call to emending the vocalization to the expected ʿôśeʰ.[48]

I take a different approach. This vocalization of the m. sg. participle of IIIy verbs is common in reliable manuscripts of the Mishna. For example, Gideon Haneman listed numerous examples in his detailed work on the Parma manuscript.[49] Accordingly, I interpret this feature as a dialectal variation of IH transmitted accurately by the Masora.

[11]

Verse 43 contains wayyēlek melek yiśrā'ēl ʿal bêtô "the king of Israel went to his house," with the preposition ʿal instead of the expected 'el. See our discussion above, at 1 Kings 13 [4].

---

47. Burney, Kings, 242.

48. See also GKC, 358, n. 1.

49. G. Haneman, Torat ha-Ṣurot shel Leshon ha-Mishna ʿal pi Mesorat Ketav-Yad Parma (De Rossi 138) (Tel-Aviv: Tel-Aviv University, 1980) 357–58.

I KINGS 21

In v. 1 the word *hêkāl* is used to mean "palace," referring to the palace of the Israelian king Ahab, as opposed to its usual meaning "temple."[1] An examination of the other biblical attestations of *hêkāl* = "palace" reveals this to be a northern usage.

Psalm 45 is clearly a northern psalm[2] and therein occur two examples of *hêkāl* = "palace," in the expressions *hêkĕlê šēn* "palaces of ivory" in v. 9 and *hêkāl melek* "palace of the king" in v. 16. The contexts of Hos 8:14 and Amos 8:3 imply that *hêkāl(ôt)* in these passages refers to royal palaces, not sacred temples. This usage occurs in Joel 4:5 in a prophetic address to Tyre and Sidon, where addressee-switching is clearly in effect. The expression *hêkĕlê melek* in Prov 30:28 occurs in a book with many Phoenician affinities and, in particular, in a section between the two Massa segments (see Prov 30:1, 31:1). Massa is no doubt to be found in the region northeast of traditionally Israelite territory.[3]

Elsewhere in the Bible, *hêkāl* refers to the palaces of either Assyrian or Babylonian kings (2 Kgs 20:18, Isa 13:22, 39:7, Nah 2:7, Dan 1:4, 2 Chr 36:7), which is logical given the Mesopotamian origin of the Hebrew word *hêkāl* = Akkadian *ekallu* = Sumerian É.GAL. This leaves only Ps 144:12, where *hêkāl* = "palace," though this usage may be attributed to the presumed post-exilic date of this psalm.

In Ugaritic, the word *hkl* also means "palace." It is used in *UT* 1 Aqht 172 to refer to the home of King Danel. In *UT* 33:9 it appears in a text that, most likely, refers to the royal family; note the expressions *ksu b'lt* "throne of the mistress (=queen?)" in l. 7 and *bt gdlt* "eldest daughter (=ranking princess?)" in l. 8. All other attestations of *hkl* are in *UT* 51, the famous description of the construction of a palace for Baal. The meaning "palace" for *hykl* is attested

---

1. BDB, 228; and KB, 230–31.

2. See Rendsburg, *Psalms*, 45–50.

3. Eph'al, *The Ancient Arabs*, 218–19.

in Aramaic as well, specifically in Ahiqar 9, 17, 23, 44 (though more frequently in Aramaic the word means "temple").[4]

In sum, internal biblical evidence and cognate data from Ugaritic and Aramaic indicate the use of *hêkāl* for "palace" (as opposed to "temple") as a feature of northern Hebrew.[5]

[2]

In v. 6, we read *kî ʾădabbēr ʾel nābôt hayyizrĕʿēʾlî* "because I spoke to Naboth the Jezreelite," spoken by Ahab to Jezebel as he relates to her his conversation with Naboth. Above, at 1 Kings 20 [8], we noted that the preterite use of the prefix conjugation in narrative prose is an IH trait. The present passage is a specific case of this usage, because it occurs in a causal clause introduced by *kî*. S. R. Driver called this an instance "of an exceptional character," and offered the suggestion that the verb is a frequentative here.[6] Burney, however, noted correctly that Driver's "suggestion of a *frequentative* force for the imperf....is less probable, there being no hint of this in the preceding narrative."[7]

Fortunately, we are able to turn to cognate usage from Moabite for a precise parallel to this passage. In Mesha Stele lines 5–6 we read *ky yʾnp kmš bʾrṣh* "because Kemosh was angry with his land" with reference to the past. J. C. L. Gibson was the first, as far as I know, to point out the parallel between Mesha Stele lines 5–6 and 1 Kgs 21:6: "For a rare example of the imperf. with past meaning in a causal clause in Hebr. see 1 Kgs. xxi 6."[8]

---

4. See *DNWSI*, 1.278, for examples culled mainly from texts from Palmyra and Hatra.

5. Schniedewind and Sivan ("Elijah-Elisha Narratives," 314–15) included this word in their list of problematic items, though they also stated that "its use in some texts dealing with the northern kingdom only reflects the literary stylizing of the narrative."

6. S. R. Driver, *A Treatise on the Use of the Tenses in Hebrew* (Oxford: Clarendon Press, 1892) 32.

7. Burney, *Kings*, 244. In place of Driver's analysis, Burney offered the following interpretation: "The use of the imperf. is here somewhat strange, but may perhaps be explained as laying pictorial stress upon the *commencement* of the king's overtures, a usage resembling the Eng. *historical present*; 'I *speak*' or '*begin to speak*,' when immediately negotiations are cut short by a definite refusal." I make no attempt to judge this understanding of the verse, but note that in the parallel to be deduced below in Mesha Stele lines 5–6 the prefixed verb *yʾnp* also commences the telling of the historical narrative after the general introduction of the first few lines of the inscription.

8. Gibson, *Textbook of Syrian Semitic Inscriptions*, 1.78.

The general point was made above in our earlier discussion; in this case we are able to establish a very specific isogloss shared by Moabite and IH.[9]

[3]

Twice in the chapter, in vv. 8 and 11, the word *ḥōrîm* "nobles, freemen" is used. S. R. Driver already identified this word as a northern feature in the stories of the northern kings.[10] Burney concurred, with the simple statement, "The word doubtless belongs to the N. Pal. dialect."[11]

Both the noun form *ḥōr* "noble, freeman" and the verbal root *ḥrr* "set free, liberate" are common in Aramaic throughout antiquity (Official, Nabatean, Palmyrene, Galilean, Mandaic, etc.).[12] The same holds true for MH.[13] This pattern of a rare word in a northern biblical text and a common word in Aramaic and MH points to the correctness of Driver's position.

The picture is more complicated, however, since the word *ḥōr* occurs in other biblical texts as well.[14] Qoh 10:17 is explicable as another example of a northern text. The common use of this noun in Nehemiah (2:16, 4:8, 4:13, 5:7, 6:17, 7:5, 13:17), on the other hand, may be explained as a true Aramaism; accordingly, these usages do not affect our conclusion.

But the presence of *ḥōr* in Isa 34:12, Jer 27:20, 39:6 requires special comment. Jer 27:20 may be explained by the fact that Jeremiah's Anathoth dialect included this word in its lexicon. However, this solution does not resolve Jer 39:6. This section of the book of Jeremiah is an historical account and there is nothing in it to suggest that the prophet is the author. Perhaps this usage can be ascribed to Aramaic influence beginning to exert itself in the early sixth century BCE.

The meaning of *ḥōr* in Isa 34:12 is unclear, though probably polysemy is at work. In a section that deals with Edom, *ḥōrehā* could mean "her caves" (note the general description of desolation), "her Hurrians" (recall Genesis

---

9. The three examples in 1 Kgs 21:6, 2 Kgs 8:29, 9:15 (on the latter two, see below at the appropriate places) were treated by E. J. Revell, "The System of the Verb in Standard Biblical Prose," *HUCA* 60 (1989) 12. Although Revell understood that these verses did not fit the standard pattern of the Hebrew verbal system, he did not connect that observation to IH.

10. Driver, *Introduction*, 188, n.*.

11. Burney, *Kings*, 244 (see also p. 209).

12. *DNWSI*, 1.401–2; Beyer, *Aramäische Texte*, 585; Sokoloff, *Dictionary*, 216; Jastrow, *Dictionary*, 1.439, 1.506; and Drower and Macuch, *Mandaic Dictionary*, 126.

13. *HDHL*, 044/8838–40.

14. BDB, 359; and KB, 329.

36, Deut 2:22), or "her nobles" (note *mĕlûkā^h* "kingdom" and *śāreha* "her princes" in the same verse). Thus, although "her nobles" is possible in our passage, it may be only the secondary or tertiary meaning coming through. Regardless of how one explains *ḥôr* "noble, freeman" in these two passages, the general picture demonstrates that the lexeme is a feature of IH.

[4]

Twice in this chapter, in vv. 20 and 25, and again in 2 Kgs 17:17, we encounter the Hitpaʿel form of *mkr*. The expressions are all similar:

1 Kgs 21:20: *yaʿan hitmakkerĕkā laʿăśôt hāraʿ bĕʿênê YHWH*
> "because you decided to do evil in the eyes of YHWH" (Elijah to Ahab)

1 Kgs 21:25: *ʾăšer hitmakkēr laʿăśôt hāraʿ bĕʿênê YHWH*
> "who decided to do evil in the eyes of YHWH" (narrator about Ahab)

2 Kgs 17:17: *wayyitmakkĕrû laʿăśôt hāraʿ bĕʿênê YHWH*
> "they decided to do evil in the eyes of YHWH" (narrator about northern Israel).[15]

These usages are not related to the usual meaning of the verb *mkr* "sell" or to the Hitpaʿel of this root in Deut 28:68: *wehitmakkartem šām lĕʾōyĕbekā laʿăbādîm wĕlišĕpāḥôt* "There you shall sell yourselves to your enemies as male slaves and female slaves." Instead, as J. C. Greenfield noted, the three cases above are to be derived from a second root *mkr* "advise, counsel."[16] This root with this meaning occurs in Ethiopian.[17] Therefore, in 1 Kgs 21:20, 21:25, and 2 Kgs 17:17 the reflexive intent would be "take under advice, accept counsel" > "decide." Note that Targum Yonatan and the Peshitta under-stood this, with their use of the verb *ḥšb* in their translations of *hitmakkēr*.

---

15. In the first two verses, the root *mkr* was chosen by the author of 1 Kings 21 specifically to produce the alliteration with the word *kerem* "vineyard," which is so central to the entire episode (vv. 1, 2[2×], 6[3×], 7, 15, 16, 18). I owe this observation to my son David E. Rendsburg. I shall discuss this example further in my monograph on alliteration currently in preparation.

16. J. C. Greenfield, "Etymological Semantics," *ZAH* 6 (1993) 32–33.

17. E. Ullendorff, "The Contributions of South Semitics to Hebrew Lexicogra-phy," *VT* 6 (1956) 194, explained *mĕkērôtêhem* in Gen 49:5 thus, but I still prefer to see this word as "their swords," with the derivation from Greek *makhaira*. I admit, however, that the poet, at the same time, may have had the idea of "their counsels" in mind, especially in light of the following verse with its words *bĕsôdām* "in their counsel" and *biqhālām* "in their gathering."

There is no cognate evidence from Phoenician, Aramaic, or elsewhere that can be used to support our claim that IH lexical development is involved here. But the fact that this rare biblical usage occurs only in northern contexts (Ahab in the present chapter and the general Israelian population in 2 Kings 17) is sufficient grounds to justify our conclusion.

Potential cognate support is forthcoming from the verb *mlk* "advise, counsel." This usage, which is well known from MH and Aramaic (as well as Akkadian),[18] occurs once in the Bible, as an Aramaism in Neh 5:7.[19] According to Greenfield, "we have then *mkr/mlk*, which involves admittedly both a metathesis and an interchange of consonants."[20] If this view is accepted, we can then identify a lexical isogloss linking IH *mkr* and MH/Aramaic *mlk*.

18. Jastrow, *Dictionary*, 2.790–91; and Sokoloff, *Dictionary*, 310.

19. BDB, 576; and KB, 530.

20. Greenfield, "Etymological Semantics," 33, n. 36.

1 Kings 22

[1]

On the use of inflected forms of the *nota accusativi* (*ʾōt*-forms) to replace inflected forms of the preposition *ʾet* (*ʾitt*-forms) in vv. 7, 8, 24 (paralleled in 2 Chr 18:6, 18:7, 18:23), see our discussion above, at 1 Kings 20 [5].

[2]

On the use of "one" for the indefinite article in *sārîs ʾeḥād* "a eunuch" in v. 9, see our discussion above, at 1 Kings 13 [3].

[3]

In v. 16, the unnamed Israelian king, presumably Ahab, says *kammeʰ pěʿāmîm* "how many times?" On the use of *meʰ* before a non-laryngeal consonant, see our discussion above, at 1 Kings 14 [4].

[4]

In v. 24 the northern prophet Zedekiah asks Micaiah *ʾê zeʰ ʿābar rûaḥ YHWH mēʾittî lědabbēr ʾōtāk* "Which way did the spirit of YHWH pass from me to speak with you?" Typically in BH, the interrogative *ʾê zeʰ* "which?" governs a following noun, e.g., 1 Sam 9:18, 1 Kgs 13:12. Indeed, in the parallel to our verse in 2 Chr 18:23, the Judahite editor of Chronicles altered the received Kings text to include the noun *derek* "way" after *ʾê zeʰ* "which?"[1]

Only in 1 Kgs 22:24 and Qoh 11:6 does *ʾê zeʰ* govern a following verb; note that the latter example occurs in a northern composition as well. Furthermore, this usage is regular in MH.[2] On the basis of the distribution of *ʾê zeʰ* + verb in 1 Kgs 22:24 and Qoh 11:6, coupled with its more regular usage in

---

1. As noted by Burney, *Kings*, 255.

2. Segal, *Grammar*, 44–45; and Segal, *Diqduq*, 59–60. HDHL, 018/3557–73, counts 554 cases of the masculine form (018/3557–67) and 296 cases of the corresponding feminine form (018/3568–73), although not all these are the specific usage under discussion here.

MH, I conclude that this syntagma was a feature of IH. In JH, as the Chronicles passage demonstrates, this construction was not tolerated.

[5]

In v. 28 the northern prophet Micaiah says *lô² dibbēr YHWH bî* "YHWH has not spoken to me." Normally the verb *dbr* governs by the preposition *lĕ-* or *²el*. When the preposition *bĕ-* is used, it means "speak about, speak against, speak through."[3] In the present example, this last interpretation ("speak through") is possible, but the more likely understanding is as translated above. That is to say, in 1 Kgs 22:28 the preposition *bĕ-* is used following *dbr*, but the sense is equivalent to the normal usage with the prepositions *lĕ-* or *²el* following *dbr*. This usage appears in the Bible in only two other places, both in northern contexts: 2 Sam 23:2[4] and Hos 1:2.[5] Although we have no cognate evidence to support our conclusion, the distribution of *dbr b-* "speak to" in the Bible points to its identification as an IH feature.

[6]

In v. 30 there are two instances of the infinitive absolute used as a finite verb. The Israelian king (again, presumably Ahab) says *hithappeś wābô² bammilḥāmā^h* "I shall disguise myself and go into the battle."[6]

This usage has engendered much discussion over the years, but rarely has it been noted that this syntagma is in origin a northern feature. The cognate evidence certainly points in that direction, since it is more common in Ugaritic,[7] Phoenician,[8] and the Amarna letters from Byblos and other north-

3.   BDB, 181.

4.   G. A. Rendsburg, "The Northern Origin of 'The Last Words of David' (2 Sam 23,1–7)," *Biblica* 69 (1988) 119.

5.   Driver, *Notes on the Hebrew Text of the Books of Samuel*, 274–75, suggests other attestations in which *dbr b-* means "speak to." However, further examination reveals the presence of other nuances, e.g., Hab 2:1, where *lir²ōt ma^h yĕdabbēr bî* must mean "to see what he will speak against me," especially in light of the following stich *ûmā^h ²āšîb ʿal tôkaḥtî* "and how I shall respond upon my reproof."

6.   In theory, these forms could be imperatives (thus NJPSV), with Ahab instructing Jehoshaphat to disguise himself. But this interpretation leads to a difficult reading, because (1) immediately following, Ahab tells Jehoshaphat to wear his regular clothes, and (2) the second half of the verse states explicitly that Ahab disguised himself and then went into battle.

7.   *UT*, 80; and S. Segert, *A Basic Grammar of the Ugaritic Language* (Berkeley: University of California Press, 1984) 93.

8.   J. Friedrich and W. Röllig, *Phönizisch-punische Grammatik*, 2nd ed. (Rome:

ern sites,[9] than it is in other varieties of Canaanite.[10] The distribution of this usage in pre-exilic biblical texts also points to this conclusion (see below).

Pontifical Biblical Institute, 1970) 135–36; and Segert, *A Grammar of Phoenician and Punic*, 197.

9. Ten examples from Byblos (EA 89:38–39, 109:44–46, 113:40–42, 116:27–28, 118:36–39, 129:32–34, 129:40–42, 132:30–35, 137:49, 362:25–29) were identified by W. L. Moran, "The Use of the Canaanite Infinitive Absolute as a Finite Verb in the Amarna Letters from Byblos," *JCS* 4 (1950) 169–72. In a follow-up article, Moran put forward an additional example, EA 287:46, in a letter from Jerusalem ("'Does Amarna Bear on Karatepe?'—An Answer," *JCS* 6 [1952] 76–80). Concerning this last example, it is apposite to cite Moran's conclusion that the scribe of the Jerusalem letters hailed from Syria to the north ("The Syrian Scribe of the Jerusalem Amarna Letters," in *Unity and Diversity: Essays in the History, Literature, and Religion of the Ancient Near East* [eds. H. Goedicke and J. J. M. Roberts; Baltimore: Johns Hopkins University Press, 1975] 146–66).

Three additional examples (EA 173:12, 185:72, 364:21) were identified in an unpublished paper by S. Izre'el, "Ve-shuv ʿal *(y)qtl* ʾnk u-Maqbilav ba-Leshonot ha-Knaʿaniyot." All three are from northern letters: EA 173 mentions Amqi, i.e., the Beqaʿ; EA 185 is from Hazi in the Beqaʿ; and EA 364 is from Ashtaroth in Bashan. Some of these examples may be open to alternative readings and interpretations, especially EA 173:12, which occurs in a broken context. For further study, see W. L. Moran, *The Amarna Letters* (Baltimore: Johns Hopkins University Press, 1992).

In summary, it is clear that the evidence of the Amarna tablets supports the conclusion that the syntagma of the infinitive absolute as a finite verb is used intensively in the northern dialects of Canaan.

My thanks to Shlomo Izre'el for sharing with me his aforecited unpublished paper.

10. For general discussion, see J. Huesman, "Finite Uses of the Infinitive Absolute," *Biblica* 37 (1956) 271–84; and W. R. Garr, *Dialect Geography of Syria-Palestine 1000-586 B.C.E.* (Philadelphia: University of Pennsylvania Press, 1982) 183–84. For a brief statement, see W. L. Moran, "The Hebrew Language in Its Northwest Semitic Background," in *The Bible and the Ancient Near East: Essays in Honor of William Foxwell Albright* (ed. G. E. Wright; Garden City, N.Y.: Doubleday, 1961) 61–62.

In the Ugaritic, Phoenician, and Amarna examples, the subject (be it noun or pronoun) always is expressed. But in many of the biblical examples to be presented here, the subject is not expressed. Thus, there is a slight difference in usage, but I follow the lead of almost all scholars in the field in subsuming all varieties of the phenomenon under one syntagma.

In my treatment of this usage I do not distinguish between those instances that have a pronominal subject and those that have a nominal subject. Ugaritic and Amarna Canaanite afford examples of both types. Phoenician has yielded cases only of the former, but this may be due to the defective orthography. That is to say, a case such as *wbn ʾnk* "and I built" can be interpreted only as an infinitive absolute serving as a finite verb. But in a case such as *wbn hmlk* "and the

I have compiled the following lists of biblical examples from previous work on the subject conducted by A. Rubenstein,[11] J. Huesman,[12] and, more recently, B. Waltke and M. O'Connor.[13] From the examples presented in these sources, I exclude from consideration Num 30:3, Deut 14:21, 15:2, Josh 9:20, 2 Kgs 19:29, Isa 8:6, 21:5, 22:13, Jer 7:9, Ezek 1:14, and Joel 2:26, since in these cases either the infinitive absolute is used as an imperative (as reflected in the standard translations) or other phenomena are present.

From pre-exilic books, the following are northern examples: Judg 7:19, 1 Sam 2:28, 22:13, 1 Kgs 9:25, 22:30(2×), 2 Kgs 3:16, 4:43, Amos 4:5, Prov 12:7, 15:22, 17:12; and the following are southern examples: Exod 8:11, Lev 25:14, 1 Sam 25:26, Isa 5:5, 37:19. The southern provenance of the latter list is clear. The northern origin of the former list can be demonstrated. Judg 7:19 is part of the Gideon cycle; the two passages from 1 Samuel concern Eli (in Shiloh in the territory of Ephraim) and Saul (a Benjaminite); 1 Kings 9 concerns Solomon—where again we posit the work of Phoenician scribes; the two passages from 2 Kings 3–4 are part of the Elisha cycle; Amos is a northern prophet; and Proverbs is a northern composition.

Accordingly, of the seventeen pre-exilic attestations of the infinitive absolute as a finite verb, only five occur in Judahite sections of the Bible, whereas twelve are in Israelian portions.[14] The distribution of this usage in the Bible accords with the cognate evidence from Phoenician, Ugaritic, and

---

king built," the verb could be either the 3 m. sg. *qtl* form or the infinitive absolute. Clearly, with no evidence to the contrary, scholars would parse *wbn hmlk* as a *qtl* form of the verb with subject. In my decision not to distinguish between the usage with pronominal subject and the usage with nominal subject, I again follow the lead of almost all scholars who have studied this syntagma.

11. A. Rubenstein, "A Finite Verb Continued by an Infinitive Absolute in Biblical Hebrew," *VT* 2 (1952) 362–67.

12. Huesman, "Finite Uses of the Infinitive Absolute," 284–86. I exclude from consideration the passages adduced by Huesman through emendation of the Masoretic Text. Thus, on pp. 286–95 of the above article and in the following: J. Huesman, "The Infinitive Absolute and the Waw + Perfect Problem," *Biblica* 37 (1956) 410–34.

13. B. Waltke and M. O'Connor, *An Introduction to Biblical Hebrew Syntax* (Winona Lake, Ind.: Eisenbrauns, 1990) 594–97.

14. I have omitted the data from the book of Jeremiah, which contains more examples (10) of this syntagma than does any other biblical work: 3:1, 7:18, 13:16Q, 14:5, 19:13, 22:14, 32:33, 32:44, 36:23, 37:21. But, as noted earlier, although most of the events described in the book of Jeremiah occurred in Jerusalem, Jeremiah hailed from Anathoth, a city in Benjamin, and, thus, his dialect was non-Judahite.

Byblos Amarna. The lines of evidence converge to demonstrate that the use of the infinitive absolute as a finite verb was characteristic of northern dialects of Canaanite, including IH.

The use of the infinitive absolute as a finite verb appears more frequently in exilic and post-exilic books:[15] Isa 42:20, 59:4, Ezek 23:30, 23:36, 23:47, Hag 1:6, 1:9, Zech 3:4, 7:5, 12:10, Job 15:35, Qoh 4:2, 8:9, 9:11, Esth 2:3, 3:13, 6:9, 8:9, 9:1, 9:6, 9:12, 9:16–18, Dan 9:5, 9:11, Neh 7:3, 8:8, 9:8, 9:13, 1 Chr 5:20, 16:36, 2 Chr 28:19, 31:10. Even here, it should be noted, some of the sources are northern, namely, Qohelet and Nehemiah 9. But the majority, of course, stems from clear Judahite material, i.e., either from Judah itself or from Judean exiles. Once more we see at work the influence of IH on JH during the 500s and beyond in the wake of the reunification of northern and southern exiles in Mesopotamia.

The general picture that emerges from this survey of the data is clear: the use of the infinitive absolute as a finite verb was a feature of IH.[16]

[7]

The syntax of the phrase *hammelek hāyāʰ māʾŏmād bammerkābāʰ* "the king was propped up in the chariot" in v. 35 includes the syntagma of *hyh* + participle, labelled the "progressive tense" or the "periphrastic perfect construction." This is a distinctively MH usage.[17] It appears commonly in Aramaic[18] and frequently in northern settings in the Bible. 2 Sam 3:6 and 3:17 concern Abner of the house of Saul; our verse, 1 Kgs 22:35, describes the king of Israel (which one is not clear); 2 Kgs 6:8, 17:33(2×), 17:41, 2 Chr 18:34 all concern the northern kingdom of Israel; and Job 1:14 is in a non-Judahite setting.[19] This evidence indicates that this construction is a grammatical feature linking Israelian and Aramean territory.[20]

---

15. GKC, 345; Rubinstein, "A Finite Verb," 363; and Waltke and O'Connor, *Syntax*, 595.

16. See also Schniedewind and Sivan, "Elijah-Elisha Narratives," 332.

17. Segal, *Grammar*, 156; and Segal, *Diqduq*, 182.

18. See the survey by J. C. Greenfield, "The 'Periphrastic Imperative' in Aramaic and Hebrew," *IEJ* 19 (1969) 206–7.

19. The many examples in post-Exilic books (Dan 8:5, 8:7, 10:2, 10:9, Neh 3:26, 5:18, 6:14, 6:19[2×]) are to be considered true Aramaisms.

20. Schniedewind and Sivan ("Elijah-Elisha Narratives," 319) labeled this feature "problematic" vis-à-vis the issue of northern Hebrew, although they added the suggestion that "in these particular cases (1 Kgs 22:35, 2 Kgs 6:8) the use of the Aramaizing periphrastic may be a stylistic choice conditioned by the fact that both passages deal with a battle against the Aramaeans" (*ibid.*).

2 KINGS 1

[1]

The expression *ḥŏlî zeʰ* "this illness" in v. 2 (see also 2 Kgs 8:8, 8:9), in the mouth of Ahaziah, lacks the expected definite article on both the noun and the modifying demonstrative pronoun. This usage is common in MH, Phoenician, and occurs elsewhere in BH in northern texts.

Segal did not discuss this phenomenon specifically, but he did note several examples in the Mishna within the course of a general discussion on the demonstrative pronoun: M. Shevuʿot 3:7 *kikkar zô* "this loaf" and M. Menahot 13:9 *šôr zeʰ* "this bull."[1] Burney's statement that this feature "is regular in Rabbinic Heb." is essentially accurate.[2]

The same is true about Phoenician. In Segert's words, "The substantive which is followed by an adjectival demonstrative pronoun is often not provided with the article," e.g., *KAI* 29:1 *ʾrn zn* "this box"; *KAI* 26:A:III:8–9 *ʿm z* "this people"; Poenulus 930 *macom syth* "this place."[3]

In the Bible this usage appears elsewhere: Mic 7:12 *yôm hûʾ* "that day," and Ps 80:15 *gepen zôʾt* "this vine." The former occurs in the section of Micah 6–7 attributed to a northern source,[4] and the latter occurs in the collection of northern Asaph psalms.[5]

1. Segal, *Grammar*, 201.

2. Burney, *Kings*, 261.

3. Segert, *A Grammar* of *Phoenician and Punic*, 177. The first and third examples above are brought by Segert, the second is my own contribution. See also Friedrich and Röllig, *Phönizisch-punische Grammatik*, 152, with the note that the usage here discussed appears "nicht selten." Note that, in general, Phoenician uses the definite article more sparingly than does BH. Thus, even when the noun is definite by virtue of the presence of the definite article, the demonstrative pronoun lacks the definite article, e.g., *KAI* 26:A:II:9: *hqrt z* "this city" (and several more times in the same inscription).

4. See F. C. Burkitt, "Micah 6 and 7: A Northern Prophecy," *JBL* 45 (1926) 159–61; and Ginsberg, *The Israelian Heritage* of *Judaism*, 25–26. For recent discussion, though without accepting the hypothesis, see S. Vargon, *Sefer Mikha: ʿIyyunim ve-Perushim* (Ramat-Gan: Bar-Ilan University Press, 1994) 165–66.

5. Rendsburg, *Psalms*, 73–81.

The cognate evidence and the distribution of this usage in the Bible converge to demonstrate its northern quality.

[2]

In v. 7, the Israelian king Ahaziah says, *me^h mišpaṭ hā$^{\,\prime}$îš* "What is the manner of the man?" The use of *me^h* before a non–laryngeal consonant, as in the *mem* of *mišpaṭ*, is a feature of IH. See our discussion above, at 1 Kings 14 [4].

[3]

On the use of inflected forms of the *nota accusativi* (*$^{\prime}$ôt*-forms) to replace inflected forms of the preposition *$^{\prime}$et* (*$^{\prime}$itt*-forms) in v. 15(2×), see our discussion above, at 1 Kings 20 [5].

2 Kings 2

[1]

The verb *glm* "roll up (a garment)" is predicated of Elijah in v. 8. This is the only occurrence of the verb in the Bible; it is attested once more in MH (Sifra, Behar 5:5).[1] A nominal form occurs in the expression *gělômê tĕkēlet* "blue cloaks" in Ezek 27:24 as part of the prophet's words to Tyre. Although this word is unattested in Phoenician, it may have been selected by Ezekiel as part of the technique of addressee-switching. Support for this conclusion is forthcoming from MH, where the noun *gělôm* (presumed vocalization) is attested five times (all in Sifre Bemidbar).[2]

The verb *glm* "roll up" occurs also in Aramaic,[3] which attests also to a nominal cognate *gělîmāʾ* "cloak."[4]

The evidence indicates that the root *glm* is a feature of IH.[5]

[2]

In v. 20 the unique form *ṣělôḥît* "dish" occurs in the mouth of Elisha. The more typical form *ṣallaḥat* "dish" occurs in 2 Kgs 21:13, Prov 19:24, 26:15, and a plural form *ṣēlāḥôt* "dishes" appears in 2 Chr 35:13. This suggests that *ṣallaḥat* was distributed throughout the language in its various dialects, for Proverbs is a northern book and 2 Kings 21 (also 2 Chronicles 35) has a Judahite setting. By contrast, the form *ṣělôḥît* was limited to IH.

---

1. *HDHL*, 032/6303; see also Jastrow, *Dictionary*, 1.250.
2. *HDHL*, 032/6303.
3. Jastrow, *Dictionary*, 1.250.
4. Jastrow, *Dictionary*, 1.249; Sokoloff, *Dictionary*, 130; and C. Brockelmann, *Lexicon Syriacum* (Halle: Max Niemeyer, 1928) 118.
5. In contrast to Schniedewind and Sivan ("Elijah-Elisha Narratives," 320), who identified the root only as a unique linguistic feature in the story and not to be utilized for the purpose of identifying northern Hebrew, I am inclined not to relate the Hebrew noun *golem* "formless mass" in Ps 139:16. Although it is possible that this meaning derives from the root *glm* "roll up," the semantics of "formless mass" and "roll up" are sufficiently distant from each other to preclude consideration of the former in our discussion of the latter.

The form ṣĕlôḥît occurs only here in the Bible, but it is very common in MH, attested 58 times in Tannaitic texts.[6] In fact, it is the only form that occurs in MH (ṣallaḥat is wanting). Furthermore, the cognate form ṣĕlûḥîtāʾ occurs in some Aramaic dialects (Targum Yonatan, Galilean Aramaic, Christian Palestinian Aramaic).[7]

For my theory to be applicable here, ṣĕlôḥît and ṣallaḥat must denote the same vessel using alternative names, as opposed to two words for two separate pottery types. Support for the former assumption is found in Targum Yonatan, which uses ṣĕlûḥîtāʾ to translate ṣallaḥat in 2 Kgs 21:13.

---

6. *HDHL*, 077/15752–53; see also Jastrow, *Dictionary*, 2.1282.
7. Jastrow, *Dictionary*, 2.1282; Sokoloff, *Dictionary*, 465; and Schulthess, *Lexicon Syropalaestinum*, 171.

2 KINGS 3

[1]

Much has been written about the word *nôqēd* in v. 4, especially regarding its specific meaning.[1] I am content to use the English term "shepherd foreman" for lack of anything more specific, though simple "shepherd" cannot be excluded in certain contexts.[2] Unnoticed in all discussion is the fact that *nôqēd* is attested only in northern contexts and, therefore, should be considered an element of IH.[3] Elsewhere in the Bible, the word occurs in Amos 1:1, and although this superscription most likely is a Judahite addition to a book of northern prophecy, it may utilize a northern term to describe the professional activity of a prophet from the northern part of the country (see the Introduction for a brief discussion on the location of the Tekoa of Amos). In addition, the word occurs three times in MH;[4] it is attested in Syriac as *nāqdāʾ*,[5] and it appears relatively frequently in Ugaritic as *nqd*.[6]

[2]

On the use of inflected forms of the *nota accusativi* (*ʾôt*-forms) to replace inflected forms of the preposition *ʾet* (*ʾitt*-forms) in vv. 11, 12, 26, see our discussion above, at 1 Kings 20 [5].

---

1. For a recent discussion and rich bibliography, see Paul, *Amos*, 34–35. Because Mesha is called *nôqēd* in 2 Kgs 3:4, some scholars have attempted to restore *nqdy* "my shepherd foremen" in Mesha Stele, ll. 30–31, thus, e.g., Gibson, *Textbook of Syrian Semitic Inscriptions*, 1.75, 1.82. But extreme caution is advised here; very little of the passage is legible.
2. See BDB, 667; and KB, 632.
3. Thus also Schniedewind and Sivan, "Elijah-Elisha Narratives," 328.
4. *HDHL*, 065/13348; see also Jastrow, *Dictionary*, 2.890.
5. Payne Smith, *Dictionary*, 350.
6. *UT*, 447; and *DLU*, 2.329–30.

[3]

Verse 16 contains another instance of the infinitive absolute used as a finite verb: *ʿāśôʰ hannaḥal hazzeʰ gēbîm gēbîm* "This wadi shall be full of pools," in the mouth of Elisha as he quotes God. For this usage, see our discussion above, at 1 Kings 22 [6].

[4]

Verse 19 contains one of the two biblical occurrences of *mibḥōr* "choicest," in contrast to the standard term *mibḥār*. This example is placed in the mouth of Elisha. The second attestation is in 2 Kgs 19:23, a decidedly Judahite text, but placed in the mouth of Rabshakeh, who, most likely, was an Israelian or an Aramean.[7] The form *mibḥōr* "choicest" reflects the shift of /á/ > /o/ (length uncertain) characteristic of Phoenician and IH (or at least some sub-dialects thereof). For this phonological issue, see our discussion below, at 2 Kings 6 [4].

[5]

The verb *ḥrb* "slay, slaughter, fight" occurs in v. 23 in the phrase *hāḥŏrēb neḥerbû hammĕlākîm* "the kings must have fought" in the mouth of the Moabites. The noun form *ḥereb* "sword," related to this verb, is exceedingly common in BH. But the verb is very rare. It occurs again only in Jer 50:21 and 50:27, in the prophetic oracle against Babylon.[8] The latter two attestations are part of the technique of addressee-switching in the prophet's words to the Aramaic-speaking Neo-Babylonians. Note that the verb *ḥrb* "slay, kill" is particularly frequent in Syriac.[9] As Burney noted, the Peshitta uses *ḥrb* regularly to render Hebrew *hikkāʰ* "slay, strike."[10] In summary, the root *ḥrb* "slay, slaughter, fight" was a trait of IH.[11]

---

7. See above, at 1 Kings 13, n. 19.
8. BDB, 352; and KB, 329–30.
9. Payne Smith, *Dictionary*, 155.
10. Burney, *Kings*, 271.
11. We cannot determine the existence of the verb *ḥrb* "slay, slaughter, fight" in Moabite—our knowledge of this language is too limited. Nonetheless, we wonder if the author of 2 Kings 3 did not place this verb in the mouth of the Moabites intentionally.

2 KINGS 4

[1]

On the use of "one" for the indefinite article in *ʾiššāʰ ʾaḥat* "a woman" in v. 1, see our discussion above, at 1 Kings 13 [3].

[2]

Four times in this chapter—in each case in the Ketiv—the 2 f. sg. pronominal suffix is *-kî* instead of the usual form *-ēk*.[1] The four cases are in vv. 2, 3, 7(2×). The suffix *-kî* occurs in other northern texts: Song 2:13K, Ps 116:7(2×), 116:19. These seven attestations represent sufficient grounds to label the usage an IH morpheme.

Although absolute proof is lacking, we assume that the proto-Semitic morpheme *-kî* was the norm in second-millennium Northwest Semitic, including Ugaritic (whose orthography can indicate only *-k*).[2] As regards first-millennium dialects, the suffix *-kî* is attested in Aramaic,[3] and we can be reasonably sure that this form was continued in Phoenician. It appears as *-ky* in Official Aramaic[4] (examples may be found in *BMAP* 9[5] and in Cowley 8[6]) and in Qumran Aramaic (e.g., Genesis Apocryphon 19:19, 20[2×][7]). More-

---

1. Burney (*Kings*, 208) already identified this as a northern feature. See also Cogan and Tadmor, *II Kings*, 60.

2. *UT*, 36, 149.

3. For a thorough examination of all the evidence, see S. E. Fassberg, "The Pronominal Suffix of the Second Feminine Singular in the Aramaic Texts from the Judean Desert," *DSD* 3 (1996) 10–19.

4. S. Segert, *Altaramäische Grammatik* (Leipzig: VEB Verlag, 1975) 170–71; and P. Leander, *Laut- und Formenlehre des Ägyptisch-aramäischen* (Göteborg: Elanders, 1928) 27–32.

5. E. G. Kraeling, *The Brooklyn Museum Aramaic Papyri* (New Haven: Yale University Press, 1953) 238.

6. Cowley, *Aramaic Papyri*, 22.

7. J. A. Fitzmyer, The *Genesis Apocryphon of Qumran Cave I* (Rome: Biblical Institute Press, 1971) 115; and B. Jongeling, C. J. Labuschagne, and A. S. van der Woude, *Aramaic Texts from Qumran* (Leiden: E. J. Brill, 1976) 91, n. 20.

over, although many of the later dialects attest -*k* or -*yk*,[8] the form -*ky* is still used, perhaps vestigially, in Syriac.[9] For Phoenician, we can point to a Punic spelling with -*ky*.[10] The presence of -*kî* in IH, therefore, creates an isogloss linking IH with Aramaic and Phoenician used to the north of Israel. All these languages/dialects retained the proto-form. In JH, on the other hand, uncharacteristically the final long vowel -*î* was dropped; the addition of a helping vowel created the standard BH form -*ēk*.

The other attestations of 2 f. sg. pronominal suffix -*kî* in the Bible are Jer 11:15, Ps 103:3(2×), 103:4(2×), 103:5, 135:9, 137:6. The presence of -*kî* in Jeremiah may be due to the local dialect of Anathoth also employing this suffix. Ps 137:6 most likely is to be explained by the theory of the reunion of northern and southern exiles during the sixth century BCE, the date of this poem's composition.[11] Psalms 103 and 135 are post-exilic compositions,[12] so in these cases Aramaic influence is the most likely explanation.

[3]

Twice in this chapter, in vv. 13 and 14, we encounter the expression *me*[h] *laʿăśôt* "What can be done?" in the mouth of Elisha. This vocalization reflects the use of *me*[h] before a non-laryngeal consonant, in this case the *lamed* of *laʿăśôt*. On this usage as a feature of IH, see our discussion above, at 1 Kings 14 [4].

8. E. Y. Kutscher, *Meḥqarim ba-ʾAramit ha-Gelilit* (Jerusalem: Hebrew University, 1969) 22 = E. Y. Kutscher, *Studies in Galilean Aramaic* (trans. M. Sokoloff; Ramat-Gan: Bar-Ilan University, 1976) 31; and D. M. Golomb, *A Grammar of Targum Neofiti* (Chico, Calif.: Scholars Press, 1985) 48–49, 51–52.

9. C. Brockelmann, *Syrische Grammatik* (Leipzig: Reuther & Reichard, 1960) 49; and T. Nöldeke, *Compendious Syriac Grammar* (London: Williams & Norgate, 1904) 46.

10. Friedrich and Röllig, *Phönizisch-punische Grammatik*, 47; and Segert, *A Grammar of Phoenician and Punic*, 96. The only form attested is suffixed to a noun, but probably the pronominal suffix following a verb was the same.

11. On this and other aspects of this poem, see G. A. Rendsburg and S. L. Rendsburg, "Physiological and Philological Notes to Psalm 137," *JQR* 83 (1993) 385–99.

12. On Psalm 103, see the detailed study of A. Hurvitz, *Beyn Lashon le-Lashon* (Jerusalem: Bialik, 1972) 107–52, with specific treatment of 2 f. sg. pronominal suffix -*kî* on pp. 116–19. Virtually all scholars view Psalm 135 as post-exilic, especially as it is constructed mainly from other biblical passages; see, e.g., A. Cohen, *The Psalms* (London: Soncino, 1945) 441.

[4]

In v. 13 we read *hăyēš lĕdabbēr lāk ʾel hammelek ʾô ʾel śar haṣṣābāʾ* "Can we speak on your behalf to the king or to the commander of the army?" In this clause the interrogative *hă-* is continued not by the usual *ʾim* but by the unexpected *ʾô*.[13]

This syntagma occurs in the Deir 'Alla dialect in II,9: *hlʿš h bk lytʿṣ ʾw lmlkh lytmlk* "Will he not take counsel with you, or will he not ask advice (of you)?" In the Bible this usage is attested only in non-Judahite settings:[14] Judg 18:19, 2 Kgs 4:13, 6:27, Job 16:3, 38:28, 38:31, Qoh 2:19, 11:6.[15] Job and Qohelet require no comment; the Judges passage occurs in the story of the Danites' finding their new home in the north; and the two passages from 2 Kings occur within the history of the northern kingdom (the former in the mouth of Elisha, the latter in the mouth of the Israelian king). It is clear that the use of *hă-...ʾô* in an extended question is a feature of IH.

[5]

Verses 16 and 23 contain the Ketiv *ʾty* for the 2 f. sg. independent personal pronoun. See our discussion above, at 1 Kings 14 [2].[16]

[6]

In the Ketiv of v. 23 the word *hlkty* (presumably to be vocalized *hôlāktî*) "you (f. sg.) are going," is spoken by the man from Shunem in the territory of Issachar. This form reveals an inflected participle, with the pronominal indicator imported from the *qtl* form. Moreover, the pronominal indicator is the proto-Semitic and IH form *-tî*, not the SBH form *-t* for 2 f. sg. Although one must be careful in judging a single usage preserved in a Ketiv, in the present instance I elect to include this example as another feature of IH in the Israelian material of the book of Kings.[17]

---

13. For examples of the standard usage, see *DCH*, 1.304–5.

14. For further discussion, see J. C. Greenfield, "Philological Observations on the Deir 'Alla Inscription," in *The Balaam Text from Deir 'Alla Re-evaluated* (eds. J. Hoftijzer and G. van der Kooij; Leiden: E. J. Brill, 1991) 116, where, however, only 2 Kgs 6:27 is cited. See my earlier treatment in G. A. Rendsburg, "The Dialect of the Deir 'Alla Inscription," *BO* 50 (1993) 322.

15. The examples in Gen 44:19 and Deut 4:32 represent different syntagmas.

16. Cogan and Tadmor, *II Kings*, 60, noted this example as evidence for IH.

17. See my earlier treatment in Rendsburg, "Morphological Evidence for Regional Dialects in Ancient Hebrew," 82–84. Schniedewind and Sivan ("Elijah-Elisha Narratives," 332) also posited a northern feature here, though they understood the Ketiv as a *qtl* form with 2 f. sg. suffix *-tî*.

The above example is one of nine instances in the Bible where participles (both active and passive) are inflected with the suffixes normally attached to *qtl* verbs. Most scholars subsume this usage under the phenomenon known as the *ḥireq compaginis*.[18] I prefer, however, to treat these nine instances as a separate phenomenon.

This usage is paralleled in certain dialects of Aramaic.[19] G. Dalman presented about a dozen examples, of which I cite three for purposes of illustration: Targum Pseudo-Yonatan Gen 15:12: *mtrmyyt* "sie wurde geworfen"; Targum Pseudo-Yonatan Num 22:30: *mthnyyty* "ich wurde benutzt"; and Y. Ketubbot 11:5: *myṭznt* "du wirst ernährt."[20] In his monograph on the language of the Babylonian Talmud, M. Margolis noted that although the m. pl. participle is paradigmatically *yhby(n)*, the form *yhbw* also appears, with "the ending imported from the perf."[21]

The Aramaic evidence helps us explain the nine examples of inflected participles in the Bible. Three occur in pre-exilic texts. The aforecited example in 2 Kgs 4:23 occurs in a northern geographical setting. Gen 31:39(2×) *gĕnûbtî* "I was robbed," spoken by Jacob to Laban, appears in an Aramaic-speaking environment.[22] The remaining six instances appear in books written *c.* 586 BCE, when Aramaic influence began to exert itself upon Hebrew: Jer 10:17K, 22:23K(2×), 51:13K, Ezek 27:3K, Lam 4:21. Moreover, in some of these passages style-switching is evident. Although Jer 22:23 occurs in a speech addressed to Jehoiakim in Jerusalem, the prophet evokes the imagery of far northern Israel ("Lebanon" and "cedars"). Jer 51:13 occurs in the

---

18. GKC, 253–54; and D. A. Robertson, *Linguistic Evidence in Dating Early Hebrew Poetry* (SBLDS 3; Missoula, Mont.: Scholars Press, 1972) 69–76.

19. The use of inflected participles is not to be confused with another, quite widespread, phenomenon in Aramaic, namely, the attachment of the independent pronouns (or shortened forms thereof) to the participle. This is an altogether different feature. See T. Nöldeke, *Mandäische Grammatik* (Halle: Waisenhaus, 1875) 230–33; Nöldeke, *Compendious Syriac Grammar*, 45; and C. Brockelmann, *Grundriss der vergleichenden Grammatik der semitischen Sprachen*, 2 vols. (Berlin: Reuther & Reichard, 1908–13) 1.582.

20. G. Dalman, *Grammatik des jüdisch-palästinischen Aramäisch* (Leipzig: Hinrichs, 1905) 284.

21. M. Margolis, *A Manual of the Aramaic Language of the Babylonian Talmud* (Munich: C. H. Beck, 1910) 40. For more examples, see J. N. Epstein, *Diqduq ʾAramit Bavlit* (Jerusalem: Magnes, 1960) 39.

22. For additional Aramaisms in the chapters narrating the dealings of Jacob and Laban, see Greenfield, "Aramaic Studies and the Bible," 129–30; and Rendsburg, "Linguistic Variation and the 'Foreign' Factor in the Hebrew Bible," 182–83.

address to Babylon, a country that at this time was speaking Aramaic. Ezek 27:3 is in a context concerning Tyre and, although we have no evidence for inflected participles in Phoenician, we are once again in a northern setting.

The evidence, then, allows us to conclude that the use of inflected participles was another isogloss linking IH and Aramaic.

[7]

In v. 24 we read *ʾal taʿăṣor lî lirkōb* "Do not prevent me from riding," with the preposition *l-* instead of the expected preposition *m(n)*. Related to this usage is the ablative use of both *l-* and *b-* instead of *m(n)*.

Although many scholars are of the opinion that this interchange of prepositions is a standard feature of the entire biblical corpus,[23] Z. Zevit raised some serious objections to this view.[24] Among his observations, Zevit noted that it is not until the fourth century BCE that the first appearance of ablative *m(n)* occurs in Phoenician, suggesting that *b-* and *l-* served to express "from" in Phoenician prior to that time. Biblical evidence suggests that the same situation holds for IH. I cannot claim to have conducted an exhaustive search, but it is apparent that a good number of the biblical instances of *b-/l-* = "from" appear in northern contexts. Note the following examples:

Josh 3:16K: *harḥēq mĕʾōd bĕʾādām* (Q: *mēʾādām*)
            "very far from Adam"

2 Kgs 14:13:   *bĕšaʿar ʾeprayim ʿad šaʿar happinnāh*
            "from the gate of Ephraim unto the corner gate"

2 Kgs 14:28:   *hēšîb ʾet dammeśeq wĕʾet ḥămāt lîhûdāh bĕyiśrāʾēl*
            "He retrieved Damascus and Hamath from Yehuda (=Samʾal)
            for Israel."

Ps 10:1:   *lāmāh YHWH taʿămōd bĕrāḥôq*
            "Why, O YHWH, do you stand from afar?"

Ps 29:10:   *YHWH lammabbûl yāšāb*
            "YHWH has reigned from (=since) the flood."

Ps 140:11:   *bĕmahămôrôt bal yāqûmû*
            "From the deep pits they will not arise."

All these passages have northern settings. The two passages in 2 Kings 14 occur in the records of the Israelian kings Jehoash and Jeroboam II, respec-

---

23. The standard treatment is N. M. Sarna, "The Interchange of the Prepositions *Beth* and *Min* in Biblical Hebrew," *JBL* 78 (1959) 310–16.

24. Zevit, "The So-Called Interchangeability of the Prepositions *b*, *l*, and *m(n)* in Northwest Semitic."

tively; Josh 3:16 concerns a city in the territory of Manasseh; and all three examples from Psalms are in northern compositions.

Ps 10:1 deserves special comment. The preposition that usually is governed by the verb ʿmd in such contexts is m(n) "from" (see Exod 20:18, 20:21, 1 Sam 26:13, 2 Kgs 2:7, Isa 59:14, Ps 38:12), but in the present instance it is b-. In the past, scholars have been apt to emend Ps 10:1 to read mērāḥôq. However, this is clearly a case of the use of the preposition b- or l- for an expected m(n). Therefore, no emendation is necessary.

[8]

In v. 28 the Shunammite woman says to Elisha hălôʾ ʾāmartî lôʾ tašleh ʾōtî "Did I not say, 'Do not mislead me'?" These words refer back to the woman's earlier statement to the prophet in v. 16: ʾal tĕkazzēb bĕšipḥātĕkâ "Do not deceive your maidservant." The form tašleh in v. 28 is unique in the Bible, both in form and in meaning.[25] First, it is the only Hiphʿil of the root šly in the Bible. Second, unlike all other attestations of the root (and its byform šlw), which mean "be at rest, be at ease, be peaceful," in this instance the root means "mislead, cause to err."

This usage occurs in Aramaic, where the root appears in the Peʿal form, meaning "err, forget, be negligent," and in the ʾAphʿel form "cause to err, mislead."[26] This latter meaning fits the context of 2 Kgs 4:28 perfectly.

Accordingly, Brown-Driver-Briggs labeled this usage a "strong Aramaism"[27] and Burney included it in his list of lexical items in Kings "which betray the influence of Aram."[28] The methodology of this study was anticipated by Cogan and Tadmor, who stated that this verb "is part of the patois of north Israel which permeates the prophetic literature of Kings."[29] IH, like Aramaic, knew the root šly "err" and utilized this verb, at least in the Hiphʿil conjugation, with the meaning "cause to err, mislead." Some JH equivalents are the roots kzb, tʿy, and šgg/šgy.

[9]

On the verb ghr "bend, crouch" in vv. 34–35, see our discussion above, at 1 Kings 18 [3].

---

25. BDB, 1017; and KB, 972.

26. Jastrow, *Dictionary*, 2.1582; and Sokoloff, *Dictionary*, 553. Nominal forms from the same root are also attested.

27. BDB, 1017

28. Burney, *Kings*, 209.

29. Cogan and Tadmor, *II Kings*, 58. See their further comment on p. 60. See now also Schniedewind and Sivan, "Elijah-Elisha Narratives," 331.

[10]

The *hapax legomenon* zrr "sneeze" occurs in v. 35 in the phrase *wayzōrēr hanna*ʿar ʿad šebaʿ pĕʿāmîm "The lad sneezed seven times." There is only one other attestation of this root in all ancient Northwest Semitic.[30] The noun form *zrynwy* (apparently a variant of *zrynwhy*) is used in Aramaic, in the Targum to Job 41:10, to translate the Hebrew ʿăṭîšōtāw "his sneezes."[31] Although this is slender evidence, it points to the root *zrr* being a feature of IH, with its lone cognate in Aramaic.[32]

[11]

The rare noun ʾōrōt, the plural of a singular noun ʾōrā[h] known from post-biblical Hebrew (see below), occurs in v. 39. Although the word is variously translated as "herbs," "sprouts," "growth," and so on, "the exact identification of this wild plant remains uncertain."[33] This noun occurs in one other biblical passage, Isa 26:19, in the expression *ṭal ʾōrōt* "the dew on fresh growth" (NJPSV).[34] The latter passage appears in a section of Isaiah with a high

---

30. I disassociate our root from the form *zōrû* "pressed" in Isa 1:6, thus BDB, 266–67, 284; and *HALOT*, 1.283. KB, 269, on the other hand, lists *zōrû* and *wayzōrēr* together.

31. This point was noted by Burney, *Kings*, 276; Montgomery and Gehman, *Kings*, 372; and Cogan and Tadmor, *II Kings*, 58.

32. Although it has little or no effect on the above conclusion, a word about the etymology of *zrr* "sneeze" is appropriate. G. R. Driver, "Some Hebrew Medical Expressions," *ZAW* 65 (1953) 258 n. 4, appears to have been the first to connect this root with Arabic *ḏrr* "scatter, sprinkle" (see also *HALOT*, 1.283), which in turn seems to be a byform of the more widespread Semitic root *ḏry* "scatter." This latter root is known from Ugaritic *ḏry*, Aramaic *ḏry*, and Hebrew *zry*. But if this etymology is accepted for Hebrew *zrr* "sneeze," then we would expect *⋆drynwy* (*⋆drynwhy*) for *zrynwy* (*⋆zrynwhy*) in the Targum to Job 41:10 (compare the aforementioned root *ḏry* yielding Hebrew *zry*, Aramaic *ḏry*). The counter argument could claim that either (1) the presence of two *reš* in the root *ḏrr* affected the outcome of this root, so that even in Aramaic the root emerged as *zrr*, as in Hebrew; or (2) *zrynwy* (*⋆zrynwhy*) is a Hebraism in the Aramaic of the Targum to Job. Alternatively, one could dismiss Driver's etymology altogether—after all, "sneeze" is not exactly the same as "scatter, sprinkle"—and simply posit a root *zrr* attested once in Hebrew and once in Aramaic.

33. Cogan and Tadmor, *II Kings*, 58.

34. See also KB, 90. Other dictionaries, incorrectly in my opinion, list ʾōrōt in Isa 26:19 under ʾōrā[h] "light"; see BDB, 21; *HALOT*, 1.25; and *DCH*, 1.164.

concentration of IH features and, although it is not clear what is "northern" about Isaiah 26, the linguistic evidence is indisputable.[35]

The word *ʾôrā^h* is attested also in MH, albeit only in Amoraic sources, and rarely at that. It occurs in B. Yoma 18b to explain the plant name *gargîr*; and Bereshit Rabba 20 uses the masculine form *ʾôr* as a homiletical play on *ʿôr* "leather" in Gen 3:21 (referring to Adam and Eve's garments).[36]

Confirmation for the northern home of this word is forthcoming from its attestation in Ugaritic.[37] The form *ur* (in the masculine; note the aforecited text in Bereshit Rabba 20!) occurs twice, in *UT* 1 Aqht 66, 73.[38] The context makes it very clear that it is the name of a plant (see also below under *bṣql* in v. 42). In fact, both in our Kings passage and in the Aqht passage the context concerns drought.

Furthermore, it is very likely that the noun *ʾôrā^h* is related to the verb *ʾry* (*ʾrh*) "pluck." Note the following examples of nouns of the same *mišqal* as *ʾôrā^h* derived from IIIy verbs: *gôlā^h* "exile" from *gly*; *ʿôlā^h* "offering" from *ʿly*; and *sôʾā^h* "devastation" from *šʾy*. Thus, it is germane to point out that the verb *ʾry* "pluck" is, itself, a northern lexeme. It occurs in the Bible only in Ps 80:13 and Song 5:1, both northern compositions,[39] and it is more common in MH, though once more attested only in Amoraic sources.

Thus the evidence demonstrates that *ʾôrôt* in v. 39, to be translated as "herbs, sprouts, growth" or the like, is a northern feature.[40]

[12]

Another unusual plant name in v. 39 is *paqqûʿôt*, typically rendered "wild gourds" (thus NJPSV). This is the sole biblical reference to the word, whereas it is attested four times in the MH corpus (e.g., M. Shabbat 2:2).[41] In addition, cognate forms are known in most Aramaic dialects.[42]

Also germane is the noun *pĕqāʿîm* in 1 Kgs 6:18, 7:24, referring, most likely, to gourd-shaped carvings adorning the Temple. As noted previously, from

---

35. See S. Noegel, "Dialect and Politics in Isaiah 24–27," *AuOr* 12 (1994) 177–92.

36. Jastrow, *Dictionary*, 1.32–33.

37. For extensive discussion with ample bibliography, see B. Margalit, *The Ugaritic Poem of AQHT* (BZAW 182; Berlin: Walter de Gruyter, 1989) 394–96.

38. The word *ur* occurs also in *UT* 76:1:11, but the text is badly broken and does not allow a certain interpretation.

39. I neglected to include this evidence vis-à-vis Psalm 80 in my *Psalms* book.

40. Jastrow, *Dictionary*, 1.118.

41. HDHL, 076/15450; see also Jastrow, *Dictionary*, 2.1208.

42. Brockelmann, *Lexicon Syriacum*, 590; and Sokoloff, *Dictionary*, 443.

the high concentration of Phoenician forms in 1 Kings 6–8, it is apparent that Phoenician scribes were responsible for the Temple-building account. And, although *pĕqāʿîm* is not attested in Phoenician, the evidence points to a northern home for this lexeme.

Moreover, it is clear that the verb *pqʿ* "split"—unattested in the Bible—was characteristic of northern Hebrew. It is relatively common in MH, occurring fourteen times in the Qal (e.g., M. Zevahim 9:6[3×]) and nine times in the Hiphʿil (e.g., T. Yadayim 1:14).[43] It was used widely in Aramaic as well.[44] The noun *paqqûʿôt* "wild gourds" most likely gained its name from the manner in which the vegetable was split open to cook and eat it.

The evidence presented here demonstrates that this is a northern usage.

[13]

The verb *plḥ* "cut, split" in v. 39 occurs in the Bible only in northern compositions. Apart from the present passage, it appears in Ps 141:7, Prov 7:23, Job 16:13, 39:3.[45]

A cognate appears in Aramaic, where the root *plḥ* occurs occasionally with the meaning "cut, split," e.g., B. ʿAvoda Zara 18a.[46] (A verb *plḥ* "work, worship" is very common in Aramaic, but the two verbs should be kept distinct.) JH has several equivalent verbs, most prominently *ntḥ* distributed throughout the corpus, but also *btr*, though attested only in Gen 15:10(2×). The evidence points to the northern home of this lexical feature.[47]

[14]

A famous instance of an Ugaritic-Hebrew correspondence is the identification of Ugaritic *bṣql* with Hebrew *bṣqlnw*, thus the consonantal text in v. 42. The Masoretic text vocalizes the latter as *bĕṣiqlônô*, as the tradents appear to have understood the initial *bet* as the preposition "in." U. Cassuto was the first

---

43. *HDHL*, 076/15449–50; see also Jastrow, *Dictionary*, 2.1210; and M. Moreshet, *Leqsiqon ha-Poʿal she-Nitḥadesh bi-Lshon ha-Tannaʾim* (Ramat-Gan: Bar-Ilan University Press, 1980) 286–87. The noun *peqaʿat* "coil of rope," occurring nine times in MH, e.g., M. Kelim 10:4, appears to be unrelated. For citations, see *HDHL*, 076/15550; and Jastrow, *Dictionary*, 2.1211.

44. Jastrow, *Dictionary*, 2.1210; and Sokoloff, *Dictionary*, 443.

45. BDB, 812; and KB, 761. For fuller treatment, see *HALOT*, 3.930. I neglected to include this lexeme in my discussion of Psalm 141 in Rendsburg, *Psalms*, 99–102.

46. Jastrow, *Dictionary*, 2.1178.

47. The noun form *pelaḥ* "millstone, slice of fruit," by contrast, was used throughout ancient Hebrew.

to show the connection between the two literatures.[48] Ugaritic *bṣql* occurs in *UT* 1 Aqht 62, 63, 64, 65 (and elsewhere),[49] where it clearly means "ear of grain" (it is replaced by the well-known word *šblt* in lines 69, 70, 71, 72). Furthermore, as was the case with *'ōrōt* above, the context in the Aqhat epic, as in our Kings pericope, concerns drought. The lexeme *běṣiqlōnô* in 2 Kgs 4:42 must also mean "ear of grain," in which case the form needs to be revocalized in some manner with the *bet* as an integral part of the word.

The pronunciation of the word is unknown, although **baṣqel* is an educated guess (cf. similar forms such as the immediately preceding word *karmel*).

I take this opportunity to propose an explanation for the final *-nw* of the Masoretic text. Most likely this is an example of final *-m* being confused with the ligature *-nw*.[50] If this is correct, we can assume an original reading *bṣqlm*, that is, the plural form of *bṣql*. We would then have a trio of phrases, *leḥem bikkûrîm*, *'eśrîm leḥem śĕ'ōrîm*, and *karmel baṣqelîm* (the last word with reconstructed vocalization), each having a singular noun followed by a plural noun ending in *-îm*.

Regardless of the details involved in the equation of Ugaritic *bṣql* and Hebrew *bṣqlnw*, it is quite clear that the latter represents an IH lexical feature in the biblical text.

[15]

Verse 43 contains two instances of the infinitive absolute used as a finite verb: *'ākôl wĕhôtēr* "They shall eat and have some left over" in the mouth of Elisha quoting God. For this usage see our discussion above, at 1 Kings 22 [6].

---

48. U. Cassuto, "Daniele e le spighe. Un episodio della tavola ID di Ras Shamra," *Orientalia* 8 (1939) 238–43 (English version in U. Cassuto, *Biblical and Oriental Studies*, 2 vols. [trans. I. Abrahams; Jerusalem: Magnes Press, 1975] 2.193–98). For recent treatments, see H. R. (C.) Cohen, *Biblical Hapax Legomena in the Light of Akkadian and Ugaritic* (SBLDS 37; Missoula, Mont.: Scholars Press, 1978) 112–13; and Margalit, *The Ugaritic Poem of AQHT*, 389–92.

49. *UT*, 375; and *DLU*, 1.118.

50. See R. Weiss, "On Ligatures in the Hebrew Bible (*nw* = *-m*)," *JBL* 82 (1963) 188–94.

2 KINGS 5

[1]

The word *ʾahălê* "would that" in v. 3 occurs in the mouth of a north Israelite girl captured by the Arameans. It is a rare word in the Bible, occurring again only in Ps 119:5, with the variant pronunciation *ʾahălay*. The form is attested twice in Ugaritic, in *UT* 1 Aqht 64, 71.[1] The combination of rare usage in the northern stories in Kings and the twofold attestation in Ugaritic points to this form being a northern vocable. Of course, such a statement ignores the presence of *ʾahălay* in Ps 119:5. Note, however, that Psalm 119 is a post-exilic composition;[2] most likely we are dealing with a northern lexeme that found a home in LBH upon the reunion of the northern and southern exiles.[3]

[2]

The form *běhištahăwāyātî* "in my bowing down" in v. 18, in the mouth of Naaman the Aramean army commander, bears an ending akin to Aramaic morphology.[4] The expected Hebrew form would be *běhištahăwôtî*. This may be an attempt at style-switching, i.e., the speech of Naaman the Aramean has been colored by an Aramaic form, in which case this example may not belong properly to the present study (i.e., a Judahite author could have used the term as easily as an Israelian author). However, since it is possible that a Hebrew subdialect of the north utilized the ending known from Aramaic, I include this example in the present study.

---

1. *UT*, 354; and *DLU*, 1.16.

2. Hurvitz, *Beyn Lashon le-Lashon*, 130–52.

3. Schniedewind and Sivan ("Elisha-Elijah Narratives," 320) included this form in their list of unique linguistic features that could not, however, be utilized for identifying northern Hebrew.

4. See Burney, *Kings*, 208. For the Aramaic evidence of a general nature, see Dalman, *Grammatik*, 349–50, 393, 406–7. However, an exact counterpart to the form in 2 Kgs 5:18 is not presented in Dalman; that is, there are no examples of a T-stem infinitive of a IIIy verb with the 1st person common singular pronominal suffix. Nevertheless, it is clear what such a form would have looked like.

96

[3]

In v. 25 the interrogative "whence" occurs in the Ketiv as *m'n* = *mēʾān*. The Qeri reads the standard form *mēʾayin*. The proposed vocalization *mēʾān* can be inferred on the basis of two other occurrences in the Bible: 1 Sam 10:14 *ʾān* "where?" and Job 8:2 *ʿad ʾān* "how long?" In addition, note the common MH interrogative *lĕʾān* "whither?" The passage in 1 Kings is in the mouth of Elisha; the passage in 1 Samuel is in the mouth of Saul's uncle, presumably a Benjaminite; and the Job passage occurs in a book with its well-known Transjordanian setting. This distribution, coupled with the MH form *lĕʾān*, demonstrates the northern nature of *ʾān* as a free-standing form or with prepositions attached.

The phonology behind this form fits within a much larger understanding of the phonology of IH. The proto-form includes the diphthong *ay* (cf. Arabic *ʾayna* "where?"), which, in this case, is contracted not to the usual *ê* but to *ā*. This feature is attested in other non-Judahite contexts, for example, Job 9:9 *ʿāš* "Ursa Major" and Ps 141:5 *yānî* "my wine." The feature is more common in Aramaic dialects (and also stretches back in the general area of Syria to Amorite in the second millennium BCE and to Eblaite in the third millennium BCE) and, in fact, can be witnessed to this day in certain Arabic dialects of Lebanon and northern Israel. All this demonstrates that *ʾān*, in particular, and the monophthongization of *ay* > *ā*, in general, is characteristic of IH.[5]

---

5. For a detailed treatment, see G. A. Rendsburg, "Monophthongization of *aw/ ay* > *ā* in Eblaite and in Northwest Semitic," *Eblaitica* 2 (1990) 91–126. See now also Schniedewind and Sivan, "Elijah-Elisha Narratives," 333.

2 KINGS 6

[1]

The root *gzr* "cut" is attested throughout BH. But with the specific meaning of cutting down trees, it occurs only here, in v. 4. Cogan and Tadmor already commented: "The use of the verb here may reflect northern dialectal usage."[1] Although this verbal usage does not continue in MH, two nominal forms from this root, *gezer* and *gāzîr*, both meaning "log, club," are well attested in Tannaitic sources (10 times and 9 times, respectively).[2]

The JH equivalent is the root *krt*, which is well distributed throughout the Bible in a variety of connotations, including the cutting down of trees or the cutting of wood (e.g., Deut 19:5, 20:19, 20:20, 1 Kgs 5:20[2×], 6:36, 7:2, 7:12, 2 Kgs 19:23 = Isa 37:24, Isa 14:8, 44:14, Jer 6:6).

Aramaic utilizes the root *gzr* in a variety of contexts where Hebrew prefers *krt*.[3] The best known of these is covenant terminology. Whereas Hebrew uses *kārôt běrît* "cut a covenant," Aramaic uses *gězar ʿădāyāʾ* "cut a covenant."[4] Although I have not found an example of the Aramaic verb *gzr* in the context of cutting wood (the Targumim use *qṣṣ* to render Hebrew *krt* in such cases),[5] Aramaic does utilize the noun form *gizrāʾ* for "log, club."[6]

The evidence points to the correctness of Cogan and Tadmor's statement.[7]

---

1. Cogan and Tadmor, *II Kings*, 69.

2. *HDHL*, 031/6251–53. Sample attestations are, respectively, M. Sheqalim 6:6 and T. Sheqalim 1:12.

3. For a sampling of usages, see Jastrow, *Dictionary*, 1.231–32; *DNWSI*, 1.220; and Beyer, *Die aramäischen Texte vom Toten Meer*, 542.

4. As noted by Cogan and Tadmor, *II Kings*, 69.

5. The root is used thus also in MH. For both the MH and Aramaic evidence, see Jastrow, *Dictionary*, 2.1407–8.

6. Jastrow, *Dictionary*, 1.232.

7. See also Schniedewind and Sivan, "Elijah-Elisha Narratives," 330–31.

[2]

In the same story as the above example, the verb *qṣb* "cut," again referring to the cutting of wood, occurs in v. 6. This verb appears only here and in Song 4:2 in BH; in the latter passage the context is shorn sheep. The derived noun *qeṣeb* means "shape," that is, "something cut," in 1 Kgs 6:25, 7:37. These passages occur in the description of the construction of the Temple, a section of the Bible in which one finds a good number of Phoenicianisms, thus yielding the conclusion that these chapters were composed by Phoenician scribes. Although the context is not perfectly clear, the root *qṣb* occurs in one Punic text, *KAI* 145:9.[8] In MH the root is more common; it occurs 17 times in the corpus (12 times in the Qal, 5 times in the Piʿel), with a wide range of meanings, not only "cut," but also "decide, determine."[9] All of this suggests that *qṣb* is an IH feature.[10]

[3]

On the syntagma *hyh* + participle in the phrase *ûmelek ʾărām hāyāʰ nilḥām bĕyiśrāʾēl* "and the king of Aram was fighting against Israel" in v. 8, see our discussion above, at 1 Kings 22 [7].

[4]

Scholars are in agreement that the word *taḥănôtî* in v. 8 is a most unusual form. The typical approach is textual emendation.[11] However, as Burney pointed out,[12] Targum Yonatan understood the word as "my camp" with its rendering *byt mšrnʾ*. There is no reason to reject this understanding. Therefore, alongside the common noun *maḥăneʰ* "camp," formed by preformative *m-* affixed to the root *ḥnh*, Hebrew admitted the variant form with preformative *t-*. There are no parallels to this lexeme in all ancient Hebrew or Northwest Semitic.

---

8.   Scholars disagree as to whether *qṣb* here (actually the word is *ʿqṣb*) is a noun ("carved stone," "statue," or the like) or a verb (that is, "cut") in this text. For discussion, see *DNWSI*, 2.1021.

9.   *HDHL*, 080/16284–85; see also Jastrow, *Dictionary*, 2.1404.

10. The sole remaining instance of the root in BH, namely, *qiṣbê hārîm* "extremities of the mountains" in Jon 2:7, is most likely from the same root but with a very specific meaning. Accordingly, one should not attempt to relate this usage to the present discussion.

11. See Burney, *Kings*, 285; Montgomery and Gehman, *Kings*, 382; and *HALOT* 4.1719, for a sampling of possibilities.

12. Burney, *Kings*, 285.

As noted in the Introduction, uniqueness alone does not allow us to claim that a rare feature in a northern text is automatically a northern trait. But in the present instance this would seem to be the best solution, that is, to assume that the word is an IH vocable.[13] I incline toward this conclusion for the lexical aspect of this word because of the stronger evidence vis-à-vis the morphology of *taḥănôtî*. I refer to the fact that the pronominal suffix *-î* instructs us that the base noun *taḥănôt* is singular, specifically feminine singular. If the form were plural, the pronominal suffix would be *-ay*. Especially comparable to *taḥănôtî* "my camp" in 2 Kgs 6:8 is the form *ʿēdôtî* "my testimony" in Ps 132:12, also with the pronominal suffix *-î*, appearing in a northern poem.[14]

The f. sg. suffix *-ôt* is part of a much larger context in Hebrew. The original form of the ending is *-at*. However, in this case, unlike the normal shift of *-at* > *-āʰ*, the shift of *-at* > *-ot* (*-ôt*) transpired.

The ending *-ôt* is the result of two phenomena known from Phoenician. First, the f. sg. nominal ending *-at* does not shift to *-āʰ* as in Hebrew. Second, the short *a*-vowel when accented shifts to *ō* (I use the macron because we are unsure of the quantity of the Phoenician vowel [long or short], though I use the circumflex in transliterating Hebrew words because the laws of Hebrew phonology inform us that the vowel is treated as if it were long).[15] Accordingly, we are able to place the IH feature *-ôt* in f. sg. nouns into a larger context.

Biblical examples include the following forms:[16] Judg 5:29, Prov 14:1 *ḥakmôt* "wise lady"; Ps 16:11, 45:16 *śĕmāḥôt* "joy"; Ps 45:1 *yĕdîdôt* "love"; Ps 53:7 *yĕšûʿôt* "salvation"; Ps 73:22 *bĕhēmôt* "beast" (and probably always when the word refers to the hippopotamus, an animal native to the northern Jordan Valley); Ps 76:11, Prov 22:24 *ḥēmôt* "wrath"; Ps 132:12 *ʿēdôt* "testimony";

---

13. Schniedewind and Sivan ("Elijah-Elisha Narratives," 322), by contrast, included this word in their list of unique linguistic features, without assigning it as a northernism.

14. Rendsburg, *Psalms*, 87–90.

15. For the f. sg. nominal ending in Phoenician, see Segert, *A Grammar of Phoenician and Punic*, 110, 114–15. For the shift of accented short *a* to *ō*, see Friedrich and Röllig, *Phönizisch-punische Grammatik*, 29–30, 106–7. For a full discussion of all the pertinent data relevant to this shift, notwithstanding a contrary conclusion, see A. Dotan, "Stress Position and Vowel Shift in Phoenician and Punic," *IOS* 6 (1976) 71–121. Finally, see now J. Fox, "A Sequence of Vowel Shifts in Phoenician and Other Languages," *JNES* 55 (1996) 37–47.

16. See already Rendsburg, *Psalms*, 32; and Rendsburg, "Morphological Evidence," 79–80. However, in these earlier treatments I did not include the examples from Kings presented here.

Prov 1:20, 9:1 *ḥokmôt* "wisdom"; Prov 28:20 *ʾĕmûnôt* "faith"; Qoh 1:17, 2:12, 7:25, 9:3 *hôlēlôt* "madness." These Psalms are all northern poems; Judges 5 is one of the most widely recognized northern compositions; and Proverbs and Qohelet are two books of northern provenance.

In summary, although I cannot demonstrate that the base noun of *taḥănôtî* is clearly an IH trait, I surmise that it is.[17] More certain is the conclusion that the f. sg. nominal ending *-ôt* is an IH element, representing an important isogloss with Phoenician.

For an additional example of this phenomenon in Kings, see our discussion below, at 2 Kings 10 [3].

[5]

Another unique usage is the word *nĕḥittîm* "descending" in v. 9. Many scholars emend the word to a vocable based on the root *ḥbʾ* "hide" or with a more specific military meaning "ambush," with support from the ancient versions.[18] But there is no need for such a major manipulation of the Masoretic Text. P. Joüon offered a less drastic emendation, positing an active participle *nôḥătîm* "descending."[19] Although I reject the need for Joüon's emendation as well, his proposal is most helpful in pointing the direction to the proper solution.

In Aramaic the passive participle of the verb takes the *qĕtîl* form; moreover, the passive participle often carries active meaning.[20] In MH, the passive participle is, as in BH, of the *qātûl* form, but the same syntactic development can be seen regularly.[21] One such example occurs in IH as well, namely Song 3:8 *ʾăḥûzê ḥereb* "skilled in the sword."[22]

---

17. Most likely, whether this form is an IH feature or not, it was chosen to enhance the alliteration with *nĕḥittîm* "descending" in v. 9, on which see immediately below. Note that *taḥănôtî* echoes all three consonants of *nĕḥittîm*, whereas SBH *maḥăneh* would echo only two of them.

18. See, e.g., Burney, *Kings*, 285; and the discussion in Montgomery and Gehman, *Kings*, 382.

19. P. Joüon, "Notes de critique textuelle (AT) 2 Rois 6, 8–10," *MUSJ* 5 (1911–12) 477.

20. Nöldeke, *Compendious Syriac Grammar*, 220; and Margolis, *A Manual of the Aramaic Language of the Babylonian Talmud*, 82.

21. Segal, *Grammar*, 160–61; and Segal, *Diqduq*, 133–34. The most detailed treatment is that of Y. Blau, "Benoni Paʿul be-Horaʾa ʾAqtivit," *Leshonenu* 18 (1952–53) 67–81.

22. See M. V. Fox, *The Song of Songs and the Ancient Egyptian Love Songs* (Madison: University of Wisconsin Press, 1985) 124. Blau, "Benoni Paʿul be-Horaʾa

In light of this information, I propose that *nĕḥittîm* "descending" in 2 Kgs 6:9 is a form akin to the Aramaic passive participle, but with active sense.

One problem remains, namely, the presence of the *dagesh* in the *taw* of *nĕḥittîm*. However, there are parallels to this phenomenon. David Qimhi pointed out long ago that "a Dagesh in the final consonant sometimes replaces the long vowel of the second radical, e.g., *šĕʿippîm* Jb 4:13, *nĕḥittîm* 2K 6:9, *ḥăbittîm* 1 Chr 9:31."[23] Although there may not be another example of the m. pl. passive participle receiving this treatment (Qimhi's example of Prov 24:31 *ḥărullîm* is not totally convincing), the doubling is present in similar forms, e.g., *ʾădummîm* and *nĕquddîm*.

Alternatively, one may wish to posit a confusion between *nĕḥittîm* and the Niphʿal of the root *ḥtt* "terrorize" (attested once in Mal 2:5), a meaning that fits the context of 2 Kgs 6:9 as well. This confusion would have led to the doubling of the *taw* in *nĕḥittîm* and the concomitant shortening of the preceding vowel from *î* to *i*.

On the lexical side, it is noteworthy that the root *nḥt* appears in the Bible, with the exception of the present instance, only in poetic texts. It should, therefore, be considered an element of "Hebrew poetic diction," that is, of a word that is common in Aramaic but that is reserved in Hebrew for poetic usage.[24] However, when such a word occurs in prose, as it does in 2 Kgs 6:9, it is proper to see the presence of the root *nḥt* "descend," instead of SBH *yrd* "descend," as evidence for IH. Furthermore, we may note, following Montgomery and Gehman, that the root *nḥt* is frequently used in military

---

ʾAqtivit," 72, proposed two other examples, in Isa 46:1 and Neh 4:12, but I do not find either example convincing. In the former, it is not clear if the word in question refers to the idols or to the animals (as Blau admitted); see NJPSV as an example of interpreting the word as passive. And without wishing to think in English, note that the second example is the exact equivalent of English "girded," expressed in the passive. But even if Blau were granted his point, I would explain these two examples as Aramaisms in the language of the exilic prophet and the post-exilic Nehemiah, both members of the Aramaic-speaking Babylonian Jewish community.

23. W. Chomsky, *David Kimhi's Hebrew Grammar (Mikhlol)* (New York: Bloch, 1952) 244.

24. See the classic statement by G. R. Driver, "Hebrew Poetic Diction," *Congress Volume Copenhagen 1953* (SVT 1; Leiden: E. J. Brill, 1953) 26–39, with this specific example noted on p. 30. Wagner, *Aramaismen*, 82–83, included *nḥt* in his list of Aramaisms, but the issue is more complicated than that simple statement. For examples of *nḥt* "descend" in Aramaic, see *DNWSI*, 2.726–27; and Jastrow, *Dictionary*, 2.897.

contexts in Syriac.[25] Finally, it is apposite to note the presence of the Ugaritic cognate *nḫt* "descend" (*UT* 52:37, 68:11, 68:18).[26]

In summary, the identification of *nĕḥittîm* in 2 Kgs 6:9 as an IH feature rests on three points: (1) the presence of the root *nḫt* in a prose text; (2) the *qĕtîl* form of the passive participle; and (3) the use of the passive participle in an active sense.[27]

[6]

In v. 11 the form *miššellānû* "from among us" includes the relative pronoun *še-*, appearing within the independent possessive pronoun *šel*.

The origin of the form *še-* has been widely discussed,[28] but one will agree with E. Y. Kutscher that "its use was common in the vernacular of Northern Palestine."[29] This conclusion is based on the cognate evidence and on the distribution of this form in IH texts. The cognate form *ʾš* occurs in Phoenician and Ammonite.[30] In pre-exilic biblical texts, *še-* is limited to northern contexts: the Song of Deborah (Judg 5:7[2×]), the Gideon cycle (Judg 6:17, 7:12, 8:26), and the aforecited example from the Elisha cycle (2 Kgs 6:11). Not until exilic and post-exilic times did *še-* penetrate to Judah (e.g., Lam 2:15, 2:16, 4:9, 5:18, Jon 1:7, 1:12, Ezra 8:20, 1 Chr 5:20, 27:27, various late psalms). Even in the later period, however, its most frequent appearance is in the northern compositions Qohelet and Song of Songs, as well as in the northern poem Psalm 133 (2 times [vv. 2 and 3]). Finally, in MH, representing a northern dialect of post-biblical times, *še-* is the only relative pronoun used.

As noted above, the form *miššellānû* in 2 Kgs 6:11 includes the independent possessive pronoun *šel* as well. This, in fact, is the earliest attestation of this usage in the Bible. Later occurrences are: Jon 1:7, 1:12, Song 1:6, 3:7, 8:12, Qoh 8:17. Again the usage is standard in MH. A parallel occurs in Aramaic *zyl/dyl*, thus also pointing to the northern nature of *šel*.[31]

---

25. Montgomery and Gehman, *Kings*, 382. See Payne Smith, *Dictionary*, 336, with "march, besiege" included among the more common definitions.

26. *UT*, 443.

27. Schniedewind and Sivan ("Elijah–Elisha Narratives," 325) included this item in their list of examples introduced into the text to provide an Aramaic setting.

28. I have discussed this form already in Rendsburg, *Psalms*, 91–92; and Rendsburg, "The Galilean Background of Mishnaic Hebrew," 228.

29. Kutscher, *A History of the Hebrew Language*, 32. See, earlier, Burney, *Kings*, 208; and recently Schniedewind and Sivan, "Elijah–Elisha Narratives," 328–30, though with some qualification.

30. See Garr, *Dialect Geography*, 85–86.

31. Avi Hurvitz *apud* Rendsburg, *Diglossia in Ancient Hebrew*, 123 n. 29, suggested

In sum, we accept the view expressed by Montgomery and Gehman that *še-* (and by extension *miššellānû*) is a "good N Israelite" usage.[32]

[7]

The unique form *ʾêkōʰ* "where?" appears in v. 13. Closely related is the form *ʾêkāʰ* "where?" appearing in the northern composition Song 1:7(2×) (see below for a possible additional example). Earlier in the century, Brown-Driver-Briggs and Burney identified this item as a northern lexeme,[33] and, more recently, Rabin concurred, labeling it a *milla ṣefonit muvheqet*.[34] The cognate evidence is forthcoming from Aramaic-Syriac, where the form *ʾêkāʾ/ hêkāʾ* "where?" occurs.[35] Also related, as Rabin posited, is the exceedingly common MH form *hêkān* "where?" attested 212 times in Tannaitic literature (including spellings with an *ʾaleph*, that is, *ʾêkān*).[36]

Rabin pointed to one additional biblical passage.[37] In Judg 20:3 the Israelites gathered at Mizpah ask, *ʾêkāʰ nihyātāʰ hārāʿāʰ hazzōʾt* "ʾêkāʰ did this evil happen?" The Levite who hailed from *har ʾeprayim* "the mount of Ephraim" (Judg 19:1) begins his response to this question with geographical information: *haggibʿātāʰ ʾăšer lĕbinyāmîn* "to Gibeah of Benjamin [I and my concubine came]" (Judg 20:4). For Rabin this exchange points to an understanding of the word *ʾêkāʰ* as "where?" again set in a northern context. I am not as convinced. However, if this interpretation is correct, then we have another attestation of *ʾêkāʰ* "where?" in northern Hebrew.

Regardless of the example of Judg 20:3, the evidence is clear that *ʾêkōʰ/ ʾêkāʰ*, attested for certain in 2 Kgs 6:13 and Song 1:7(2×), is an IH trait.[38]

---

that since *miššellānû* occurs in the mouth of the king of Aram, it operates as a calque on the Aramaic *zyl/dyl* in an attempt to capture the foreignness of the monarch's native Aramaic speech (what I have called style-switching). This is an alternative explanation of the presence of *miššellānû* in 2 Kgs 6:11.

32. Montgomery and Gehman, *Kings*, 383. Thus also Cogan and Tadmor, *II Kings*, 72.

33. BDB, 32; and Burney, *Kings*, 209. Both spoke of the Ketiv form *ʾêkāʰ* in 2 Kgs 6:13, though neither the Aleppo Codex nor the Leningrad Codex marks a Ketiv/Qeri pair at this verse.

34. Rabin, "Leshonam shel ʿAmos ve-Hosheaʿ," 123.

35. Jastrow, *Dictionary*, 1.47, 1.345; and Payne Smith, *Lexicon*, 13.

36. HDHL, 018/3573–77; see also Jastrow, *Dictionary*, 1.48, 1.345.

37. Rabin, "Leshonam shel ʿAmos ve-Hosheaʿ," 123–24.

38. Schniedewind and Sivan ("Elijah-Elisha Narratives," 324) opined that "the use of this term reflects the fact that the speaker is an Aramean." This is possible, but the fact that it occurs in other contexts points to a different conclusion.

[8]

On the use of the inflected form of the *nota accusativi*, namely *ʾôtām*, to replace the inflected form of the preposition *ʾet*, namely *ʾittām*, in v. 16, see our discussion above, at 1 Kings 20 [5].

[9]

In v. 19 the f. sg. demonstrative pronoun appears as *zôʰ* instead of the standard form *zôʾt*. Previous scholars have commented on the northern origin of this form (and its alternative spelling *zô*).[39] As *zôʰ*, the form appears in Qohelet six times (2:2, 2:24, 5:15, 5:18, 7:23, 9:13) and in Ezek 40:45. As *zô*, it appears in Hos 7:16 and Ps 132:12. With one exception, all these instances are in northern texts. Hosea is the best example of a northern prophet in the Bible; Qohelet is a book replete with northern elements; and Psalm 132 has a similar concentration of northern forms.[40] Only Ezekiel is not a northern composition, though this example could be explained by the reunion of northern and southern exiles in the sixth century BCE.

The cognate evidence supports the conclusion that *zô/zôʰ* is the IH counterpart to JH *zôʾt*. Cognate forms are attested in Phoenician and Aramaic,[41] and MH uses only the form *zô*. In light of this evidence, it is not surprising to find *zôʰ* used as the f. sg. demonstrative pronoun in 2 Kgs 6:19.[42]

[10]

The root *kry* (*krh*) occurs in v. 23 as a verb "make a feast" and as a noun "feast": *wayyikreʰ lāhem kērāʰ* "and he made for them a feast." The SBH equivalent

---

39. See, e.g., Burney, *Kings*, 208; Segal, *Grammar*, 41 (but no such statement in Segal, *Diqduq*, 49); and Kutscher, *A History of the Hebrew Language*, 31. See now also Schniedewind and Sivan, "Elijah-Elisha Narratives," 327.

40. Rendsburg, *Psalms*, 87–90.

41. The evidence for both languages is presented by Garr, *Dialect Geography*, 85.

42. I have excluded from consideration the three cases of the expression *kāzôʰ wĕkāzeʰ* "like this and like that" in Judg 18:4, 2 Sam 11:25, 1 Kgs 14:5. I judge this idiom to be a colloquialism that permeated spoken Hebrew irrespective of geography; see Rendsburg, *Diglossia in Ancient Hebrew*, 134.

Schniedewind and Sivan ("Elijah-Elisha Narratives," 327), by contrast, included these verses in their discussion of the northern quality of *zôʰ/zô*. I suspect they were driven by the fact that two of the three appear in northern contexts: Judg 18:4 in the story of Micah set in Ephraim and 1 Kgs 14:5 in the story of Ahijah of Shiloh. However, note that the former appears in the mouth of a Levite who was not native to the region of Ephraim (see v. 3) and the latter appears in the speech of YHWH to the prophet. Finally, the example of 2 Sam 11:25 is placed in the mouth of David.

ʿāśāʰ mišteʰ "made a feast" is well distributed throughout the corpus (Gen 19:3, 26:30, 40:20, Judg 14:10, 2 Sam 3:20, 1 Kgs 3:15, Esth 1:3).[43] The only other occurrence of this root in the Bible is in Prov 16:27, where the context indicates that kôreʰ means "cook" or the like.[44] The opposition with an SBH usage and the attestation of the verb in Proverbs combine to demonstrate that the root kry (krh) is an IH lexical item.

[11]

The measurement qāb occurs in v. 25 as a *hapax legomenon*. Its exact size is unknown and, therefore, we cannot identify with any certainty its JH equivalent. However, the word is extremely common in MH, attested 189 times,[45] and it is widespread in Aramaic.[46] This evidence alone points to the conclusion that qāb is an element of IH.[47]

[12]

In v. 27 we read mēʾayin ʾōšîʿēk hămin haggōren ʾô min hayyāqeb "From where could I save you? From the threshing floor? Or from the winepress?" The syntagma of hă-... ʾô in an extended question is an element of IH, as discussed above, at 2 Kings 4 [4].

[13]

The syntagma zôʾt hārāʿāʰ "this evil" in v. 33 has been discussed above, at 1 Kings 14 [3].

---

43. See also Schniedewind and Sivan, "Elijah-Elisha Narratives," 321.

44. See Chen, *Israelian Hebrew in the Book of Proverbs*, 139. See also M. Dahood, *Proverbs and Northwest Semitic Philology* (Rome: Pontifical Biblical Institute, 1963) 37.

45. *HDHL*, 078/15857–60.

46. *DNWSI*, 2.977; Jastrow, *Dictionary*, 2.1307; and Sokoloff, *Dictionary*, 472.

47. Schniedewind and Sivan ("Elijah-Elisha Narratives," 324) included this word in their list of features due to Aramaic influence.

2 KINGS 7

[1]

On the expression ʿal napšām "for their life" in v. 7, with the preposition ʿal for an expected ʾel, see our discussion above, at 1 Kings 13 [4].

[2]

On the use of "one" for the indefinite article in ʾōhel ʾeḥād "a tent" in v. 8, see our discussion above, at 1 Kings 13 [3].

[3]

The form bhśdh "in the field" in the mouth of an Israelian king (which one is not altogether certain) occurs in the Ketiv of v. 12. This usage reflects non-elision of the definite article (h) following a uniconsonantal prefixed preposition (b, l, k). This irregularity occurs elsewhere in the Bible: 1 Sam 13:21, Ezek 40:25, 47:22, Ps 36:6, Qoh 8:1, Neh 9:19, 12:38, 2 Chr 10:7, 25:10, 29:27.[1] The only parallel usage to the non-elision of he in this environment within the Canaanite sphere is its appearance in Punic, where it occurs eight times, e.g., *KAI* 130:3: bhšt "in the year."[2] Although this phenomenon does not occur in any standard Phoenician texts, we, nevertheless, suspect that it was native to some northern Canaanite dialects.[3]

---

1. I exclude from consideration 2 Sam 21:20, 21:22 lĕhārāpāʰ = 1 Chr 20:6, 20:8 lĕhārāpāʾ, where the he is apparently considered part of the title; Dan 8:16 lĕhallāz, where the he is an essential part of the demonstrative pronoun; and the eight cases of kĕhayyôm "on this particular day," which is used to distinguish it from kayyôm "now."

2. Friedrich and Röllig, *Phönizisch-punische Grammatik*, 53; and Segert, *A Grammar of Phoenician and Punic*, 108 (I do not understand what Segert meant by "in these instances the article was probably restored").

3. See already Burney, *Kings*, 209; and R. C. Steiner, *The Case for Fricative-Laterals in Proto-Semitic* (AOS 59; New Haven: American Oriental Society, 1977) 43 and 55 n. 42. For my earlier treatments, see Rendsburg, *Psalms*, 40; and Rendsburg, "The Northern Origin of Nehemiah 9," 356. For an alternative view, see Schniedewind and Sivan, "Elijah-Elisha Narratives," 317–18.

In 1 Sam 13:21 the action occurs in the territory of Benjamin and the story concerns the kingship of Saul; Ps 36:6 occurs in a psalm with many northern affinities;[4] Qoh 8:1 appears in a northern book; and Neh 9:19 occurs in a chapter whose northern provenance has been demonstrated.[5] When we add 2 Kgs 7:12K to our list, we note that five of the eleven biblical attestations of this usage occur in northern texts, a sufficient proportion to enable us to identify this phenomenon as a characteristic of IH.

The remaining six passages are in exilic or post-exilic compositions. Here we may appeal again to Gordon's hypothesis that late biblical literature evinces northern grammatical features due to the reunion of Israelian exiles and Judahite exiles in Mesopotamia in the sixth century BCE. In addition, two of these passages, though in clear Judahite contexts, may utilize the form with non-elision of the *he* for literary purposes to indicate foreignness or northernness. Ezek 47:22 *ûlĕhaggērîm* "and for the foreigners" presumably refers to specific Canaanite (Phoenician?) elements in the land of Canaan, especially in light of the northern boundary postulated in Ezek 47:15–17. 2 Chr 25:10 *lĕhaggĕdûd* "for the company" refers specifically to an Ephraimite military unit.

---

4. Rendsburg, *Psalms*, 37–43.

5. Rendsburg, "The Northern Origin of Nehemiah 9."

2 KINGS 8

[1]

On the Ketiv *'ty* for the 2 f. sg. independent personal pronoun in v. 1, see our discussion above, at 1 Kings 14 [2].

[2]

Twice in v. 3, we find the preposition *'el* for an expected *'al: wattēṣē' liṣ'ōq 'el hammelek 'el bêtāh wĕ'el śādāh* "She went out to scream at the king about her house and about her field." See our discussion above, at 1 Kings 13 [4].

[3]

On the use of "one" as the indefinite article in *sārîs 'eḥād* "a eunuch" in v. 6, see our discussion above, at 1 Kings 13 [3].

[4]

On the use of the inflected form of the *nota accusativi*, namely *mē'ōtô*, to replace the inflected form of the preposition *'et*, namely *mē'ittô*, in v. 8, see our discussion above, at 1 Kings 20 [5].

[5]

Twice in this chapter, in vv. 8 and 9, King Ben-Hadad of Aram uses the expression *ḥŏlî ze*^{h} "this illness." In the first case, he speaks these words directly to Hazael and, in the second case, Hazael quotes the king in speaking to Elisha. On this usage, with the expected definite article lacking from both the noun and the modifying demonstrative pronoun, see our discussion above, at 2 Kings 1 [1].

[6]

On the preterite use of the *yqtl* form of the verb in v. 29, in the phrase *'ăšer yakkûhû 'ărammîm* "which the Arameans had inflicted upon him," see our discussion above, at 1 Kings 20 [8]. Many exegetes propose emending the prefix conjugation form *yakkûhû* to the suffix conjugation form *hikkûhû*,[1] and, indeed, that is how the parallel passage in 2 Chr 22:6 reads. But in light of the distribution of this usage, along with the cognate evidence, we accept the text as an accurate reflection of the northern dialect of ancient Hebrew. Centuries after this text was written, the thoroughly Judean redactor of Chronicles altered the form to the expected *qtl* verb.

This passage does not occur within the story about a northern king, but is introduced here, in 2 Kgs 8:29, within the context of the reign of Ahaziah king of Judah. Note the following, however: (1) the subject of the sentence is Joram king of Israel; (2) the line is repeated virtually verbatim in 2 Kgs 9:15 (see below) within a purely Israelian context; and (3) Ahaziah is the Judahite king with the most intimate contacts with the north, viz., his mother was Athaliah daughter of Omri. In short, there is sufficient evidence to permit the above conclusion that the preterite use of the *yqtl* form *yakkûhû* in 2 Kgs 8:29 is a feature of IH.

---

1. E.g., Montgomery and Gehman, *Kings*, 398; and *BHS, ad loc.*

2 KINGS 9

[1]

The confusion of *ʾel* and *ʿal* occurs four times in this chapter. In v. 3 we read: *mĕšaḥtîkā lĕmelek ʾel yiśrāʾēl* "I anoint you as king over Israel"; in the first part of v. 6 we read *wayyíṣoq haššemen ʾel rôʾšô* "and he poured the oil on his head"; and in the latter part of v. 6 we read *mĕšaḥtîkā lĕmelek ʾel ʿam YHWH ʾel yiśrāʾēl* "I anoint you as king over the people of YHWH, over Israel" (with two examples). On this usage, see our discussion above, at 1 Kings 13 [4].

[2]

In vv. 10, 36, 37, the word *ḥēleq* is used as "field" in the expression *ḥēleq yizrĕʿeʾl* "field of Jezreel," referring to the locale of Jezebel's death.[1] The normal meaning of this word is "lot, fate, portion, allotment." The only clear occurrences of *ḥēleq* = "field" in the Bible are the three instances here in 2 Kings 9 and one in Amos 7:4.[2] The Amos passage is in a northern context.

Two additional passages in which *ḥēleq* may mean "field" are Hos 5:7 and Mic 2:4. If the former is understood in this manner, then once more we are dealing with a northern composition. In the Micah passage, most likely the surface meaning of *ḥēleq* is "fate," since *ḥēleq ʿammî* "fate of my people" is an expected phrase. However, since the prophet uses *śādênû yĕḥallēq* "our field he divides" later in the verse, the meaning *ḥēleq* = "field" also can be sensed.

---

1. There are difficulties in placing Jezebel's death in a "field," because she meets her death when her eunuchs throw her from a palace window, after which her blood splatters on a *qîr* "wall" and her body is trampled by horses. I would explain *ḥēleq* here not as "field" in the sense of "open field," but rather as "courtyard," the open area in the palace complex that included the royal stables. Other scholars prefer to emend *ḥēleq* to *ḥēl* "rampart," as in 1 Kgs 21:23 (see the discussion in Cogan and Tadmor, *II Kings*, 112–13). But the text should stand and be explained as above. See further the next note.

2. BDB, 324; and KB, 307. Another possible attestation is achieved through emending *ḥēl* in 1 Kgs 21:23 (see previous note) to *ḥēleq*, in accordance with some Hebrew manuscripts and Targum Yonatan (thus, for example, NJPSV). If this emendation is correct, note that once more the context is Israelian.

Micah is a Judahite author, so, in his poetry, the prophet may be taking advantage of a meaning not used in Judah regularly, but one that was recognizable to his Judahite audience through contact with Israelians. Thus, regardless of how one interprets Mic 2:4, the overall picture shows that *ḥēleq* = "field" is a northern usage.

Support for this view is forthcoming from Aramaic, in which the metathesized form *ḥql* is the standard word for "field" (see also Akkadian *eqlu*). This is true for all Aramaic dialects in antiquity.[3] Note, for example, that the Targumim regularly translate Hebrew *śādeʰ* with Aramaic *ḥql*.

To complete the discussion it is necessary to note that one other Hebrew text uses *ḥēleq* as "field," namely, 1QM 12:12: *ḥmwn mqnh bḥlqwtykh* "hordes of cattle in your fields." There is nothing in the War Scroll specifically nor in the Dead Sea Scrolls generally that points to a northern context; furthermore the scrolls were discovered in the Judean Desert. The best explanation for this usage is Aramaic influence.

[3]

The word *gerem* in the phrase *gerem hammaʿălôt* in v. 13 has engendered much discussion. The simplest solution is to recognize that "*gerem*, 'bone,' like its synonym *ʿeṣem*, may mean 'substance, self'; thus 'the steps themselves' (so Ibn-Janah) or the 'bare steps' (Gesenius, Ewald)."[4] I accept this opinion and, thus, view the word *gerem* here as "substance, self," derived from its base meaning "bone."

Elsewhere in the Bible *gerem* means just "bone," but the distribution points clearly to a northern home. In Gen 49:14 the word occurs in Jacob's blessing to Issachar, one of the northern tribes.[5] The additional attestations in Prov 17:22, 25:15, Job 40:18 are in non-Judahite settings.

Moreover, the cognate *garmāʾ* is the standard word for both "bone" and "self" in Aramaic.[6] Hence, once more we have an excellent example of a lexical feature shared by IH and Aramaic. It is, therefore, not surprising to encounter *gerem* in a portion of Kings relating the story of King Jehu.

---

3. *DNWSI*, 1.401; Beyer, *Die aramäischen Texte vom Toten Meer*, 584; Sokoloff, *Dictionary*, 213; Jastrow, *Dictionary*, 1.497; and Payne Smith, *Dictionary*, 252.

4. Cogan and Tadmor, *II Kings*, 108. See also Montgomery and Gehman, *Kings*, 404–5.

5. For my earlier treatment, see G. A. Rendsburg, "Israelian Hebrew Features in Genesis 49," in *Let Your Colleagues Praise You: Studies in Memory of Stanley Gevirtz*, 2 vols. (eds. R. J. Ratner, L. M. Barth, M. L. Gevirtz, and B. Zuckerman) = *Maarav* 7–8 (1991/92) 2.163–64.

6. KB, 1062; Jastrow, *Dictionary*, 1.270; and Sokoloff, *Dictionary*, 136.

[4]

On the use of the prefix-conjugation form *yakkûhû* with preterite meaning in v. 15, see our discussion above, at 2 Kings 8 [6].

[5]

The word *šipʿat* "multitude" in v. 17(2×) occurs in a story about the northern kings Jehoram and Jehu. The second of these, placed in the mouth of an Israelian scout, appears in the absolute state. The morphology of this word retains the f. sg. nominal ending -*at* in the absolute state, as occurs in most Canaanite dialects (JH and Deir ʿAlla are two exceptions), in Aramaic in nouns derived from IIIw/y roots,[7] and in biblical passages with an overwhelmingly Israelian distribution.[8] The Masora retains the ending in one of two forms: -*āt* with *qameṣ* or -*at* with *pataḥ*.

Five examples appear in northern psalms: *gaʾăwat* "haughtiness" in Ps 10:2,[9] *mĕnāt* "portion" in Ps 16:5, *naḥălāt* "heritage" in Ps 16:6, *ḥayyat* "beast" in Ps 74:19, and *šĕnat* "sleep" in Ps 132:4. The musical instruments *maḥălat* in Ps 53:1, 88:1 and *nĕgînat* in Ps 61:1 may have been borrowed from Canaanites who preserved the -*at* suffix. The form *mĕʾat* "hundred" in Qoh 8:12 appears in a northern composition. There has been much discussion about the word *pōrāt* in Gen 49:22, though most of it has concentrated on the meaning of the word—I follow S. Gevirtz's translation of *pōrāt* as "she-ass."[10] Of particular interest is the fact that this word, which retains the -*at* ending, appears specifically in Jacob's blessing to Joseph, who represents a significant segment of northern Israel. In addition, Jeremiah utilizes the words *yitrat* "abundance" in Jer 48:36 and *tĕhillāt* "praise" in Jer 49:25Q in speeches aimed at Moab and Damascus, respectively.

The evidence from toponyms that retain -*at*/-*āt* is also germane, in that they are concentrated in the north: two in Asher (*ḥelqat*, *libnāt*), three in Naphtali (*ḥammat*, *ʾănāt*, *raqqat*), one in Issachar (*ʾănāḥărāt*), one in Zebulun (*dābrat*), one in Ephraim (*mikmĕtāt*), and two in Transjordan (*tabbāt*, *qĕnāt*).

---

7. Garr, *Dialect Geography*, 59–60, 93–94; and Segert, *Altaramäische Grammatik*, 206–7.

8. For earlier treatments, see Rendsburg, *Psalms*, 23–24; and Rendsburg, "Israelian Hebrew Features in Genesis 49," 167–68; Schniedewind and Sivan ("Elijah-Elisha Narratives," 334) concurred.

9. See R. Gordis, "Psalm 9–10 — A Textual and Exegetical Study," *JQR* 48 (1958) 112.

10. S. Gevirtz, "Of Patriarchs and Puns: Joseph at the Fountain, Jacob at the Ford," *HUCA* 46 (1975) 35–40.

Other forms with the ending *-at/-āt* are to be explained by different means. The vocables *māḥŏrāt* "morrow" (25 times) and *rabbat* "much" (7 times) are adverbs for which the ending *-at/-āt* was felt to have an adverbial function and, thus, did not shift to *-āʰ*.[11] The form *zimrat* "strength/song" in Exod 15:2 appears in an early poem, dating presumably from a time before the shift of *-at >-āʰ*.[12] Other nouns are borrowings, e.g., *qēṣāt* "end" in Dan 1:2, 1:5, 1:15, 1:18, Neh 7:20, is an Aramaism, and *barqat* "emerald" in Ezek 28:13 is most likely an Akkadianism (cf. Akkadian *barraqtu*).

In summary, the f. sg. nominal ending *-at/-āt* is a feature shared by IH and Phoenician, Ammonite, etc.[13]

[6]

Apropos to the word just discussed, the root *špʿ* itself is an IH lexeme. The noun *šipʿāʰ* "multitude" (or as just noted, even as *šipʿat* in the absolute state) occurs twice in 2 Kgs 9:17, twice in Job (22:11, 38:34), once in the prophet Ezekiel's oracle to Tyre (26:10), and once in Second Isaiah (60:6). With the exception of the last case, all are in non-Judahite contexts. Even the last one can be incorporated into our schema, because the exilic prophet may have been influenced by Aramaic (for the Aramaic evidence, see below). Finally, another nominal form from this root, *šepaʿ* "abundance," occurs once in the Bible, specifically in Deut 33:19 within the joint blessing to Issachar and Zebulun.

The two noun forms are attested, though admittedly not very widely, in MH: *šepaʿ* occurs six times in Sifre Devarim 354 (and only here); *šipʿāʰ* occurs twice in the corpus, in parallel texts M. Sota 8:1 and Sifre Devarim 192.[14]

More generous evidence is forthcoming from Aramaic, in which the root is common, generating both nouns and verbs. In Galilean Aramaic, *špʿ* occurs

---

11. J. Blau, "The Parallel Development of the Feminine Ending *-at* in Semitic Languages," *HUCA* 51 (1980) 18.

12. On the early date of Exodus 15, see Robertson, *Linguistic Evidence in Dating Early Hebrew Poetry*, 153–56. The word *zimrāt* appears also in Isa 12:2, Ps 118:14 in the expression *ʿozzî wĕzimrāt yāh*. However, one can surmise that it is merely a fossilized form in the three-word phrase that apparently became a byword in ancient Israel.

13. Numerous scholars elect to emend *šipʿat* in 2 Kgs 9:17; thus, for example, *BHS*, *ad loc*. Cogan and Tadmor (*II Kings*, 109–10) resisted emendation and proposed an attractive alternative, namely, "the form might reflect the excited speech of the lookout" (p. 110).

14. *HDHL*, 089/18258. For additional attestations in Amoraic sources, see Jastrow, *Dictionary*, 2.1618–19.

in the ʾAphʿel form, meaning "give in abundance"; also attested are two nominal forms meaning "abundance, overflowing portion."[15] Babylonian Aramaic presents similar evidence, in addition to which there are several attestations of the verb in the Peʿal, meaning "flow, overflow."[16]

Examples from the Targumim include Targum Neofiti to Exod 26:12–13, with five instances of the root špʿ "overflow, abundant" (3× in the text, 2× in the margin) to render the Hebrew root srḥ. Targum Yonatan incorporates the root špʿ into its rendering of Hebrew nāhār "River (Euphrates)" when the context is the strong flow of the river, as in Isa 48:18, 59:19, 66:12: kišĕpaʿ nĕhar pĕrāt "like the flow of the River Euphrates."

In addition, the word špʿt occurs in a Punic inscription, most likely with the meaning "abundance, wealth," though some scholars debate this point.[17]

We conclude that the root špʿ "flow, overflow, give in abundance, etc." is an IH lexical trait.[18]

[7]

In v. 18 a unique 3 m. pl. pronominal suffix occurs in the expression ʿad hēm "unto them."[19] The typical reaction of exegetes to this usage is emendation to the expected form ʿădêhem.[20] However, this apparent anomaly in BH is paralleled in another Canaanite dialect. In the Mesha Stele, line 18, we read wʾsḥb.hm "I dragged them," with a very clear word divider separating the two words. W. R. Garr commented that "the objective suffix was probably a form of the independent pronoun in Moabite; the plural suffix had not yet been fused to the verb."[21] Furthermore, as J. C. L. Gibson noted, also in Aramaic and Syriac "'them' after a verb is regularly written separately."[22]

---

15. Sokoloff, *Dictionary*, 563–64.

16. Jastrow, *Dictionary*, 2.1618–19.

17. See *DNWSI*, 2.1184.

18. Schniedewind and Sivan ("Elijah-Elisha Narratives," 334) are "less certain" on this point.

19. The following discussion is anticipated in Rendsburg, "Morphological Evidence for Regional Dialects in Ancient Hebrew," 74.

20. Thus, e.g., GKC, 108; Burney, *Kings*, 299; *BHS, ad loc.*; and J. Gray, *I and II Kings* (OTL; Philadelphia: Westminster, 1970) 545. Note, however, that Burney (*Kings*, 209) suggested that the unusual ʿad hēm is a northern feature. For a most detailed treatment, also ending in emendation, see H. M. Orlinsky, "The Biblical Prepositions *tāḥat, bēn, báʿad*, and Pronouns ʾᵃnū́ (or ʾanū̄), zōʾtāh," *HUCA* 17 (1942) 283 n. 23.

21. Garr, *Dialect Geography*, 112.

22. Gibson, *Textbook of Syrian Semitic Inscriptions*, 1.81.

In light of this evidence, there is no reason to emend MT at 2 Kgs 9:18. Rather, we are dealing with an IH form, one that we might be able to localize to a Transjordanian subdialect. The context of 2 Kings 9 places us in that region. Although the specific words ʿad hēm are spoken by a watchman from Jezreel, the central character of this pericope is Jehu. And although we do not know exactly whence Jehu hailed, it is clear that he has Transjordanian connections. For example, in 1 Kgs 19:16 the Gileadite prophet Elijah is instructed by God to anoint Jehu; and in 2 Kgs 9:1–6 Jehu eventually is anointed king by Elisha in Ramoth-gilead. In short, it is not coincidental that ʿad hēm occurs in an Israelian story and that it is most closely paralleled by Moabite (and Aramaic) usage.[23]

[8]

Two verses later, in v. 20, another unusual prepositional usage appears: ʿad ʾălêhem "unto them."[24] This formation, with the preposition ʿad followed immediately by a declined form of the preposition ʾel, is closely related to the expression ʿad lĕ- in 1 Kgs 18:29. The discussion there, at 1 Kings 18 [1], is relevant for the phenomenon here as well.

[9]

The preposition ʿad typically means "until," but in a few instances in the Bible the meaning "while" is present. In Aramaic, by contrast, the preposition ʿad serves both meanings regularly.[25] A good example of Aramaic ʿad = "while" (or, for smoother English in this case, "during") is Dan 6:8, 6:13 ʿad yômîn tĕlātîn "during (the next) thirty days."

When Hebrew ʿad bears the connotation "while," we may suspect northern dialect. A sure instance of this usage is 2 Kgs 9:22 ʿad zĕnûnê ʾîzebel "while the harlotries of Jezebel (continue)."[26] Other examples occur in Judg 3:26, in a story about the Benjaminite hero Ehud; 1 Sam 14:19, in the account of

---

23. Schniedewind and Sivan ("Elijah-Elisha Narratives," 323) included this item in their list of unique linguistic features, with the suggestion that it may "reflect the narrative styling of the colloquial as opposed to the literary vernacular" (*ibid.*).

24. See already Burney, *Kings*, 209. On proposals to emend, see Montgomery and Gehman, *Kings*, 405. Again, for fullest treatment, see Orlinsky, "The Biblical Prepositions *tāḥat*, *bēn*, *báʿad*, and Pronouns ʾaʿnū (or ʾanū), zōʾtāh," 283 n. 23.

25. BDB, 1105; and Sokoloff, *Dictionary*, 395.

26. Burney (*Kings*, 299) felt the need to comment on this usage and to present parallel examples, but apparently he did not consider it to be a sign of northern Hebrew.

King Saul from the tribe of Benjamin; and Ps 141:10, a poem that exhibits an array of IH features.[27] It occurs also in Jon 4:2, for which several explanations are possible: (1) direct Aramaic influence is at work; (2) the scene is in Nineveh and the author has Jonah speaking an Aramaic-tinged Hebrew at this point; or (3) the historical Jonah was an Israelian prophet (see 2 Kgs 14:25) and thus his speech is presented as IH.[28]

[10]

The form *wayyirmĕsennāʰ* "and he trampled her" in v. 33 is one of a small group of exceptions to a rule of Hebrew grammar. Hebrew possesses two pairs of 3 sg. pronominal suffixes attached to verbs: those with *nun* (3 m. sg. *-ennû*, 3 f. sg. *-ennāʰ*) and those without (3 m. sg. *-ēhû*, 3 f. sg. *-ehā*).[29] Among the rules governing their distribution is the use of the latter set with *waw*-consecutive.[30] The exceptions are:[31] Judg 15:2 *wāʾettĕnennāʰ* "and I gave her," Job 7:18 *wattipqĕdennû* "and you inspected him," Job 20:15 *wayĕqiʾennû* "and he vomits it," Job 33:24 *wayĕḥunnennû* "and he was gracious to him," Lam 1:13 *wayyirdennāʰ* "and he ruled it" (thus rendering MT, though the context is difficult and many prefer to repoint and to derive the verb from the root *yrd* "go down"), and our example from 2 Kgs 9:33.

We note that Hebrew also possesses two forms of the 2 m. sg. pronominal suffix attached to verbs, both with and without *nun* (though in the former, the *nun* is assimilated to the following *kaf*). Again, the same pattern obtains, that is, one finds the forms without *nun* used with the *waw*-consecutive. However, there are a handful of exceptions: Isa 49:7 *wayyibḥārekkā* "and he chose you," Ps 81:8 *wāʾăḥallĕṣekkā* "and I rescued you," Prov 7:15 *wāʾem-ṣāʾekkā* "and I found you."

---

27. Rendsburg, *Psalms*, 99–102, though I neglected to include this item in my treatment.

28. The dictionaries and grammars suggest other examples (see, e.g., BDB, 724–15), but in those instances the meaning "until" is equally or more likely the case and, therefore, I have excluded them from consideration here.

29. For the proto-Semitic background of these forms, see R. Hetzron, "Third Person Singular Pronoun Suffixes in Proto-Semitic," *Orientalia Suecana* 18 (1969) 101–27.

30. The seminal article is M. Lambert, "De l'emploi des suffixes pronominaux avec *noun* et sans *noun* au futur et à l'imperátif," *REJ* 46 (1903) 178–83. See also T. Muraoka, "The *Nun Energicum* and the Prefix Conjugation in Biblical Hebrew," *AJBI* 1 (1975) 63–71.

31. See Muraoka, "The *Nun Energicum* and the Prefix Conjugation in Biblical Hebrew," 64–65, for this list of exceptions.

The distribution of these forms suggests that in IH it was possible to employ the suffixes with *nun* with the *waw*-consecutive. Judg 15:2 is in the mouth of a Philistine (Samson's father-in-law); Psalm 81 and Proverbs are northern compositions; and Job presents style-switching at work. The examples from Lamentations and Second Isaiah are due to the influence of the reunion of northerners and southerners during the Exile. The example from 2 Kgs 9:33, therefore, is to be explained as a feature of IH.[32]

[11]

In the Ketiv of v. 37, the form *hyt* as the 3 f. sg. suffix-conjugation form of the verb "to be" occurs in a story set in the Jezreel Valley (the Qeri reads the standard form *hāyĕtā^h*). The Ketiv form aligns with the 3 f. sg. *qtl* of IIIy verbs in MH, which bears the termination *-at* (as opposed to BH *-ā^h*).[33] In addition, the ending *-at* is standard in Aramaic.[34] The evidence indicates a northern setting for this atypical BH termination.[35]

However, the issue is more complicated. Other IIIy verbs that retain the ending *-at* in BH appear in Lev 25:21, 26:34, Jer 13:19, Ezek 24:12, and in the Siloam Tunnel inscription, line 3. The date of Leviticus is a moot point, but I tentatively explain the two forms from this book as archaic survivals.[36]

---

32. Muraoka, "The *Nun Energicum* and the Prefix Conjugation in Biblical Hebrew," 65, n. 2, stated that one should "Read with Qere *wayyirmĕsūhā*," that is, "and they trampled her." But neither the Leningrad Codex nor the Aleppo Codex includes such a Qeri. Presumably Muraoka intended an emendation, with a change in the consonantal text of *nun* to *waw*, with an implied subject "the horses" mentioned immediately beforehand. But the text should not be emended, since, apparently, the intended subject is Jehu, as suggested by David Qimhi and Ralbag in their commentaries.

33. Segal, *Grammar*, 91–92; Segal, *Diqduq*, 152; Kutscher, *History*, 128; and Haneman, *Torat ha-Ṣurot shel Leshon ha-Mishna*, 342–43.

34. R. Degen, *Altaramäische Grammatik* (Wiesbaden: Franz Steiner, 1969) 76; F. Rosenthal, *A Grammar of Biblical Aramaic* (Wiesbaden: Otto Harrassowitz, 1974) 51, 66; and Segert, *Altaramäische Grammatik*, 247.

35. See my earlier treatment in Rendsburg, "The Galilean Background of Mishnaic Hebrew," 229–30.

36. On the other hand, the possibility that this small section of Leviticus stems from northern Israel warrants investigation. Note not only these two examples of IIIy *qtl* forms with *-at*, but also (1) the use of the infinitive absolute *qānô^h* in place of the finite verb in 25:14; (2) the form *mĕ'ôt*, reflecting the Phoenician shift of *a > o* in 25:16; and (3) the lexeme *hēn* "if" in 25:20, better known from Aramaic. Accordingly, there are four IH features in the pericope of Lev 25:13–24 (one of which is repeated in 26:34).

The example in Jeremiah may be due to the prophet's Anathoth dialect and the example in Ezekiel may be an Aramaism, since both of these books have many such examples. However, in the Siloam Tunnel inscription, which is in eighth-century Jerusalemite Hebrew, a form with -*at* is totally unexpected. Perhaps the scribe was an Israelian who had come south after the fall of Samaria. Or perhaps this is an Aramaism, basing this supposition on our knowledge that Jerusalemite officials knew Aramaic by this time (2 Kgs 18:26 = Isa 36:11).[37] Regardless of these uncertainties, I still feel confident that the ending -*at* in IIIy verbs was a characteristic of IH, illustrated by 2 Kgs 9:37K, and one that persisted into MH.

Finally, of tangential interest, note that historically the ending -*at* is older than -*āʰ*. Accordingly, IH was more archaic than JH in this instance; and MH, attested at the latest period in the history of ancient Hebrew, also preserved this ancient feature.[38]

---

37. In more general terms, see Kutscher, *History*, 67.
38. See Kutscher, *History*, 128.

2 KINGS 10

[1]

Verse 7 contains the word *dûd* "pot, basket" (in the plural form *dûdîm*). The word appears in two passages with clear northern affinities: 1 Sam 2:14, describing the activity at Shiloh in the territory of Ephraim, and Ps 81:7, a northern composition.[1] In addition, the term occurs three times in the book of Jeremiah, the prophet from Benjamin (24:1, 24:2[2×]), and once in the book of Job (41:12). The only attestation that cannot be ascribed to a non-Judahite setting is 2 Chr 35:13, although here we can offer the explanation of Aramaic influence.[2]

In Aramaic, *dûd* occurs more commonly, being attested in Palmyrene,[3] Galilean Aramaic,[4] Babylonian Aramaic,[5] and Syriac.[6] The Targumim frequently use *dûd* to translate the more common Hebrew word *sîr* "pot." Thus, for example, Targum Neofiti uses *dûd* to render *sîr* in Exod 16:3, 27:3, 38:3; Targum Pseudo-Yonatan does likewise in all three passages (and also introduces *dûd* in two other places: Lev 8:31, Num 6:18); while Targum Onqelos uses *dûd* to render *sîr* only at Exod 16:3 (though it too introduces *dûd* at Num 6:18); and Targum Yonatan opts for *dûd* as the equivalent for *sîr* in 2 Kgs 4:38–41(5×), Zech 14:20–21, and elsewhere.

---

1. I neglected to include this feature in my monograph devoted to the northern Psalms. I am indebted to my graduate student Colin Smith for bringing this example to my attention.

2. The unusual plural forms attested for *dûd*, namely, the construct form *dûdāʾê* in Jer 24:1 and the absolute form *děwādîm* in 2 Chr 35:13, are not relevant to our discussion. I am interested here only in the use of the word *dûd*, in singular or plural, regardless of form. Accordingly, I refrain from commenting upon these irregular plural forms.

3. D. R. Hillers and E. Cussini, *Palmyrene Aramaic Texts* (Baltimore: Johns Hopkins University Press, 1996) 355.

4. Sokoloff, *Dictionary*, 140.

5. Jastrow, *Dictionary*, 1.283.

6. Payne Smith, *Dictionary*, 85.

In addition, *dd* is widely used in Ugaritic as the common word for "pot, vessel." As one would expect, it is especially well attested in administrative texts.[7]

We conclude that whereas Hebrew *sîr* "pot, vessel" was utilized throughout ancient Israel—note its broad distribution throughout the Bible, including northern contexts (e.g., 2 Kgs 4:38–41[5×]), the alternative term *dûd* "pot, basket" was at home only in northern Israel. Its distribution in the Bible and the Aramaic and Ugaritic cognates demonstrate the point.[8]

[2]

The noun *ṣibbûrîm* "piles, heaps" or "groups" in v. 8 appears only here in BH. The noun is extremely common in MH, appearing 542 times in the Tannaitic corpus, where the meaning, more generally, is "group of people, congregation, etc."[9] For an example of *ṣibbûr* meaning "pile" in the Mishna, see M. Peʾa 6:5 *šĕnê ṣibbûrê zêtîm* "two piles of olives." In addition, a verb *ṣbr* "join, pile up, collect" (always in the Qal) is attested 17 times in MH, e.g., M. Yoma 5:1.[10]

Cognate support is forthcoming from Ugaritic, in which both masculine *ṣbr* and feminine *ṣbrt* "team, group" occur.[11] The noun *ṣibbûr* "congregation" also occurs in Aramaic, although apparently only with this meaning.[12] But a verb *ṣbr* "pile up, collect" occurs in Aramaic; it is used by the Targum of Ruth to render Hebrew *lqṭ* "collect" in Ruth 2:7, 2:8, 2:15.[13]

It is clear that *ṣibbûrîm* in 2 Kgs 10:8 is an IH lexical item.

[3]

The noun *maṣṣĕbôt* "pillar" in v. 26 appears, at first glance, to be a plural form. However, upon closer inspection it clearly must be a singular form. Note that

---

7. *UT*, 384; and *DLU*, 1.129.

8. In the above discussion, I have not distinguished between the two meanings of *dûd*. More frequently it means "cooking pot" and, thus, one can note the clear opposition with *sîr*; less commonly, perhaps only in the Jeremiah passages (24:1–2[3×]), which refer to figs being contained in a *dûd*, does it means "basket."

9. *HDHL*, 077/15664–74; see also Jastrow, *Dictionary*, 2.1274.

10. *HDHL*, 077/15663–64; see also Jastrow, *Dictionary*, 2.1259–60. The verb occurs once in Ben Sira (47:18).

11. *UT*, 472.

12. Jastrow, *Dictionary*, 2.1274.

13. *Ibid.*, 2.1260.

the noun is resumed by a 3 f. sg. pronoun in *wayyiśrĕpûhā* "and they burnt it" later in the verse, and that the standard form *maṣṣĕbat* "pillar" (in construct) occurs in the next verse (v. 27).

Accordingly, this is another example of the feature(s) treated earlier: the retention of the f. sg. nominal ending *-at* and its shift (as in Phoenician) to *-ôt*. See our discussion above, at 2 Kings 6 [4].

[4]

In v. 30 the word for "those of the fourth generation" appears as *rĕbîʿîm*. This form occurs again in 2 Kgs 15:12.[14] This form stands in contrast to the JH term *ribbēʿîm* "those of the fourth generation," which appears in Exod 20:5, 34:7, Num 14:18, Deut 5:9. Note also the corresponding term of the same nominal formation *šillēšîm* "those of the third generation," which occurs in the same four verses and in Gen 50:23.

The form in 2 Kgs 10:30, 15:12 is an IH feature. The Targumic practice is to render the above verses from the Torah with the parallel Aramaic *qĕtîl* form (in the first group of cases with the inclusion of the word *dār* "generation"), e.g., Targum Onqelos to Exod 20:5, 34:7, Num 14:18, Deut 5:9 *dār tĕlîtay* "the third generation" and *dār rĕbîʿay* "the fourth generation." See also Targum Onqelos to Gen 50:23 for *bĕnîn tĕlîtāʿîn* "those of the third generation." These forms are the exact morphological correspondence to *rĕbîʿîm* in 2 Kgs 10:30 and 15:12.

In this instance, we are able to rely on three converging lines of evidence—distribution within the Bible, contrast with JH usage, and presence of Aramaic parallel—to defend the claim that this feature is an IH trait.

[5]

The phrase *lĕqaṣṣôt bĕyiśrāʾēl* "to reduce Israel" in v. 32 has caused difficulties for commentators. A major step toward the elucidation of this phrase was taken by Jonas Greenfield, who noted that the biblical expression is semantically linked to the use of the root *qṣy* (*qṣh*) "reduce, cut off" in Phoenician. This is seen most clearly in the Eshmunazor inscription (*KAI* 14), especially *lqṣtnm* in lines 9–10.[15] In Greenfield's words, "The verb *lqṣtnm* is not easy to translate. There can be no doubt in my mind that it must be associated with

---

14. The word *bĕnê* "sons of" appears before *rĕbîʿîm* in both places, but that issue does not concern us here. The usage with *bĕnê* can be considered standard based on Gen 50:23 *bĕnê šillēšîm*. Furthermore, our interest here is with the morphology of the single word *rĕbîʿîm*.

15. For other attestations in Phoenician, see *DNWSI*, 2.1022.

biblical Hebrew *lĕqaṣṣōt* used in II Kings 10:32.... In the biblical passage the referent is clearly the loss of territory, while in Eshmunazor it is probably loss of life."[16] The close connection between these two texts is due to the fact that 2 Kings 10 is an Israelian composition, which utilized the verb in a fashion attested in Phoenician.

The verb *qṣy* (*qṣh*) is not common in the Bible, but still we may note the following. In texts that may be identified as JH, the verb occurs in the Qal (Hab 2:10) and the Hiph'il (Lev 14:41, 14:43). It probably is not coincidental that *qṣy* (*qṣh*) occurs in the Pi'el in 2 Kgs 10:32 and again in Prov 26:6, another Israelian composition.[17]

The evidence from these two issues (the Phoenician parallel and the Pi'el usage) points to the conclusion that the phrase *lĕqaṣṣôt bĕyiśrā'ēl* "to reduce Israel" reflects IH usage.

---

16.   J. C. Greenfield, "Scripture and Inscription: The Literary and Rhetorical Element in Some Early Phoenician Inscriptions," in *Near Eastern Studies in Honor of William Foxwell Albright* (ed. H. Goedicke; Baltimore: Johns Hopkins Press, 1971) 264.

17.   The Pi'el also occurs 5 times in the Mishna, all in M. Ma'asarot (2:7, 2:8 [3×], 3:1) (thus according to the Kaufman MS; other manuscripts, including Parma, read Qal). But the meaning is totally different; the context concerns the harvesting of figs. B. Stade, cited by Montgomery and Gehman (*Kings*, 416), noted that the use of the preposition *bĕ-* in 2 Kgs 10:32 is paralleled by MH. But the only such passage is M. Ma'asarot 2:7, though, as just noted, the context is harvesting figs, so there can be no connection to the Kings usage. For all MH attestations of this root, with all conjugations, see *HDHL*, 080/16286–88. Cogan and Tadmor (*II Kings*, 117) suggested a general connection between the MH usage and 2 Kgs 10:32.

2 KINGS 13

[1]

Verse 21 concerns the dead man who was tossed into the tomb of Elisha, with the result that the corpse of the deceased touched the bones of Elisha: *wayĕḥî wayyāqom ʿal raglāw* "and he revived and arose on his feet." The collocation of the two verbs *ḥyy* "live" and *qwm* "arise" occurs elsewhere in the Bible only in northern contexts.[1] The two verbs occur in poetic parallelism in Hos 6:2, a northern prophetic book, and in Isa 26:14, 26:19, in a section of Isaiah replete with IH features.[2]

In addition, the two verbs are collocated in an Aramaic text, the Genesis Apocryphon from Qumran, 20:29. In this passage, Abram removes the evil spirit from Pharaoh, about whom it is then written, *wḥy wqm* "and he revived and arose."[3]

The distribution of this usage in the Bible and the Aramaic cognate demonstrate that the pairing of these two verbs is an IH trait.

---

1. See already Y. J. Yoo, *Israelian Hebrew in the Book of Hosea* (Ph.D. dissertation, Cornell University, 1999) 76–78.

2. See Noegel, "Dialect and Politics in Isaiah 24–27."

3. For the text, see J. A. Fitzmyer, *The Genesis Apocryphon of Qumran Cave I* (Rome: Biblical Institute Press, 1971) 66. Fitzmyer rendered the passage differently (p. 67), understanding *wḥy* as the end of one sentence ("and he was cured") and *wqm* as the beginning of the next ("And the king rose..."). But in light of the usage in 2 Kgs 13:21, it is better to treat the two verbs in 1QapGen 20:29 as a single phrase.

2 KINGS 14

[1]

Burney astutely observed that the expression *bêt šemeš ʾăšer lîhûdāʰ* "Beth-shemesh, which is to Judah" in v. 11 points to a northern perspective.[1] For a related example, see above, at 1 Kings 19 [1].

[2]

This chapter contains two examples of the ablative use of the prepositions *l-* and *b-* instead of the usual preposition *min*:

2 Kgs 14:13   *bĕšaʿar ʾeprayim ʿad šaʿar happinnāʰ*
           "from the gate of Ephraim unto the corner gate"

2 Kgs 14:28   *hēšîb ʾet dammeśeq wĕʾet ḥămāt lîhûdāʰ bĕyiśrāʾēl*
           "He retrieved Damascus and Hamath from Yehuda (=Samʾal) for Israel."[2]

On these passages, see our discussion above, at 2 Kings 4 [7].

---

1. Burney, *Kings*, 207, 215.

2. For the proper understanding of this verse, see *UT*, 92; and C. H. Gordon and G. A. Rendsburg, *The Bible and the Ancient Near East* (New York: W. W. Norton, 1997) 241–42.

2 Kings 15

The phrase *qābol ʿām* "before the people" in v. 10 has been challenged by most scholars. The typical reaction is textual emendation, with or without versional support.[1] The statement in BDB "the Aram. is surprising"[2] provides the solution to the problem. In Aramaic the root *qbl* provides the form of the preposition "before" (alongside *qdm*). Many examples are attested in Official Aramaic, especially in the Elephantine papyri.[3] In Biblical Aramaic, see Dan 2:31, 3:3, 5:1 (and many other passages with other nuances of the preposition *qābēl*).[4] In the Targumim, forms of *qbl* (with or without *l*) are used to render the Hebrew preposition *neged*, e.g., Targum Pseudo-Yonatan to Exod 19:2 *qbl ṭwwrʾ* = Hebrew *neged hāhār*, Targum Pseudo-Yonatan to Exod 34:10 *qbl kl ʿmk* = Hebrew *neged kol ʿamměkā*, Targum Onqelos to Num 25:4 *lāqăbēl šimšāʾ* = Hebrew *neged haššāmeš*, Targum Yonatan to Josh 8:11 *lāqăbēl qartāʾ* = Hebrew *neged hāʿîr*.

In light of the evidence put forth in this monograph, it is not surprising to find an Aramaic-like usage in a section of Kings detailing the history of the northern kingdom. Clearly, *qābol* "before" in 2 Kgs 15:10 is an IH feature, linking this dialect of ancient Hebrew with the Aramaic dialects spoken to the northeast.[5]

Another issue arising from *qābol ʿām* "before the people" is the lack of the expected definite article. But article usage is notoriously subject to change from dialect to dialect (see, for example, 2 Kgs 1:2, 8:8, 8:9), and in this case one must assume a standard phrase or standard usage in IH that did not require

---

1. For a sampling of proposals, see Burney, *Kings*, 321–22; and Montgomery and Gehman, *Kings*, 455.

2. BDB, 867.

3. See *DNWSI*, 2.981, for references.

4. BDB, 1110; and KB, 1117.

5. On Ezek 26:9 *qābŏllô*, see M. Greenberg, *Ezekiel 21–37* (AB 22A; New York: Doubleday, 1997) 533.

the definite article. This, however, is a secondary point that does not affect the main conclusion reached above that the preposition *qābol* is an IH trait.

[2]

On *běnê rěbîʿîm* "those of the fourth generation" in v. 12, see our discussion above, 2 Kings 10 [4].

[3]

The noun *yeraḥ* "month" occurs in v. 13. The standard Hebrew word for "month" is *ḥōdeš*, attested 28 times in the Bible; clearly it was used in all strata of ancient Hebrew. The alternative noun *yeraḥ*, on the other hand, occurs only twelve times, with a distribution pointing to its home in northern Israel.

The clearest examples are the following: our passage in 2 Kgs 15:13; Deut 33:14 in the context of the blessing to Joseph; 4 times in Job (3:6, 7:3, 29:2, 39:2) (against only two occurrences of *ḥōdeš* in the book [14:5, 21:21]); and 3 times in the account of the construction of the Temple (1 Kgs 6:37, 6:38, 8:2)—always in conjunction with month names known from Phoenician (respectively, Ziv, Bul, Ethanim), a usage attributable to the fact that Phoenician scribes recorded the building activity.

We are left with three other instances: Exod 2:2, Deut 21:13, Zech 11:8. In Exod 2:2, there are no other signs of IH in the story of Moses's birth. However, the exigencies of alliteration directed the author to use the dialectal word in its plural form *yěrāḥîm* because of the expression *wattaḥměrāh baḥēmār* "she smeared it with bitumen" in the next verse—note the presence of the consonants *ḥet, mem,* and *reš* in all three words. Concerning Deut 21:13, scholars have suggested that the book of Deuteronomy is a northern composition.[6] At first glance the linguistic evidence does not support this conclusion, but a full-scale study of the question is certainly a desideratum. Finally, note that Zech 11:8 is post-exilic and, thus, Aramaic influence may be at work. But regardless of how we judge these three passages, the overall distribution points to *yeraḥ* as an IH lexical item.

This conclusion is supported by the cognate evidence from Ugaritic, Phoenician, and Aramaic. In Ugaritic, *ḥdt* is limited to "new moon," whereas

---

6. See, among others, E. Nielsen, "Historical Perspectives and Geographical Horizons: On the Question of North-Israelite Elements in Deuteronomy," *ASTI* 11 (1977/78) 77–89; and M. Weinfeld, *Deuteronomy 1–11* (AB 5; New York: Doubleday, 1991) 44–50. I have addressed the issue of Deuteronomy, in words similar to what I have written here, in G. A. Rendsburg, "Notes on Israelian Hebrew (II)," *JNSL* 26 (2000) 33–45, especially pp. 35–36, 42.

yrḥ is employed for "month."[7] The same situation obtains in Phoenician: *ḥdš* is restricted to "new moon,"[8] while *yrḥ* is used for "month."[9] In Aramaic, *yrḥ* is attested in all dialects (e.g., Official Aramaic, Nabatean, Palmyrene, Hatran, Galilean, Jewish Babylonian, Syriac) as the word for both "month" and "new moon."[10] Because examples are so widespread, one hardly needs to note that the Targumim employ this term as the translational equivalent of Hebrew *ḥōdeš*.

The Gezer Calendar (*KAI* 182) utilizes the word *yrḥ* repeatedly. Given the location of Gezer in the territory of Judah, this presents a problem for my thesis. While some *ad hoc* explanations could be offered (perhaps the inscription is Canaanite, that is, authored by a non-Israelite; perhaps the dialect boundary in this particular case linked Gezer with the north; and so on), I prefer not to follow such potential lines of argument and simply admit that the Gezer evidence does not support my conclusion. I remain convinced of my approach, nonetheless, based on the overriding argument forthcoming from (1) the distribution of *yrḥ* in the Bible, (2) the opposition of this term to SBH *ḥdš*, and (3) the cognate data from Ugaritic, Phoenician, and Aramaic.

[4]

The expression *hôṣiʾ kesep*, literally "bring out silver," more idiomatically "levy," appears in v. 20 and nowhere else in the Bible. Montgomery and Gehman cited Paul Haupt's comparison of the MH usage of *hôṣiʾ* in the sense of "collect" and the parallel Aramaic usage of the root *npq*.[11] As the illustrations below demonstrate, the MH and Aramaic usages are not exactly the same as the biblical idiom—generally, the former mean "pay, expend," whereas the latter has the specific connotation "levy"—but to the extent that both refer to monetary issues, the phrases are comparable.

The MH evidence may be exemplified by M. Ketubbot 8:5 *hammôṣiʾ hôṣāʾôt ʿal niksê ʾištô* "he who expends expenditures on his wife's property," where both the Hiph ʿil verb and the derived noun *hôṣāʾāh* appear.[12]

---

7. *UT*, 414; and *DLU*, 1.173–74.

8. *DNWSI*, 1.350–51.

9. *Ibid.*, 1.469–71.

10. *DNWSI*, 1.469–71; Sokoloff, *Dictionary*, 245; Jastrow, *Dictionary*, 1.596; and Payne Smith, *Dictionary*, 197.

11. Montgomery and Gehman, *Kings*, 455. Cogan and Tadmor (*II Kings*, 172) noted the parallel with Akkadian *šūṣû* "take out, bring out," > "deliver, make payment."

12. For additional passages, especially with the noun form *hôṣāʾāh* "expenditure,"

Aramaic witnesses this usage for the ʾAphʿel of *npq* (the translational equivalent of Hebrew *yṣʾ*) in a variety of dialects. Note especially the following from Galilean Aramaic: Y. Gittin 46d(23) *ʾpyq ʾrbʿh dynryn* "He invested four dinars"; Vayyiqraʾ Rabba 797:3 *kmn ʾpqtwn* "How much did you spend?"; and Bereshit Rabba 1003:1 *wlʾ mpqyn bydyh klwm* "They do not pay him anything."[13] From Palmyrene Aramaic we may cite the expression *ʾpq mn kysh npqn rbrbn* "He spent from his own pocket great expenses" (Inv 10 44:5–6), with both the verb *ʾpq* (ʾAphʿel of *npq*) and the plural noun *npqn*.[14]

Once more a unique usage in the Bible has parallels in MH and Aramaic. The conclusion is clear: the idiom *hôṣîʾ kesep* "bring out silver" = "levy" was a characteristic of IH.

[5]

The noun *ʾarmôn* "palace" occurs in v. 25. See our discussion above, at 1 Kings 16 [1].

[6]

The word *ʾargôb* in v. 25 remains enigmatic for most biblical exegetes.[15] The full phrase is: *wayyakkēhû bĕšōmrôn bĕʾarmôn bêt hammelek* (thus Q; the K reads *mlk*) *ʾet ʾargôb wĕʾet hāʾaryēʰ* "and he [Pekah] slew him [Pekahiah] in Samaria, in the palace, the house of the king by *ʾargôb* and by the lion." The best and most convincing interpretation of this passage was put forward by M. J. Geller,[16] who compared our word to Ugaritic *hrgb ab nšrm* "*hrgb* the father of the eagles" mentioned in the Aqhat epic (*UT* 1 Aqht 121, etc.). According to Geller, *ʾargôb* thus refers to an eagle, and the whole phrase "the eagle and the lion" is a circumlocution for sphinxes that, presumably, were an architectural motif of the royal palace in Samaria. Sphinxes are amply attested in the Samaria ivories, and one can assume their presence in palace architecture as well (already Rashi suggested that "a golden lion stood in that palace").

---

see Jastrow, *Dictionary*, 1.340. Lacking from Jastrow's examples is Sifre Devarim 306, which I identified from the list in *HDHL*, 049/9853–54 (however, most of the 31 examples given there bear other meanings, e.g., "carrying out, transferring, transporting").

13.   All cited from Sokoloff, *Dictionary*, 358.

14.   See *DNWSI*, 2.743. The original publication is in J. Starcky, ed. *Inventaire des inscriptions de Palmyre*, vol. 10 (Damascus: Direction generale des antiquites de Syrie, 1949); see now Hillers and Cussini, *Palmyrene Aramaic Texts*, 203, 390.

15.   See the survey of opinions gathered in Cogan and Tadmor, *II Kings*, 173.

16.   M. J. Geller, "A New Translation for 2 Kings xv 25," *VT* 26 (1976) 374–77.

Colossal figures representing protective deities are known from Mesopotamia. Ashurbanipal informs us that his grandfather Sennacherib, in fact, was assassinated by them. All of this evidence leads Geller to conclude that ʾargôb means "eagle."

Of course, to accept the equation of Hebrew ʾargôb and Ugaritic hrgb, one must reckon with an interchange between ʾ and h. But such interchanges are well attested in Semitic, especially in initial position. Thus, I do not consider this problem a major barrier for accepting Geller's proposal.

Although I cannot speak to the Assyrian parallel noted above, I would suggest that theological reasons explain the inclusion of this information in the biblical account. The individual responsible for the final version of Kings, and perhaps his northern source as well, is telling us, in so many words, "See, even the protective sphinxes could not prevent Pekahiah's death; he was murdered right next to them." In his view, these devices are pagan in origin and have no role in Israelite palace architecture (notwithstanding the fact that the cherubim of the ark are the same or similar item).

Second, the Ugaritic evidence suggests that hrgb is not so much a common noun for "eagle," but rather a proper name for "the father of the eagles." This explains the absence of the definite article in the word ʾargôb as compared to its presence in the word hāʾaryēh.

To relate all this material to the subject of our investigation, I assume that it is not by chance that the word ʾargôb appears in the description of the reign of an Israelian king. The form represents a northern lexical item with a cognate in Ugaritic.

Further questions, all unanswerable due to a lack of sufficient evidence, suggest themselves. Is it coincidental that hrgb is attested only in the Aqhat epic, whose geographical background is that of the Sea of Galilee region (that is, relatively close to Samaria)? Should we also relate ʾargôb "Argob," a toponym associated with Bashan, to our discussion? If so, note its northern setting. Is it coincidental that to this day eagles are prominent in the Bashan/Golan region (at Gamla in particular)?

While we can proceed no further with this discussion, I am convinced by Geller's argumentation and I conclude that ʾargôb is an IH element.

[7]

Another IH feature occurs in v. 25, namely, the double plural construction exemplified by bĕnê gilʿādîm "sons of Gilead," that is, "Gileadites." Note that not only is the *nomen regens* plural, as is to be expected, but that the *nomen rectum* is also, quite against the norm. This is made even more striking by the fact that the second element in this construct chain is a toponym, normally *gilʿād* "Gilead," but here the plural *gilʿādîm*. Obviously, the norm in Hebrew is represented by such expressions as *běnê yěhûdāʰ* "sons of Judah," that is, "Judahites" (e.g., 2 Sam 1:18, Hos 2:2), *běnê dān* "sons of Dan," that is, "Danites" (e.g., Judg 18:2), *běnê ḥēt* "sons of Heth," that is, "Hittites" (e.g., Gen 23:3), and many others.

Double plural constructions are found predominantly in northern contexts in the Bible. Examples from the northern Psalms include: Ps 29:1 *běnê ʾēlîm* "sons of the gods," that is, "deities"; Ps 45:10 *běnôt mělākîm* "daughters of kings," that is, "princesses"; Ps 47:10 *nědîbê ʿammîm* "princes of the peoples" (contrast Num 21:18 *nědîbê hāʿām*, Ps 113:8 *nědîbê ʿammô*); Ps 74:13 *rāʾšê tannîmîm* "heads of the sea monsters" (note that in the mythic conflict Yahweh defeats only one sea monster, as indicated by the parallel term *yām* "Sea" in v. 13a, the term *liwyātān* "Leviathan" in v. 14a, and the 3 m. sg. pronominal suffix on *tittěnennû* "you give him" in v. 14b; because the *nomen regens rāʾšê* "heads of" is plural [indicating the many heads of the creature], the *nomen rectum tannîmîm* "monsters" also is in the plural); Ps 77:6 *šěnôt ʿôlāmîm* "years of eternities"; Ps 78:49 *malʾăkê rāʿîm* "messengers of evils"; Ps 116:9 *ʾarṣôt haḥayyîm* "lands of the living" (in this case the *nomen rectum* must be plural, causing the *nomen regens* to shift from an expected *ʾereṣ* "land" [thus "land of the living"] to the unexpected plural *ʾarṣôt* "lands").[17]

Cognate evidence for this usage was offered by S. Gevirtz, who assembled Phoenician, Ugaritic, and Byblos Amarna examples.[18] In addition, the double plural construction is extremely common in Mishnaic Hebrew.[19]

The double plural syntagma occurs in other contexts in the Bible as well, for example, in Chronicles.[20] The relative frequency of this usage in Chronicles most likely should be explained by Gordon's theory whereby northern features entered LBH upon the reunion of Israelians and Judahites in exile. The overall evidence strongly indicates a northern origin for this usage.

---

17. Rendsburg, *Psalms*, 35–36, 48, 57, 70, 78, 84.

18. S. Gevirtz, "Of Syntax and Style in the 'Late Biblical Hebrew' – 'Old Canaanite' Connection," *JANES* 18 (1986) 28–29.

19. Segal, *Grammar*, 187; and Kutscher, *A History of the Hebrew Language*, 129. There are ample illustrations of this usage in Segal, *Diqduq*, 97–100, though there is no explicit statement concerning the phenomenon. See further Rendsburg, "The Galilean Background of Mishnaic Hebrew," 230–31.

20. R. Polzin, *Late Biblical Hebrew: Toward an Historical Typology of Biblical Hebrew Prose* (HSM 12; Missoula, Mont.: Scholars Press, 1976) 42.

[8]

Verse 28 concerns King Pekah: *lōʾ sār min ḥaṭṭōʾt yārobʿām ben nĕbāṭ* "he did not sway from the sins of Jeroboam ben Nebat." The phrase *min ḥaṭṭōʾt* "from the sins of" is an example of the preposition *min* before an anarthrous noun. The norm in Hebrew calls for the *nun* of the preposition *min* to assimilate before a noun without the definite article.

Cognate evidence and the distribution of this phenomenon in the Bible indicate that this feature is a trait of IH.[21] In Aramaic the norm is the retention of the full form *mn* (especially since the definite article is postpositive, not prepositive). The same holds true for the Deir ʿAlla dialect, in which it is attested five times, e.g., I, 3 *mn mḥr* "on the morrow."

In the Bible the use of *min* before an anarthrous noun is well attested, 98 times to be exact.[22] Of these 98 occurrences, 51 are in Chronicles, and a few additional ones appear in Daniel and Nehemiah. There can be little doubt that the widespread appearance of this usage in Chronicles and the other late books is due to Aramaic influence over LBH.[23]

But what of the earlier attestations of *min* before an anarthrous noun? Although I readily admit to not being able to account for every instance of this usage in earlier parts of the Bible, a pattern is discernible. As the following listing of examples indicates, *min* before an anarthrous noun must have been a feature of IH.[24] Num 23:7 places us in the Balaam oracles and so serves to portray the foreignness of this non-Israelite prophet. Judg 5:20, 7:23(2×), 10:11(2×), 19:16 are all in northern settings. Jer 7:7, 17:5, 25:3, 25:5, 44:18, 44:28 aid us in aligning the Benjaminite dialect with IH. Ps 45:9, 73:19, 116:8 are in northern poems. Prov 27:8 and Song 4:15 occur in northern books. Finally, Job 30:5, 40:6 place us in a book with a strong Transjordanian influence.

In summary, the usage under discussion is a trait of IH, Aramaic, and the Deir ʿAlla dialect. Under the influence of Aramaic, it became more common in LBH as well.

---

21. See my earlier discussion in Rendsburg, "The Dialect of the Deir ʿAlla Inscription," 314–15.

22. For a complete list of occurrences, see E. König, *Historisch-kritisches Lehrgebäude der hebräischen Sprache*, 2 vols. (Leipzig: J. C. Hinrichs, 1895) 2.292.

23. Polzin, *Late Biblical Hebrew*, 66; and G. A. Rendsburg, "Late Biblical Hebrew and the Date of 'P'," *JANES* 12 (1980) 72.

24. I omit from consideration Deut 33:11, where *min* is an interrogative pronoun. Also, *min hûʾ* in Isa 18:2 and 18:7 is not to be considered in this regard, though clearly it represents a dialectal feature of some sort (perhaps addressee-switching is at work here, since Cush is addressed in this pericope).

2 KINGS 17

[1]

The presence of the Hitpaʿel of *mkr* with the meaning "decide" in v. 17 in the expression *wayyitmakkĕrû laʿăśôt hāraʿ bĕʿênê YHWH* "they decided to do evil in the eyes of YHWH," has been discussed above, at 1 Kings 21 [4].

[2]

The word *miqṣôt* "from among" in v. 32 (the actual form here is *miqṣôtām* "from among them'") is a lexical trait of IH. See our discussion above, at 1 Kings 12 [1].

[3]

The syntagma *hyh* + participle occurs three times in this chapter.[1]

> v. 33: *ʾet YHWH hāyû yĕrēʾîm*
> "they were fearing YHWH"

> v. 33: *wĕʾet ʾĕlôhêhem hāyû ʿōbĕdîm*
> "and they were worshipping their gods"

> v. 41: *wĕʾet pĕsîlêhem hāyû ʿōbĕdîm*
> "and they were worshipping their idols"

See our discussion above, at 1 Kings 22 [7].

[4]

The phrase *śām šĕmô*, literally "he placed his name," in v. 34, is paralleled elsewhere in the Bible only in Judg 8:31: *wayyāśem ʾet šĕmô* "he placed his name," and Neh 9:7 *śamtā šĕmô*, "you placed his name." Burney referred to the former as "this somewhat peculiar usage"[2] and Cogan and Tadmor characterized the phrase in 2 Kgs 17:34 as "an unusual expression."[3] The

---

1. I have translated these phrases into English with an attempt to capture the syntax of the Hebrew.

2. Burney, *Judges*, 265.

3. Cogan and Tadmor, *II Kings*, 213. They also noted the parallel in Neh 9:7.

oddity, which any seasoned reader of the Bible can sense, is to be explained by recognizing the Israelian nature of the idiom. 2 Kings 17 is a lengthy chapter dealing with the final fate of the northern kingdom of Israel. Nehemiah 9 originally was composed by a northern Israelite reflecting upon the same historical conditions. Judges 8 is part of the Gideon cycle about one of the northern judges.

The cognate evidence supports this conclusion. In Phoenician exists the very similar expression *št ʾnk šm*, literally "I placed its name," in Karatepe A ii 9–10, 17–18. Although the Phoenician phrase employs *št* instead of *śm*, the two verbs are similar. Both verbs occur in both Hebrew and Phoenician, though *śm* is more common in the former, whereas *št* is more common in the latter.[4] The evidence of Phoenician *št šm* and the distribution of *śm šm* in the Bible converge to demonstrate the Israelian Hebrew nature of this usage.

---

4. For a general idea of the relative frequency of the verbs in Phoenician, compare the lists of attestations in *DNWSI*, 2.1126 and 2.1130.

OTHER UNIQUE FEATURES

The stories of the northern kings and prophets contain numerous other unique features, especially in the area of lexicon. As noted in the Introduction, however, not every example of unique usage is automatically to be seen as evidence of IH. Such is the case with the list below; there is not enough evidence to identify these lexemes as IH traits. Schniedewind and Sivan already have noted some of these. In the list that follows, I include a number of their examples, along with others that I have isolated. It is possible that some of these items are IH characteristics, but we cannot claim them as such given our present state of knowledge. I include them here nonetheless, with the hope that future discoveries will be able either to confirm or to deny their northernness.

[1]

The difficult expression *ʿāṣûr wĕʿāzûb*, translated in NJPSV as "bond and free," appears four times in these narratives: 1 Kgs 14:10, 1 Kgs 21:21, 2 Kgs 9:8, 14:26 (in the last citation each of the two words is preceded by *ʾepes*). It appears again in the northern composition of Deuteronomy 32 (v. 36) (where the two-word phrase is preceded by a single *ʾepes*). This distribution might suggest that this phrase is an IH element. However, because we have no additional support (e.g., cognate evidence) for this conclusion, and because the very meaning of the phrase is still in doubt,[1] caution is advised. It is better to conclude that the expression is simply unique, without assigning it specifically to IH.

[2]

The word *māʿôg* "cake" occurs twice in 1 Kgs 17:12. A homonym, though apparently not related, appears in Ps 35:16. Whether this term is the equivalent of SBH *ʿûgāh* "cake" or whether it represents a specialized type of baked good cannot be determined.[2]

---

1. For recent discussion and bibliography, see Cogan and Tadmor, *II Kings*, 107.
2. This item was noted by Schniedewind and Sivan, "Elijah-Elisha Narratives," 321–22.

[3]

The root *htl* "mock" in 1 Kgs 18:27 is a *hapax legomenon*. It may be a secondary root derived from the verb *tll* "mock."[3]

[4]

The Hitpaʿel of *qdr* "be dark" occurs in 1 Kgs 18:45 (with reference to the skies darkening with clouds). The root is well attested in BH, but this is the only Hitpaʿel form.[4]

[5]

The noun *ʾăpēr* "bandage, scarf" occurs in 1 Kgs 20:38, 20:41, and nowhere else.[5]

[6]

The preposition *mēʿălê*, preserved as the Qeri in 1 Kgs 20:41 (the Ketiv reads *mʿl*), includes the only attestation of the form *ʿălê* in Biblical Hebrew prose. The other forty occurrences of this form are in poetry.[6]

[7]

The verb *yṣq*, usually meaning "pour," is used intransitively and, thus, it means "flow" in 1 Kgs 22:35. This usage occurs elsewhere only in Job 38:38.[7]

[8]

The verb *wayyaʿan* "he replied" in 2 Kgs 1:11 begins a new speech. There may be analogs to this elsewhere in the Bible and most likely in Ugaritic as well, but such examples are open to subjective interpretation.[8]

---

3. For further discussion, see Schniedewind and Sivan, "Elijah–Elisha Narratives," 322.

4. See also Schniedewind and Sivan, "Elijah–Elisha Narratives," 323.

5. See Schniedewind and Sivan, "Elijah–Elisha Narratives," 320. The BH word and its Akkadian cognate *apāru* are discussed, ever so briefly, by J. C. Green-field, "Ugaritic Lexicographical Notes," *JCS* 21 (1967) 90; the main discussion there is Ugaritic *ǵprt* "wrap, garment."

6. Chen, *Israelian Hebrew in the Book of Proverbs*, 82, noted that of the 40 poetic attestations, 28 occur in northern texts and, therefore, he classified this feature as an IH element. I prefer to be more cautious at this stage. Perhaps a future (epigraphic) discovery will reveal another instance of *ʿălê* in a northern prose context, thus solidifying the argument.

7. See BDB, 427; and Burney, *Kings*, 259.

8. Many scholars emend the text; see Cogan and Tadmor, *II Kings*, 26.

[9]

The noun *ʾāsûk* "container" in 2 Kgs 4:2, referring to a container of oil, is a *hapax legomenon*. There are no etyma in the cognate languages. Undoubtedly it is derived from the verbal root *swk* "pour, anoint."

[10]

The verb *sʿr* "storm" is used in 2 Kgs 6:11 as a "unique expression describing the king's 'storming about'."[9] If this is a northernism, it would contrast with the JH equivalent *wattippāʿem rûaḥ* "(one's) spirit was disturbed" in Gen 41:8, Dan 2:3. Targum Yonatan to 2 Kgs 6:11 rendered the expression with *wĕʾisteʿar libbāʾ*, suggesting that the usage was at home in Aramaic as well. But it occurs only in this one instance in the large Aramaic corpus and so we must proceed cautiously here. It is tempting to view this as an IH feature, but the evidence is simply insufficient.

[11]

The noun *makbēr* "netted cloth" in 2 Kgs 8:15 is a *hapax legomenon*. The root *kbr* occurs in other nominal forms in the Bible: *kābîr* (1 Sam 19:13, 19:16), *kĕbārāh* (Amos 9:9), and *mikbār* (e.g., Exod 27:4), all with similar meanings.[10]

[12]

Twice in these narratives the particle *ʾet* is used as a relative marker. In 2 Kgs 9:25 Jehu says to his officer Bidkar: *kî zĕkōr ʾānî wāʾattāh ʾēt rôkĕbîm ṣĕmādîm* "Indeed, remember how I and you were riding together?" with *ʾet* functioning as a relativizer. 2 Kgs 10:6 is an even clearer example: *ûbnê hammelek šibʿîm ʾîš ʾet gĕdôlê hāʿîr mĕgaddĕlîm ʾôtām* "and the sons of the king, seventy men whom the notables of the city were rearing," where *ʾăšer*, not *ʾet*, is expected. No parallel to this peculiar usage is attested in Northwest Semitic.

[13]

The phrase *ʾăšer ʾet yiblĕʿām* "[the ascent of Gur] which is by Ibleam" in 2 Kgs 9:27 is most unusual. The preposition *ʾet* is never used in this manner elsewhere in the Bible. But there is no cognate usage that permits us to assign this feature to IH.

---

9. Cogan and Tadmor, *II Kings*, 72.

10. See also Schniedewind and Sivan, "Elijah-Elisha Narratives," 321.

[14]

The verb śym "put, place" is predicated of Jezebel when she applies cosmetics in 2 Kgs 9:30. Normally, BH uses the verb ʿśy (ʿśh) "make, do" to express such activities.[11]

[15]

The noun meltāḥāʰ "wardrobe" in 2 Kgs 10:22 is a *hapax legomenon*. Cogan and Tadmor summarized the possible cognate evidence.[12] Note that the expression ʾăšer ʿal hammeltāḥāʰ "he who is over the wardrobe" has a counterpart in 2 Kgs 22:14 šōmēr habbĕgādîm "the guardian of the garments." Since the former occurs in a story about Jehu and the latter occurs in a story about Josiah, possibly we have here an IH-JH opposition.

[16]

The root mlṭ "escape" occurs in the Niphʿal in 2 Kgs 10:24, most inexplicably. The Piʿel is expected.[13]

[17]

The expression bāʾ šānāʰ in 2 Kgs 13:20 is extremely difficult, "meaningless," in fact, according to Cogan and Tadmor.[14] The words seem to mean "start of the year," "coming of the year," or something similar. Typically scholars repoint the Masoretic text to arrive at such an understanding.

[18]

In 2 Kgs 14:26 the word for "bitter" appears as a IIIy verb, as if derived from mry (mrh), as opposed to its usual root mrr.[15]

[19]

The meaning of the verb ḥpʾ in 2 Kgs 17:9 is difficult to determine. Cogan and Tadmor discussed the various possibilities.[16] One of their suggestions

---

11. See Cogan and Tadmor, *II Kings*, 111.

12. Cogan and Tadmor, *II Kings*, 115.

13. See Montgomery and Gehman, *Kings*, 415.

14. Cogan and Tadmor, *II Kings*, 148.

15. For comment, see Cogan and Tadmor, *II Kings*, 161.

16. Cogan and Tadmor, *II Kings*, 205.

relates the biblical attestation to the usage in Bereshit Rabba 94:8 (where the context is an explanation of the name of Huppim son of Benjamin). I have checked this passage, however, and can find nothing there that might help.

Conclusion

The evidence put forward in the preceding chapters demonstrates that the material concerning the northern kings and the northern prophets preserved in the canonical book of Kings reflects IH. These sections were composed by individuals residing in the north for whom the northern dialect of ancient Hebrew was their native tongue.[1]

We have a control by which to confirm this position. The intervening material about the kings of Judah, by and large, lacks the kind of grammatical and lexical features that have served as the database for this study. We can point to only an occasional item (e.g., the unique word *massāḥ* in 2 Kgs 11:6, which may be related to Aramaic *mishātāʾ* "balance";[2] the nominal plural ending *-în* that appears in the word *rāṣîn* "runners" in 2 Kgs 11:13; and perhaps a few others) that could be labeled an IH feature. Otherwise, not unexpectedly, the chronicles of the Judahite kings are written in pure JH.

The main goal of this study has been to identify further features of IH. As stated in the Introduction, perhaps I should have presented this research before my studies on other Israelian sections of the Bible. But regardless of the order in which my publications have appeared, the picture that emerges is ever clearer. As theorized by Hebraists in decades past—in fact, as far back as Burney in 1903, a century ago—northern Israel used a different dialect of Hebrew than did southern Judah. Moreover, the Masora has retained these

---

1. In the case of material that focuses on the actions of the kings of Israel, most likely the authors belonged to the chancellery or officialdom of the realm. In the case of the cycle(s) of stories concerning Elijah and Elisha, we probably are dealing with a product composed in popular circles in northern Israel.

2. The Hebrew term is difficult, though something like "balanced" might fit; see NJPSV "on every side." For possible relationship to the Aramaic word, see Montgomery and Gehman, *Kings*, 424. For a more critical view of the text, see Cogan and Tadmor, *II Kings*, 127. For the Aramaic term, which appears in different forms, see Jastrow, *Dictionary*, 2.805. Note that it is used in the Targumim to render Hebrew *môʾznayim* "balance, pair of scales," for example, Targum to Psalms 62:10 and Targum to Job 6:2 (see also Targum Pseudo-Yonatan's incorporation of the term into the rendering of Deut 25:15).

differences, contrary to the opinion of many eminent scholars that a certain leveling has occurred in the Masoretic text.[3]

In the Introduction, I referred to two recent studies that have treated some of the same material deduced in this monograph, namely, the articles by Young[4] and by Schniedewind and Sivan.[5] Though these two studies do not agree on every point, together they tend in the same direction. These scholars concluded that the literary dialect of the north was not significantly different from the literary dialect of the south, but that only the spoken dialects showed greater differences. Further, they stated that northern features are more likely to occur in direct discourse recorded in the Bible (thus Young more forcefully, but also Schniedewind and Sivan). We now are at the point where we can judge this position more objectively.

The following chart attempts to quantify the evidence analyzed in this study. I have listed:

(1) each chapter from 1 Kings 12 through 2 Kings 17 (except for those chapters that contain no IH material);

(2) the number of verses and IH features that occur in narration (N);

(3) the number of verses and IH features that occur in direct discourse (DD);

(4) and the total number of verses in each chapter.

If a particular IH feature occurs more than once in the same chapter, I have counted each one individually (thus the number of features in the chart does not always accord with the presentation of the evidence in each separate chapter above). For example, the word *kad* "vessel" appears three times in 1 Kings 17, used once by the woman of Zarepath (v. 12), once by Elijah (v. 14), and once by the narrator (v. 16); I have counted this as three features for statistical purposes.

I have not included the two non-linguistic features, even though they were enumerated in the treatments of the chapters above (see above, at 1 Kings 19 [1] and 2 Kings 14 [1]).

---

3. For classic statements about Masoretic leveling, with virtually verbatim wording, see E. Kautzsch, in GKC, vii; and G. R. Driver, "Hebrew Studies," *JRAS* (1948) 175. See my discussion of these two statements in G. A. Rendsburg, "The Strata of Biblical Hebrew," *JNSL* 17 (1991) 81.

4. Young, "The 'Northernisms' of the Israelite Narratives in Kings."

5. Schniedewind and Sivan, "Elijah-Elisha Narratives."

I have had to be somewhat subjective in judging those verses that are part narration and part direct discourse. If the great majority of the verse is in narration and only a small part in direct discourse, as in 2 Kgs 5:21 (with only the last word in DD), then I have counted the verse as fully narration. Similarly, if the great majority of the verse is in direct discourse and only an introductory phrase is in narration, as in 2 Kgs 7:1 (with only the first two words in N), then I have counted the verse as fully direct discourse. When a verse is more or less equally divided between narration and direct discourse, I simply counted half-verses (e.g., 1 Kgs 22:11, with the first 8 words in N and the next 9 words in DD). In addition, some verses are quite short (e.g., 2 Kgs 1:1, with only six words), whereas others are quite long (e.g., 2 Kgs 1:2, with 22 words). However, from a statistical viewpoint, the very high number of verses included in the study (700 altogether, see the chart below) levels the data and eliminates any such problems, both those resulting from my subjective decisions concerning N and DD and those resulting from verses of greatly uneven length.

We may summarize the data as follows. The corpus contains 700 verses and the total number of IH features identified in our study is 161. Of the 700 total verses, 419 or 59.9% of them occur in narration, whereas 281 or 40.1% of them occur in direct discourse. Of the 161 IH features, 80 or 49.7% of them occur in narration, whereas 81 or 50.3% of them occur in direct discourse. Or, to view these data in a different manner, overall an IH trait occurs every 4.3 verses (700 ÷ 161), in narration an IH trait occurs every 5.2 verses (419 ÷ 80), and in direct discourse an IH trait occurs every 3.5 verses (281 ÷ 81).

On the one hand, these data could be seen as confirmation of the view expressed by Young and by Schniedewind and Sivan. That is to say, there is a greater tendency for IH elements to occur in direct discourse. Note that there is a 10.2% sway from the first set of percentages to the second set of percentages (59.9% to 49.7%, or 40.1% to 50.3%). Or, using the rates presented, again, IH traits occur every 5.2 verses in narration, but more frequently, every 3.5 verses in direct discourse.

On the other hand, these data could be seen as countering Young's and Schniedewind and Sivan's position. Given the still very large number of IH elements that occur in narration, and given only a relatively small increase in the frequency with which these features appear in direct discourse, the figures allow one to conclude that, in general, the material in Kings devoted to the northern kingdom is written in northern Hebrew. In short, subjective judgment is necessary for the interpretation of these data, as typically is the case in statistical analysis. But from my vantage point, I would argue that a much larger dichotomy in the percentages would be necessary to confirm the view that the higher frequency of IH traits in direct discourse versus their less

ISRAELIAN HEBREW TRAITS IN THE BOOK OF KINGS

Chapter	N Verses	N IH Features	DD Verses	DD IH Features	Total Verses
1 Kgs 12	8.5	2	2.5	0	11
13	19.5	3	14.5	2	34
14	6.5	0	13.5	4	20
15	10	1	0	0	10
16	31	1	3	0	34
17	12.5	2	11.5	6	24
18	22.5	4	23.5	1	46
19	11.5	3	9.5	0	21
20	20	8	23	6	43
21	15	4	14	2	29
22	18.5	2	24.5	8	43
2 Kgs 1	7	1	11	3	18
2	15	1	10	1	25
3	15	2	12	5	27
4	24	8	20	14	44
5	12	0	15	3	27
6	17	6	16	8	33
7	10.5	3	9.5	0	20
8	9	4	8	4	17
9	18	6	18	11	36
10	22.5	3	12.5	2	35
13	22.5	1	2.5	0	25
14	13	2	0	0	13
15	23.5	7	0.5	1	24
17	34.5	6	6.5	0	41
Totals:	419 (59.9%)	80 (49.7%)	281 (40.1%)	81 (50.3%)	700 (100%)

DD = Direct Discourse
IH = Israelian Hebrew
N = Narrative

frequent appearance in narration was in the mind of the writer(s) as an intentional literary device.[6]

In order to illustrate the first "given" in the preceding paragraph, that is, that a large number of IH traits, both grammatical and lexical, occur in narration, I take the opportunity to list them here:[7] the roots *bdʾ, ghr, gzr, glm, zrr, ḥlṭ, kry (krh), mdd, mkr, nḥš, plḥ, qṣb,* and *šns;* the verb *lĕqaṣṣôt;* the *yqtl* preterite; the nouns *ʾargôb, ʾarmôn, ʾôrôt, gerem, dûd, hêkāl, ḥāśîp, ḥôrîm, yeraḥ, mĕdînā^h, nôqēd, pĕqûʿôt,* and *qāb;* the noun (consonantal) *bṣql;* the verbal noun *ʾăkîlā^h;* the word *miqṣôt;* the syntagma of *hyh* + participle; the prepositions *ʿad lĕ-* and *qābol;* the use of *b-* and *l-* for "from"; the non-elision of *he* after the uniconsonantal preposition *bĕ-;* the interchange of the prepositions *ʾel* and *ʿal;* the use of *min* before an anarthrous noun; the use of the numeral "one" as an indefinite article; the form *wayyirmĕsennā^h;* the f. sg. nominal suffix *-ôt;* the use of *ʾôt-* for *ʾitt;* the collocation of *ḥyh* and *qwm;* the double plural construction; and the expressions *hôṣiʾ kesep, śym šem,* and *bêt yiśśākār.* This list represents a very broad array of linguistic features. Any narrational section of the Bible (that is, material in N only, not in DD) that employs such an assemblage must be considered to be written in IH.

As another counter to the view of Young and Schniedewind and Sivan, it is striking that in a few instances, IH forms appear in the mouth of King Jehoshaphat of Judah! I refer specifically to the use of *ʾôt-* for *ʾitt-* in 1 Kgs 22:7, 2 Kgs 3:11, 3:12. If the northern author of this material was careful to place IH features only in the mouths of northern Israelites (and Arameans), then the threefold use of this feature in the mouth of the king of Judah would be inexplicable. Furthermore, in a few instances, YHWH or his angel utilizes IH features (though, in theory, this is less problematic for Young and Schniedewind and Sivan); see in particular *ʾôt-* when the angel of YHWH speaks to Elijah in 2 Kgs 1:15, and *rĕbîʿîm* spoken by YHWH himself in 2 Kgs 10:30, 15:12.

In light of this evidence, I prefer to conclude (and I admit to some subjectivity in my decision) that the Israelian material in Kings utilizes IH throughout, regardless of the presence of narration or direct discourse. The data cannot be dismissed; there is a slightly greater tendency for IH features to

---

6. I reached a similar conclusion in my work on colloquialisms in BH; they are just as likely to occur in narration as in direct discourse (though in this case the percentages correlate better than in the present study). See Rendsburg, *Diglossia in Ancient Hebrew,* 159–61.

7. The lexical features are listed in alphabetical order. The grammatical elements are presented generally in order of their appearance in Kings. Some of these items also occur in direct discourse, but the main point is that they occur in narration as well.

appear in direct discourse. But I would not accede to the claim that "these non-standard features are used in controlled environments, within a standard framework."[8] The above list demonstrates that even in narration IH features appear in large quantity.

Schniedewind and Sivan (and to some extent Young, though he focused only on those features in spoken discourse) emphasized the greater use of non-standard features in those scenes set in Aram. Clearly I am sympathetic to this view, as I already have devoted an article to the subject in general.[9] Most likely, some cases in Kings can be so explained, for example, the presence of *běhištaḥăwāyātî* in the mouth of Naaman in 2 Kgs 5:18 (I have noted others in the detailed treatment of the chapters above). But Sivan and Schniedewind went too far in stating that such scenes are more likely to produce the most examples of non-standard features. True, 1 Kings 20 and 2 Kings 6 each has 14 IH features (see the chart above), but note that 2 Kings 4 has the most IH elements of any chapter, 22 in all, with all the action set in Shunem, Carmel, and Gilgal, with no mention of Aram, and that 2 Kings 9 has 17 IH traits, with the action set in Ramoth-gilead, the area around Megiddo, and Jezreel, with only a passing reference to Aram (vv. 14–15).

To be statistically accurate, we not only should deal with the number of items in each chapter, but we also should take into account the varying lengths of each chapter. A statistical analysis produces the following results. The greatest concentration of features is in 2 Kings 4 (22 items in 44 verses, or 50%), followed by 2 Kings 9 (17 items in 36 verses, or 47.2%) and 2 Kings 8 (8 items in 17 verses, or 47.1%). Next comes one of the two chapters noted by Schniedewind and Sivan, namely, 2 Kings 6 (14 items in 33 verses, or 42%), followed by 2 Kings 15 (8 items in 24 verses, or 33.3%) and then the second chapter noted by Schniedewind and Sivan, namely, 1 Kings 20 (14 items in 43 verses, or 32.6%).[10] Of these chapters, the ones not noted in the preceding paragraph are 2 Kings 8 and 2 Kings 15. The former is set partly in Aram (vv. 7–15) and partly in Canaan (vv. 1–6, 28–29). Interestingly, the 9 verses set in Aram have 3 IH features (2 in v. 8, 1 in v. 9), thus 33%, whereas the 8 verses set in Canaan have 5 IH features (1 in v. 1, 2 in v. 3, 1 in v. 6, 1 in v. 29), thus 63%. More striking is 2 Kings 15, which is set entirely in the Land of Israel, yet contains one of the highest concentrations of IH features in the corpus.

---

8. Young, "The 'Northernisms' of the Israelite Narratives in Kings," 69–70.

9. Rendsburg, "Linguistic Variation and the 'Foreign' Factor in the Hebrew Bible," especially pp. 178–83.

10. All other chapters have a lower percentage. The overall percentage, calculated with 161 items in 700 verses, is 23%.

In other words, a setting in Aram does not necessarily produce a greater number of unusual grammatical and lexical features.

In short, a few features isolated in this study may be present in Kings as a literary device to portray the foreignness of the Arameans. However, one should not extrapolate from this phenomenon and eliminate the notion of IH as a general characteristic of the stories concerning the northern kings and the northern prophets.

Schniedewind and Sivan also suggested in passing that there "seems to be a higher concentration of linguistic anomalies in the folktales of 1 Kings 17 and 2 Kings 4–6."[11] In order not to judge which narratives are more folkloristic than others, I divided the entire corpus into those sections in which Elijah and Elisha are present (1 Kings 17–19, 1 Kings 21, 2 Kings 2, 2 Kings 4–7, and portions of other chapters) and those sections in which they are totally absent (1 Kings 12–16, 1 Kings 20, 1 Kings 22, 2 Kings 10, 2 Kings 14–15, 2 Kings 17, and portions of other chapters). Although I refrain from presenting a chart with all the data, I do present the totals here. There are 368 non-Elijah-Elisha verses, or 52.6% of the corpus, with 73, or 45.3% of the IH features compared to 332 Elijah-Elisha verses, or 47.4% of the corpus, with 88 or 54.7% of the IH features. Again, there is a slight increase, with a shift of 7.3% (that is, the difference between 52.6% and 45.3%, or between 54.7% and 47.4%). Or, to use the other method of calculation, IH features occur once every 5.0 verses in the non-Elijah-Elisha material and once every 3.8 verses in the Elijah-Elisha material. However, once more we note that the shift is not so drastic as to allow one to claim that the folktales surrounding the two prophets yield a substantially greater number of northern dialectal traits than the remaining material of a more "official" nature. A list such as the one above, delineating those features that appear in narration, could be presented here, as well, to illustrate the present issue. But there seems no need to burden the reader with a detailed list.

One additional statement made by Schniedewind and Sivan requires comment. They claimed that "more emphasis should be placed on morphological items when describing Hebrew dialects" than on lexical items.[12] On the one hand, I have no difficulty with their position, because, as the Appendix to this volume illustrates, there clearly are numerous morphological features that separate IH and JH. On the other hand, I would argue that Schniedewind and Sivan are incorrect in their view. In the Introduction to this volume, I referred to the many dialect atlases that have been produced for various languages in the world. The databases of these dialect atlases

---

11. Schniedewind and Sivan, "Elijah–Elisha Narratives," 335.

12. *Ibid.*

typically are dominated by lexical features, not morphological ones or other grammatical ones. One need think only of the German equivalents of two common words that serve to separate geographically the dialects of modern German, namely "Sonnabend" and "Samstag" for "Saturday," and "Kartoffel" and "Erdapfel" for "potato."[13]

I here note a tangential finding of this study: the main narrative in 1 Kings 22 (that is, vv. 1–38) belongs to the material emanating from the northern kingdom. This chapter has engendered much discussion, due to its uniqueness and quirky nature. I refer to the following points: (1) it deals with a northern king, namely, Ahab, but he is mentioned by name only once, in v. 20 (in the main account, that is, the aforecited verses), in contrast to Jehoshaphat king of Judah, who is mentioned by name repeatedly; (2) the chapter presents a double death notice of Ahab, one in v. 37, following a detailed description of his bloody death in battle, and one in v. 40, implying a peaceful death; and (3) unlike the remainder of the material about the northern kingdom, this chapter neither is laconic in its description of royal activities nor does it center on the prophets Elijah and/or Elisha. Scholars have proposed a variety of solutions to this problem, most of them tied to different approaches to the so-called Deuteronomistic History.[14] However one is to judge this issue, it now is clear that this chapter, like the other material about Ahab, originates in northern Israel. Note that 1 Kings 22 has seven different features delineated herein used for a total of ten times (vv. 7, 8, 9, 16, 24 [2 items], 28, 30 [1 item used 2×], 35).

Although the goal of this monograph was a contribution to the field of Hebrew linguistics, it is important to note that the main conclusion of the work has far-reaching implications for Biblical Studies in general. A number of recent studies has questioned the essential historicity of the material recorded in the book of Kings.[15] Several scholars have opined that all so-called (that is, "so-called" in the mind of these scholars) pre-exilic Israelite history is the fabrication of Persian- or Hellenistic-period Jewish scribes.

---

13. Note that the work of Avi Hurvitz toward identifying LBH (see my brief discussion in the Introduction) focuses on both grammatical and lexical features, with a heavy dose of the latter. I see no reason why lexical features cannot serve to separate IH and JH. See also the methodology employed by Ginsberg, "The Northwest Semitic Languages," to delineate his "Phoenic" group from his "Hebraic" group.

14. See the detailed study by B. Halpern and D. S. Vanderhooft, "The Editions of Kings in the 7th and 6th Centuries B.C.E.," *HUCA* 62 (1991) 179–244, with specific treatment of 1 Kings 22 on pp. 230–35.

15. The bibliography that advocates this position is ever-growing and I do not attempt here a listing of such works.

While this study hardly was necessary to show the folly of such an approach, the linguistic evidence put forward herein is one more angle by which to deny this baseless approach to the literary sources and to ancient Israelite history. That is to say, if Jewish scribes in the fifth, fourth, or even third century BCE produced the history in Kings as a fiction, one needs to ask: How is it that when writing the history of the fabricated kingdom of Judah, these scribes used JH; but when writing the history of the fabricated kingdom of Israel, these scribes used IH? One could answer that they used different dialects to produce their work—in a very clever and intelligent manner—but this seems most unlikely (notwithstanding my belief that the ancient Israelite literati engaged in style-switching very effectively).

A much simpler approach, and certainly the correct approach, is to assume, as most scholars do, that the material concerning the northern kings and the northern prophets emanates from Israelian scribes and that the material concerning the southern kings derives from Judahite scribes. Obviously, the final product is the work of Judahite hands, which incorporated the Israelian material into the canonical composition. But the Israelian material was treated with due respect; generally the northern sections of Kings were not touched—or touched up—by their southern handlers.

Such a conclusion dovetails nicely with Bin-Nun's study (discussed briefly in the Introduction), which demonstrated on independent grounds that the formulas concerning the individual kings appear in different models for Israel and Judah.[16] In other words, when the southern scribes utilized the imported northern material to create the integrated history of the two kingdoms, they not only retained the Israelian dialect, but they also left the framework formulas (introductory notices, obituary notices, etc.) intact.

In the current debate about the dating of the biblical corpus, the evidence of language either has not been utilized (thus most often) or it has been utilized in a most fanciful and farcical manner.[17] Several scholars have begun to publish serious linguistic studies to show the failings of attempts to date virtually the entire corpus to the Persian and/or Hellenistic periods.[18] I did

---

16. Bin-Nun, "Formulas from Royal Records of Israel and of Judah." For a recent attempt to argue against Bin-Nun, see K. A. D. Smelik and H.-J. van Soest, "Overlijdensteksten in het boek Koningen: De compositie van het boek Koningen (3)," *ACEBT* 13 (1994) 56–71. I have not had the opportunity to see this work; rather I cite it from the abstract that appeared in *OTA* 18 (1995) 71.

17. See, e.g., F. Cryer, "The Problem of Dating Biblical Hebrew and the Hebrew of Daniel," in *In the Last Days: On Jewish and Christian Apocalyptic and Its Period* (eds. K. Jeppesen, K. Nielsen, and B. Rosendal; Aarhus: Aarhus University Press, 1994) 185–98.

18. See, for example, A. Hurvitz, "The Historical Quest for 'Ancient Israel' and

not begin the present study as an exercise in that direction—rather, as noted above, my goal lay elsewhere—but I am happy to have it serve as a corrective to the approach that would see the material in Kings as (largely or wholly) post-exilic, indeed late post-exilic.

---

the Linguistic Evidence of the Hebrew Bible: Some Methodological Observations," *VT* 47 (1997) 301–15; A. Hurvitz, "Can Biblical Texts Be Dated Linguistically? Chronological Perspectives in the Historical Study of Biblical Hebrew," in *Congress Volume Oslo 1998* (eds. A. Lemaire and M. Sæbø; SVT 80; Leiden: Brill, 2000) 143–60; and R. M. Wright, *Linguistic Evidence for the Pre-Exilic Date of the Yahwist Source of the Pentateuch* (Ph.D. dissertation, Cornell University, 1998).

APPENDIX

FEATURES OF ISRAELIAN HEBREW
ISOLATED IN THIS STUDY

Citations are by biblical chapter and subsection,
e.g., 1K13.1 = 1 Kings 13 [1]

I. PHONOLOGY

    A. Vowels

        1. Shift of *a* to *ō* (2K3.4; see also "f. sg. nominal ending -*ôt*," below under Morphology)

    B. Diphthongs

        1. Monophthongization of *ay* > *ā* (2K5.3)

II. MORPHOLOGY

    A. Pronouns

        1. 2 f. sg. independent pronoun *ʾty* (1K14.2, 2K4.5, 2K8.1)

        2. 2 f. sg. pronominal suffix -*kî* (2K4.2)

        3. Relative pronoun *še*- (incorporated into genitive particle *šel*) (2K6.6)

        4. f. sg. demonstrative pronoun *zôʰ* (2K6.9)

        5. Interrogative pronoun *meʰ* before non-laryngeal consonants (1K14.4, 1K22.3, 2K1.2, 2K4.3)

    B. Nouns

        1. f. sg. nominal ending -*at* (2K9.5)

        2. f. sg. nominal ending -*ôt* (2K6.4, 2K10.3; see also "Shift of *a* to *ō*," above under Phonology)

        3. *qĕtîlāʰ* formation (1K19.3)

    C. Verbs

        1. 3 f. sg. *qtl* form of IIIy verbs ending in -*t*, viz., *hyt* (2K9.11)

        2. Retention of *lamed* in imperative of *lqḥ* (1K17.1)

        3. *lttn* as infinitive of *ntn* (1K17.3)

4. Irregular infinitive form $běhištaḥăwāyātî$ (2K5.2)
5. m. sg. participle of IIIy verb ending in $-ē^h$, viz., $^ɔ ōśē^h$ (1K20.10)
6. Inflected participle (2K4.6)
7. 3 sg. pronominal suffix $-ennû/-ennā^h$ attached to $wayyiqtol$ form (2K9.10)

D. Particles

1. Prepositions $b-/l-$ "from" (2K4.7, 2K14.2)
2. Preposition $^ɔ ad lě-$ (1K18.1)
3. Preposition $^ɔ ad ɔel$, viz., $^ɔ ad ɔălêhem$ (2K9.8)
4. Preposition $^ɔ ad$ with independent personal pronoun following, viz., $^ɔ ad hēm$ (2K9.7)
5. Preposition $^ɔ ad$ meaning "while" (2K9.9)
6. Preposition $qābol$ (2K15.1)
7. Non-elision of definite article he after uniconsonantal prepositions b, l, k (2K7.3)
8. Interrogative $^ɔ êkô^h$ "where" (2K6.7)

III. SYNTAX

1. $ze^h hayyôm$ "this day" syntagma (1K14.3, 2K6.13)
2. $ḥolî ze^h$ construction (definite noun with indefinite demonstrative pronoun) (2K1.1, 2K8.5)
3. Double plural construction (2K15.7)
4. Use of $^ɔ eḥād/ ^ɔaḥat$ as indefinite article (1K13.3, 1K19.2, 1K20.3, 1K22.2. 2K4.1, 2K7.2, 2K8.3)
5. $yqtl$ with past meaning (1K20.8, 1K21.2, 2K8.6, 2K9.4)
6. Passive participle with active voice (2K6.5)
7. hyh + participle formation (1K22.7, 2K6.3, 2K17.3)
8. Infinitive absolute used as narrative tense (1K22.6, 2K3.3, 2K4.15)
9. Interchange of prepositions $ɔel$ and $^ɔ al$ (1K13.4, 1K17.6, 1K18.4, 1K20.11, 2K7.1, 2K8.2, 2K9.1)
10. Preposition min followed by anarthrous noun (2K15.8)
11. Use of $ɔ ôt$-forms for expected $ɔitt$-forms (1K20.5, 1K22.1, 2K1.3, 2K3.2, 2K6.8, 2K8.4)
12. Interrogative $ɔ ê ze^h$ governing verb (1K22.4)
13. Interrogative series $hă... ɔ ô$ (2K4.4, 2K6.12)

IV. LEXICON

A. Nouns and Adjectives

1. *ʾôrôt* "herbs, sprouts, etc." (2K4.11)
2. *ʾargôb* "eagle" (2K15.6)
3. *ʾarmôn* "palace, citadel" (1K16.1, 2K15.5)
4. *bṣql* (=★*baṣqel*) "ear of grain" (2K4.14)
5. *gerem* "bone, self" (2K9.3)
6. *dûd* "pot, basket" (2K10.1)
7. *ḥāśîp* "small (flock)" (1K20.6)
8. *hêkāl* "palace" (1K21.1)
9. *ḥēleq* "field" (2K9.2)
10. *ḥôrîm* "nobles, freemen" (1K21.3)
11. *yeraḥ* "moon" (2K15.3)
12. *kad* "jar" (1K17.2, 1K18.2)
13. *kērāʰ* "feast" (2K6.10)
14. *mĕdînāʰ* "district" (1K20.4)
15. *mattat* "gift" (1K13.2)
16. *miqṣôt* "from among, some of" (1K12.1, 1K13.5, 2K17.2)
17. *nôqēd* "shepherd foreman" (2K3.1)
18. *pĕqûʿôt* "wild gourds" (2K4.12)
19. *ṣibbûrîm* "piles, heaps" (2K10.2)
20. *ṣĕlôḥît* "dish" (2K2.2)
21. *qāb* "unit of measurement" (2K6.11)
22. *rĕbîʿîm* "those of the fourth generation" (2K10.4, 2K15.2)
23. *śipʿat* "multitude" (2K9.6)

B. Verbs

1. *bdʾ* "invent, devise" (1K12.2)
2. *ghr* "bend, crouch" (1K18.3, 2K4.9)
3. *gwr* (T-stem) "dwell, reside" (1K17.4)
4. *gzr* "cut" (2K6.1)
5. *glm* "roll up (a garment)" (2K2.1)
6. *zrr* "sneeze" (2K4.10)
7. *ḥlṭ* "decide" (1K20.9)
8. *ḥrb* "slay, slaughter, fight" (2K3.5)
9. *kry* "make a feast" (2K6.10)
10. *mdd* (T-stem) "stretch oneself" (1K17.5)
11. *mkr* (T-stem) "decide" (1K21.4, 2K17.1)
12. *mnʿ* "prevent, withhold" (1K20.1)
13. *nḥš* "divine" (1K20.7)
14. *nḥt* "descend" (2K6.5)

    15. *s⁽ᶜ⁾d* "eat, dine" (1K13.1)
    16. *plḥ* "cut, split" (2K4.13)
    17. *qṣb* "cut" (2K6.2)
    18. *qṣy* (D-stem) "reduce" (2K10.5)
    19. *śpq* "be sufficient" (1K20.2)
    20. *šly* (H-stem) "mislead" (2K4.8)
    21. *šny* (T-stem) "disguise oneself" (1K14.1)
    22. *šns* "gird" (1K18.5)

C. Particles
    1. *ʾaḥălê* "would that" (2K5.1)

D. Expressions
    1. *bêt yiśśākār* "house of Issachar" (1K15.1)
    2. *dbr b-* "speak to" (1K22.5)
    3. *ḥyy* "live" and *qwm* "arise" collocated (2K13.1)
    4. *hôṣîʾ kesep* "bring out silver" > "levy" (2K15.4)
    5. *śym šēm* "place a name" > "name" (2K17.4)

V. MISCELLANEOUS
    1. *bĕʾēr šebaᶜ ʾăšer lîhûdāʰ* "Beersheba which is to Judah" (1K19.1)
    2. *bêt šemeš ʾăšer lîhûdāʰ* "Beth-shemesh which is to Judah" (2K14.1)

Afterword

After this monograph was completed, I came into contact via e-mail with Dr. Jun Ikeda of the University of Tsukuba in Tsukuba, Japan. He has turned his attention to the issue of regional dialects in ancient Hebrew in two recent articles: "Linguistic Varieties in Biblical Hebrew: An Overview and a Case Study," *Bulletin of the International Institute for Linguistic Sciences, Kyoto Sangyo University* 21 (2000) 179–204 [in Japanese]; and "Regional Dialects in Biblical Hebrew," *Studies in Language and Literature: Language* (Institute of Literature and Linguistics, University of Tsukuba) 38 (2000) 1–15 [in Japanese].

In the former, Ikeda has identified another feature of IH in Kings, namely, the omission of the *nota accusativi* ʾet. As is well known, the use of ʾet is inconsistent in the Bible, even in prose texts, so an occasional omission is nothing special. But when a pattern emerges, as it does in the material surveyed by Ikeda, one is ready to accept his conclusion. I have omitted several examples from his list that I believe can be explained according to the trends described in Joüon and Muraoka, *A Grammar of Biblical Hebrew*, 445–46 (see below). The examples that I find convincing are: 2 Kgs 3:19, 3:25(2×), 4:4, 4:5, 4:24, 4:29, 4:33, 4:36, 4:38, 5:6, 5:11, 6:4, 6:7, 6:32, 8:15, 9:1(2×), 9:3(2×), 9:6, 9:7(2×), 9:10, 9:23, 9:24, 10:15, 10:22, 13:17, 13:18, 17:12. Incorporation of these passages into our study obviously would change the statistics presented in the concluding chapter.

Among the examples put forward by Ikeda that I have omitted from this list are the following: 2 Kgs 8:12(4×), because when the object precedes the verb, the syntax "does not specifically require ʾet" (Joüon-Muraoka, §125f); and 2 Kgs 4:34(3×), because one is less likely to find ʾet "when the object designates a part of the body of the subject in an idiomatic collocation" (Joüon-Muraoka, §125ia). Notwithstanding a few examples such as these in Ikeda's list of passages, his overall conclusion is convincing.

BIBLIOGRAPHY

Academy of the Hebrew Language. *The Historical Dictionary of the Hebrew Language,* Materials for the Dictionary, Series I, 200 B.C.E. – 300 C.E., Microfiche format. Jerusalem: Academy of the Hebrew Language, 1988.

—————. *Ma'agarim: The Hebrew Language Historical Dictionary Project,* CD-ROM. Jerusalem: Academy of the Hebrew Language, 1998.

—————. *Sefer Ben Sira.* Jerusalem: Academy of the Hebrew Language, 1973.

Andersen, F. I., and D. N. Freedman. *Hosea.* AB 24. Garden City, N.Y.: Doubleday, 1980.

Andersen, T. D. "The Evolution of the Hebrew Verbal System," *ZAH* 13 (2000) 1–66.

Baltzer, D. "Literarkritische und literarhistorische Anmerkungen zur Heilsprophetie im Ezechiel-Buch," in *Ezekiel and His Book.* BETL 74. Ed. J. Lust. Leuven: Leuven University Press, 1986. Pp. 166–81.

Bauer, H., and P. Leander. *Historische Grammatik der hebräischen Sprache des Alten Testamentes.* Halle: Max Niemeyer, 1922.

Ben-Hayyim, Z. "'Ivrit Nusaḥ Shomron (Sof)," *Leshonenu* 12 (5703/4 [1942/44]) 113–26.

—————. *'Ivrit ve-'Aramit Nusaḥ Shomron.* 5 vols. Jerusalem: Bialik, 1957.

Beyer, K. *Die aramäischen Texte vom Toten Meer.* Göttingen: Vandenhoeck & Ruprecht, 1984.

Biblia Hebraica Stuttgartensia. Stuttgart: Deutsche Bibelgesellschaft, 1990.

Bin-Nun, S. R. "Formulas from Royal Records of Israel and of Judah," *VT* 18 (1968) 414–32.

Blau, J. (Y.). "Benoni Pa'ul be-Hora'a 'Aqtivit," *Leshonenu* 18 (1952/53) 67–81.

—————. "The Parallel Development of the Feminine Ending -*at* in Semitic Languages," *HUCA* 51 (1980) 17–28.

—————. *On Pseudo-Corrections in Some Semitic Languages.* Jerusalem: Israel Academy of Sciences and Humanities, 1970.

Boadt, L. "Rhetorical Strategies in Ezekiel's Oracles of Judgment," in *Ezekiel and His Book.* BETL 74. Ed. J. Lust. Leuven: Leuven University Press, 1986. Pp. 182–200.

Brinkman, J. A. "Babylonia in the Shadow of Assyria (747–626 B.C.)," *Cambridge Ancient History,* 3rd ed., III/2 (1991) 1–69.

Brockelmann, C. *Grundriss der vergleichenden Grammatik der semitischen Sprachen.* 2 vols. Berlin: Reuther & Reichard, 1908–13.

—————. *Lexicon Syriacum*. Halle: Max Niemeyer, 1928.

—————. *Syrische Grammatik*. Leipzig: Reuther & Reichard, 1960.

Brown, F., S. R. Driver, and C. A. Briggs. *A Hebrew and English Lexicon of the Old Testament*. Oxford: Clarendon Press, 1906.

Burkitt, F. C. "Micah 6 and 7: A Northern Prophecy," *JBL* 45 (1926) 159–61.

Burney, C. F. *Notes on the Hebrew Text of the Books of Kings*. Oxford: Clarendon Press, 1903.

Cassuto, U. *Biblical and Oriental Studies*. 2 vols. Trans. I. Abrahams. Jerusalem: Magnes, 1975.

—————. "Daniele e le spighe. Un episodio della tavola ID di Ras Shamra," *Orientalia* 8 (1939) 238–43.

Chen, Y. *Israelian Hebrew in the Book of Proverbs*. Ph.D. dissertation. Ithaca: Cornell University, 2000.

Chomsky, W. *David Kimḥi's Hebrew Grammar (Mikhlol)*. New York: Bloch, 1952.

Clarke, E. G. *Targum Pseudo-Jonathan of the Pentateuch: Text and Concordance*. Hoboken, N.J.: Ktav, 1984.

Clines, D. J. A., ed. *The Dictionary of Classical Hebrew*. 8 vols. Sheffield: Sheffield Academic Press, 1993-forthcoming.

Cogan M., and H. Tadmor. *II Kings*. AB 11. New York: Doubleday, 1988.

Cohen, A. *The Psalms*. London: Soncino, 1945.

Cohen, H. R. (C.). *Biblical Hapax Legomena in the Light of Akkadian and Ugaritic*. SBLDS 37. Missoula, Mont.: Scholars Press, 1978.

—————. "Neo-Assyrian Elements in the First Speech of the Biblical Rab-šaqê," *IOS* 9 (1979) 32–48.

Cowley, A. E. *Aramaic Papyri of the 5th Century B.C.* Oxford: Clarendon Press, 1923.

Cryer, F. "The Problem of Dating Biblical Hebrew and the Hebrew of Daniel," in *The Last Days: On Jewish and Christian Apocalyptic and Its Period*. Eds. K. Jeppesen, K. Nielsen, and B. Rosendal. Aarhus: Aarhus University Press, 1994. Pp. 185–98.

Dahood, M. "Canaanite-Phoenician Influence in Qoheleth," *Biblica* 33 (1952) 30–52, 191–221.

—————. *Proverbs and Northwest Semitic Philology*. Rome: Pontifical Biblical Institute, 1963.

Dalman, G. *Grammatik des jüdisch-palästinischen Aramäisch*. Leipzig: Hinrichs, 1905.

Davila, J. R. "Qoheleth and Northern Hebrew," in *Sopher Mahir: Northwest Semitic Studies Presented to Stanislav Segert*. Ed. E. M. Cook = *Maarav* 5–6 (1990) 69–87.

Degen, R. *Altaramäische Grammatik*. Wiesbaden: Franz Steiner, 1969.

DeVries, S. J. *1 Kings*. WBC. Waco, Tex.: Word Books, 1985.

Donner, H., and W. Röllig. *Kanaanäische und aramäische Inschriften*. 3 vols. Wiesbaden: Otto Harrassowitz, 1971–76.

Dotan, A. "Stress Position and Vowel Shift in Phoenician and Punic," *IOS* 6 (1976) 71–121.

Driver, G. R. *Canaanite Myths and Legends*. Edinburgh: T & T Clark, 1956.

—————. "Hebrew Poetic Diction," in *Congress Volume Copenhagen 1953*. SVT 1. Leiden: E. J. Brill, 1953. Pp. 26–39.

—————. "Hebrew Studies," *JRAS* (1948) 164–76.

—————. "Studies in the Vocabulary of the Old Testament. II," *JTS* 32 (1931) 250–57.

Driver, S. R. *An Introduction to the Literature of the Old Testament*. Oxford: Clarendon Press, 1920.

—————. *Notes on the Hebrew Text of the Books of Samuel*. Oxford: Clarendon Press, 1890.

—————. *A Treatise on the Use of the Tenses in Hebrew*. Oxford: Clarendon Press, 1892.

Drower, E. S., and R. Macuch. *A Mandaic Dictionary*. Oxford: Clarendon Press, 1963.

Eissfeldt, O. *Kleine Schriften*. 6 vols. Tübingen: J. C. B. Mohr, 1962–79.

—————. "Psalm 80," in *Geschichte und Altes Testament: Albrecht Alt zum 70. Geburtstag dargebracht*. Tübingen: J. C. B. Mohr, 1953. Pp. 65–78.

—————. "Psalm 80 und Psalm 89," *WO* 3 (1964/66) 27–31.

Eph'al, I. *The Ancient Arabs*. Jerusalem: Magnes, 1982.

Eph'al, I., and J. Naveh. "The Jar of the Gate," *BASOR* 289 (1993) 59–65.

Epstein, J. N. *Diqduq ʾAramit Bavlit*. Jerusalem: Magnes, 1960.

Even-Shoshan, A. *Qonqordanṣya Ḥadasha le-Torah Neviʾim u-Khtuvim*. Jerusalem: Kiryath Sepher, 1989.

Fassberg, S. E. "The Pronominal Suffix of the Second Feminine Singular in the Aramaic Texts from the Judean Desert," *DSD* 3 (1996) 10–19.

Fitzmyer, J. A. *The Aramaic Inscriptions of Sefire*. Rome: Pontifical Biblical Institute, 1967.

—————. *The Genesis Apocryphon of Qumran Cave I*. Rome: Biblical Institute Press, 1971.

Fox, J. "A Sequence of Vowel Shifts in Phoenician and Other Languages," *JNES* 55 (1996) 37–47.

Fox, M. V. *The Song of Songs and the Ancient Egyptian Love Songs*. Madison: University of Wisconsin Press, 1985.

Friedrich, J., and W. Röllig. *Phönizisch-punische Grammatik*. 2nd ed. Rome: Pontifical Biblical Institute, 1970.

Garr, W. R. *Dialect Geography of Syria-Palestine 1000–586 B.C.E.* Philadelphia: University of Pennsylvania Press, 1985.

Geller, M. "A New Translation for 2 Kings xv 25," *VT* 26 (1976) 374–77.

Gevirtz, S. "Of Patriarchs and Puns: Joseph at the Fountain, Jacob at the Ford," *HUCA* 46 (1975) 33–54.

—————. "Of Syntax and Style in the 'Late Biblical Hebrew' – 'Old Canaanite' Connection," *JANES* 18 (1986) 25–29.

Gibson, J. C. L. "Review of G. A. Rendsburg, *Linguistic Evidence for the Northern Origin of Selected Psalms*." in *BSOAS* 55 (1992) 543–44.

——————. *Textbook of Syrian Semitic Inscriptions*. 3 vols. Oxford: Clarendon Press, 1971–82.

Ginsberg, H. L. *The Israelian Heritage of Judaism*. New York: Jewish Theological Seminary, 1982.

——————. "The Northwest Semitic Languages," in *Patriarchs*. Ed. B. Mazar. World History of the Jewish People. New Brunswick: Rutgers University Press, 1970. Pp. 102–24, 293.

Golomb, D. M. *A Grammar of Targum Neofiti*. Chico, Calif.: Scholars Press, 1985.

Gordis, R. "Psalm 9–10 — A Textual and Exegetical Study," *JQR* 48 (1958) 104–22.

Gordon, C. H. "North Israelite Influence on Postexilic Hebrew," *IEJ* 5 (1955) 85–88.

——————. *Ugaritic Textbook*. Rome: Pontifical Biblical Institute, 1967.

Gordon, C. H., and G. A. Rendsburg. *The Bible and the Ancient Near East*. New York: W. W. Norton, 1997.

Gray, J. *I and II Kings*. OTL. Philadelphia: Westminster, 1970.

Greenberg, M. *Ezekiel 1–20*. AB 22. New York: Doubleday, 1983.

——————. *Ezekiel 21–37*. AB 22A. New York: Doubleday, 1997.

Greenfield, J. C. "Aramaic Studies and the Bible," in *Congress Volume Vienna 1980*. SVT 32. Ed. J. Emerton. Leiden: E. J. Brill, 1981. Pp. 110–30.

——————. "Etymological Semantics," *ZAH* 6 (1993) 26–37.

——————. "The 'Periphrastic Imperative' in Aramaic and Hebrew," *IEJ* 19 (1969) 199–210.

——————. "Philological Observations on the Deir ʿAlla Inscription," in *The Balaam Text from Deir ʿAlla Re-evaluated*. Eds. J. Hoftijzer and G. van der Kooij. Leiden: E. J. Brill, 1991.

——————. "Scripture and Inscription: The Literary and Rhetorical Element in Some Early Phoenician Inscriptions," in *Near Eastern Studies in Honor of William Foxwell Albright*. Ed. H. Goedicke. Baltimore: Johns Hopkins University Press, 1971. Pp. 253–68.

——————. "Ugaritic Lexicographical Notes," *JCS* 21 (1967) 89–93.

Grossfeld, B. *The Targum Sheni to the Book of Esther*. New York: Sepher-Hermon Press, 1994.

Gunkel, H. *Die Psalmen*. HKAT. Göttingen: Vandenhoeck & Ruprecht, 1926.

Halpern, B., and D. S. Vanderhooft. "The Editions of Kings in the 7th–6th Centuries B.C.E.," *HUCA* 62 (1991) 179–244.

Haneman, G. *Torat ha-Ṣurot shel Leshon ha-Mishna ʿal pi Mesorat Ketav-Yad Parma (De Rossi 138)*. Tel-Aviv: Tel-Aviv University, 1980.

Harris, Z. *Development of the Canaanite Dialects*. New Haven: American Oriental Society, 1939.

Hetzron, R. "Third Person Singular Pronoun Suffixes in Proto-Semitic," *Orientalia Suecana* 18 (1969) 101–27.

Hillers, D. R., and E. Cussini. *Palmyrene Aramaic Texts*. Baltimore: Johns Hopkins University Press, 1996.

Hoftijzer, J., and K. Jongeling. *Dictionary of the North-West Semitic Inscriptions*. 2 vols. Leiden: E. J. Brill, 1995.

Hossfeld, F. *Untersuchungen zu Komposition und Theologie des Ezechielbuches*. FzB 20. Würzburg: Echter, 1977.

Huesman, J. "Finite Uses of the Infinitive Absolute," *Biblica* 37 (1956) 271–84.

——. "The Infinitive Absolute and the Waw + Perfect Problem," *Biblica* 37 (1956) 410–34.

Hurvitz, A. *Beyn Lashon le-Lashon*. Jerusalem: Bialik, 1972.

——. "Can Biblical Texts Be Dated Linguistically? Chronological Perspectives in the Historical Study of Biblical Hebrew," in *Congress Volume Oslo 1998*. Eds. A. Lemaire and M. Sæbø. SVT 80. Leiden: Brill, 2000. Pp. 143–60.

——. "The Historical Quest for 'Ancient Israel' and the Linguistic Evidence of the Hebrew Bible: Some Methodological Observations," *VT* 47 (1997) 301–15.

Ikeda, J. "Linguistic Varieties in Biblical Hebrew: An Overview and a Case Study," *Bulletin of the International Institute for Linguistic Sciences, Kyoto Sangyo University* 21 (2000) 179–204 [in Japanese].

——. "Regional Dialects in Biblical Hebrew," *Studies in Language and Literature: Language* (Institute of Literature and Linguistics, University of Tsukuba) 38 (2000) 1–15 [in Japanese].

Izre'el, S. "Ve-shuv ʿal *(y)qtl* ʾnk u-Maqbilav ba-Leshonot ha-Knaʿaniyot." Unpublished paper.

Jastrow, M. *A Dictionary of the Targumim, the Talmud Babli and Yerushalmi, and the Midrashic Literature*. 2 vols. London: Luzac, 1903.

Jongeling, B., C.-J. Labuschagne, and A. S. van der Woude. *Aramaic Texts from Qumran*. Leiden: E. J. Brill, 1976.

Joosten, J. "The Syntax of *zeh Mošeh* (Ex 32,1.23)," *ZAW* 103 (1991) 412–15.

Joüon, P. "Notes de critique textuelle (AT) 2 Rois 6,8–10," *MUSJ* 5 (1911–12) 477–78.

Joüon, P., and T. Muraoka. *A Grammar of Biblical Hebrew*. 2 vols. Rome: Pontifical Biblical Institute, 1991.

Kaufman, S. A. "The Classification of the North West Semitic Dialects of the Biblical Period and Some Implications Thereof," in *Proceedings of the Ninth World Congress of Jewish Studies*: Panel Sessions: Hebrew and Aramaic Languages. Jerusalem: World Congress of Jewish Studies, 1988. Pp. 41–57.

Kautzsch, E. *Die Aramaismen im Alten Testament*. Halle: Max Niemeyer, 1902.

——. *Gesenius' Hebrew Grammar*. Trans. A. E. Cowley. Oxford: Clarendon Press, 1910.

Klein, S. *Sefer ha-Yishuv*. 2 vols. Jerusalem: Bialik, 5699 (1938/39).

Koehler, L., and W. Baumgartner. *Lexicon in Veteris Testamenti libros*. Leiden: E. J. Brill, 1953.

König, E. *Historisch-comparative Syntax der hebräischen Sprache*. 3 vols. Leipzig: J. C. Hinrichs, 1881–97.

————. *Historisch-kritisches Lehrgebäude der hebräischen Sprache.* 2 vols. Leipzig: J. C. Hinrichs, 1895.

Kraeling, E. G. *The Brooklyn Museum Aramaic Papyri.* New Haven: Yale University Press, 1953.

Kutscher, E. Y. "Dating the Language of the Genesis Apocryphon," *JBL* 76 (1957) 288–92.

————. *A History of the Hebrew Language.* Ed. R. Kutscher. Jerusalem: Magnes, 1982.

————. *Meḥqarim ba-ʾAramit ha-Gelilit.* Jerusalem: Hebrew University, 1969.

————. *Studies in Galilean Aramaic.* Trans. M. Sokoloff. Ramat-Gan: Bar-Ilan University, 1974.

Lambert, M. "De l'emploi des suffixes pronominaux avec *noun* et sans *noun* au futur et à l'impératif," *REJ* 46 (1903) 178–83.

Leander, P. *Laut- und Formenlehre des Ägyptisch-aramäischen.* Göteborg: Elanders, 1928.

Licht, J. *Storytelling in the Bible.* Jerusalem: Magnes, 1978.

Lipiński, E. "Banquet en l'honneur de Baal: *CTA* 3 (V AB), A, 4–22," *UF* 2 (1970) 75–88.

Macuch, R. *Grammatik des samaritanischen Aramäisch.* Berlin: Walter de Gruyter, 1982.

————. *Grammatik des samaritanischen Hebräisch.* Berlin Walter de Gruyter, 1969.

————. *Handbook of Classical and Modern Mandaic.* Berlin: Walter de Gruyter, 1965.

Malamat, A. "The Arameans," in *Peoples of Old Testament Times.* Ed. D. J. Wiseman. Oxford: Clarendon Press, 1973. Pp. 134–55.

Margalit, B. *The Ugaritic Poem of AQHT.* BZAW 182. Berlin: Walter de Gruyter, 1989.

Margolis, M. *A Manual of the Aramaic Language of the Babylonian Talmud.* Munich: C. H. Beck, 1910.

Mazurel, J. W. *De Vraag naar de Verloren Broeder: Terugkeer en herstel in de boekn Jeremia en Ezechiel.* Ph.D. dissertation. Amsterdam: Universiteit van Amsterdam, 1992.

Mitchell, H. G. "The Preposition ʾel," *JBL* 8 (1888) 43–120.

Montgomery J. A., and H. S. Gehman. *A Critical and Exegetical Commentary on the Book of Kings.* ICC. Edinburgh: T. & T. Clark, 1951.

Morag, S. "On the Historical Validity of the Vocalization of Biblical Hebrew," *JAOS* 94 (1974) 307–15.

Moran, W. L. *The Amarna Letters.* Baltimore: Johns Hopkins University Press, 1992.

————. "'Does Amarna Bear on Karatepe?'—An Answer," *JCS* 6 (1952) 76–80.

————. "The Hebrew Language in Its Northwest Semitic Background," in *The Bible and the Ancient Near East: Essays in Honor of William Foxwell Albright.* Ed. G. E. Wright. Garden City, N.Y.: Doubleday, 1961. Pp. 54–72.

─────────. "The Syrian Scribe of the Jerusalem Amarna Letters," in *Unity and Diversity: Essays in the History, Literature, and Religion of the Ancient Near East*. Eds. H. Goedicke and J. J. M. Roberts. Baltimore: Johns Hopkins University Press, 1975. Pp. 146–66.

─────────. "The Use of the Canaanite Infinitive Absolute as a Finite Verb in the Amarna Letters from Byblos," *JCS* 4 (1950) 169–72.

Moreshet, M. *Leqsiqon ha-Poʿal she-Nithadesh bi-Lshon ha-Tannaʾim*. Ramat-Gan: Bar-Ilan University Press, 1980.

Muraoka, T. "The *Nun Energicum* and the Prefix Conjugation in Biblical Hebrew," *AJBI* 1 (1975) 63–71.

Muraoka, T., and M. Rogland, "The *Waw* Consecutive in Old Aramaic? A Rejoinder to Victor Sasson," *VT* 48 (1998) 99–104.

Nielsen, E. "Historical Perspectives and Geographical Horizons: On the Question of North-Israelite Elements in Deuteronomy," *ASTI* 11 (1977/78) 77–89.

Noegel, S. "Dialect and Politics in Isaiah 24–27," *AuOr* 12 (1994) 177–92.

Nöldeke, T. *Compendious Syriac Grammar*. London: Williams & Norgate, 1904.

─────────. *Grammatik der neusyrischen Sprache*. Leipzig: T. O. Weigel, 1868.

─────────. *Mandäische Grammatik*. Halle: Waisenhaus, 1875.

del Olmo Lete, G., and J. Sanmartín. *Diccionario de la lengua ugarítica*. 2 vols. Barcelona: AUSA, 1996–2000.

Orlinsky, H. M. "The Biblical Prepositions *táhat, bēn, báʿad*, and Pronouns *ᵃnū́* (or *ʾanū*), *zōʾtāh*," *HUCA* 17 (1942) 267–92.

Pardee, D. G. "The Preposition in Ugaritic," *UF* 7 (1975) 329–78.

Paul, S. M. *Amos*. Hermenia. Minneapolis: Fortress Press, 1991.

─────────. "Cuneiform Light on Jer 9,20," *Biblica* 49 (1968) 373–76.

Payne Smith, J. *A Compendious Syriac Dictionary*. Oxford: Clarendon Press, 1903.

Polzin, R. *Late Biblical Hebrew: Toward an Historical Typology of Biblical Hebrew Prose*. HSM 12. Missoula, Mont.: Scholars Press, 1976.

Rabin, C. "The Emergence of Classical Hebrew," in *The Age of the Monarchies: Culture and Society*. Ed. A. Malamat. World History of the Jewish People. Jerusalem: Masada Press, 1979. Pp. 71–78, 293–95.

─────────. "Leshonam shel ʿAmos ve-Hosheaʿ," in *ʿIyyunim be-Sefer Tre-ʿAsar*. Ed. B. Z. Luria. Jerusalem: Kiryath Sepher, 1981. Pp. 117–36.

─────────. *A Short History of the Hebrew Language*. Jerusalem: Jewish Agency, 1973.

Ratner, R. "Morphological Variation in Biblical Hebrew Rhetoric," in *Let Your Colleagues Praise You: Studies in Memory of Stanley Gevirtz*. 2 vols. Eds. R. J. Ratner, L. M. Barth, M.L. Gevirtz, and B. Zuckerman = *Maarav* 7–8 (1991/92) 2.143–59.

Rendsburg, G. A. "Additional Notes on 'The Last Words of David' (2 Sam 23, 1–7)," *Biblica* 70 (1989) 403–8.

─────────. "Confused Language as a Deliberate Literary Device in Biblical Hebrew Narrative," *JHS* 2 (1998–99), at http://www.arts.ualberta.ca/JHS/.

─────────. "The Dialect of the Deir ʿAlla Inscription," *BO* 50 (1993) 309–29.

——————. *Diglossia in Ancient Hebrew*. AOS 72. New Haven: American Oriental Society, 1990.

——————. "Eblaite *ù-ma* and Hebrew *wm-*," in *Eblaitica: Essays on the Ebla Archives and Eblaite Language*, Vol. 1. Eds. C. H. Gordon, G. A. Rendsburg, and N. H. Winter. Winona Lake, Ind.: Eisenbrauns, 1987. Pp. 34–41.

——————. "The Galilean Background of Mishnaic Hebrew," in *The Galilee in Late Antiquity*. Ed. L. I. Levine. New York: Jewish Theological Seminary, 1992. Pp. 225–40.

——————. "Israelian Hebrew Features in Genesis 49," in *Let Your Colleagues Praise You: Studies in Memory of Stanley Gevirtz*. 2 vols. Eds. R. J. Ratner, L. M. Barth, M. L. Gevirtz, and B. Zuckerman = *Maarav* 7–8 (1991/92) 2.161–70.

——————. "*Laqṭîl* Infinitives: Yiph'il or Hiph'il?" *Orientalia* 51 (1982) 231–38.

——————. "Late Biblical Hebrew and the Date of 'P'," *JANES* 12 (1980) 65–80.

——————. *Linguistic Evidence for the Northern Origin of Selected Psalms*. SBLMS 43. Atlanta: Scholars Press, 1990.

——————. "Linguistic Variation and the 'Foreign' Factor in the Hebrew Bible," *IOS* 15 (1996) 177–90.

——————. "Monophthongization of *aw/ay* > *ā* in Eblaite and in Northwest Semitic," in *Eblaitica: Essays on the Ebla Archives and Eblaite Language*, Vol. 2. Eds. C. H. Gordon and G. A. Rendsburg. Winona Lake, Ind.: Eisenbrauns, 1990. Pp. 91–126.

——————. "Morphological Evidence for Regional Dialects in Ancient Hebrew," in *Linguistics and Biblical Hebrew*. Ed. W. R. Bodine. Winona Lake, Ind.: Eisenbrauns, 1992. Pp. 65–88.

——————. "The Northern Origin of 'The Last Words of David' (2 Sam 23, 1–7)," *Biblica* 69 (1988) 113–21.

——————. "The Northern Origin of Nehemiah 9," *Biblica* 72 (1991) 348–66.

——————. "Notes on Israelian Hebrew (II)," *JNSL* 26 (2000) 33–45.

——————. "On the Writing *bytdwd* in the Aramaic Inscription from Tel Dan," *IEJ* 45 (1995) 22–25.

——————. "Shimush Bilti Ragil shel Kinnuy ha-Remez ba-Miqra': 'Edut Nosefet le-'Ivrit Ṣefonit bi-Tqufat ha-Miqra'," *Shnaton* 12 (2000) 83–88.

——————. "The Strata of Biblical Hebrew," *JNSL* 17 (1991) 81–99.

Rendsburg, G. A., and S. L. Rendsburg. "Physiological and Philological Notes to Psalm 137," *JQR* 83 (1993) 385–99.

Revell, E. J. "The System of the Verb in Standard Biblical Prose," *HUCA* 60 (1989) 1–37.

Richardson, M. E. J., ed. *The Hebrew and Aramaic Lexicon of the Old Testament*. 5 vols. Leiden: E. J. Brill, 1994–2000.

Robertson, D. A. *Linguistic Evidence in Dating Early Hebrew Poetry*. SBLDS 3. Missoula, Mont.: Scholars Press, 1972.

Rofe, A. "La composizione di Gen. 24," *BeO* 23 (1981) 161–65.

——————. "Ephraimite Versus Deuteronomistic History," in *Storia e tradizioni di Israele: Scritti in onore di J. Alberto Soggin*. Eds. D. Garrone and F. Israel. Brescia: Paideia, 1992. Pp. 221–35.

Rosenbaum, S. N. *Amos of Israel*. Macon, Ga.: Mercer University Press, 1990.

Rosenthal, F. *A Grammar of Biblical Aramaic*. Wiesbaden: Otto Harrassowitz, 1974.

Rossell, W. H. *A Handbook of Aramaic Magical Texts*. Ringwood Borough, N.J.: Shelton College, 1953.

Rubenstein, A. "A Finite Verb Continued by an Infinitive Absolute in Biblical Hebrew," *VT* 2 (1952) 362–67.

Sarna, N. M. "The Interchange of the Prepositions *Beth* and *Min* in Biblical Hebrew," *JBL* 78 (1959) 310–16.

Schniedewind W., and D. Sivan, "The Elijah-Elisha Narratives: A Test Case for the Northern Dialect of Hebrew," *JQR* 87 (1997) 303–37.

Schulthess, F. *Lexicon Syropalaestinum*. Berlin: Georg Reimer, 1903.

Segal, M. H. (M. Z.). *Diqduq Leshon ha-Mishna*. Tel-Aviv: Devir, 1936.

——————. *A Grammar of Mishnaic Hebrew*. Oxford: Clarendon Press, 1927.

Segert, S. *Altaramäische Grammatik*. Leipzig: VEB Verlag, 1975.

——————. *A Basic Grammar of the Ugaritic Language*. Berkeley: University of California Press, 1984

——————. *A Grammar of Phoenician and Punic*. Munich: C. H. Beck, 1976.

——————. "Noch zu den assimilierenden Verba im Hebräischen," *ArOr* 24 (1956) 132–34.

Smelik, K. A. D., and H.-J. van Soest. "Overlijdensteksten in het boek Koningen: De compositie van het boek Koningen (3)," *ACEBT* 13 (1994) 56–71.

Smith, M. S. "The Baal Cycle," in *Ugaritic Narrative Poetry*. Ed. S. B. Parker. Atlanta: Scholars Press, 1997. Pp. 81–180.

Sokoloff, M. *A Dictionary of Jewish Palestinian Aramaic of the Byzantine Period*. Ramat-Gan: Bar-Ilan University Press, 1990.

Speiser, E. A. "The Etymology of ʾarmôn," *JQR* 14 (1923/24) 329.

Sperber, A. *A Historical Grammar of Biblical Hebrew*. Leiden: E. J. Brill, 1966.

Starcky, J. ed. *Inventaire des inscriptions de Palmyre*, vol. 10. Damascus: Direction generale des antiquites de Syrie, 1949.

Steiner, R. C. *The Case for Fricative-Laterals in Proto-Semitic*. AOS 59. New Haven: American Oriental Society, 1977.

Sternberg, M. *The Poetics of Biblical Narrative*. Bloomington, Ind.: Indiana University Press, 1985.

Sznycer, M. *Les passages puniques en transcription latine dans le "Poenulus" de Plaute*. Paris: C. Klincksieck, 1967.

Tadmor, H. "Rabšāqē," ʾEnṣiqlopedya Miqraʾit 7 (1976) 323–25.

Tanakh: The Holy Scriptures. Philadelphia: Jewish Publication Society, 1985.

Tawil, H. "Hebrew *slp*, Mishnaic Hebrew *ṣlp*: Akkadian *ṣalāpu/ṣullupu*: A Lexicographical Note II," *Beth Mikra* 41 (1996) 276–92.

Testen, D. "The Significance of Aramaic *r* < *⋆n*," *JNES* 44 (1985) 143–46.

Ullendorff, E. "The Contributions of South Semitics to Hebrew Lexicography," *VT* 6 (1956) 190–98.

—————. "Ugaritic Marginalia II," *JSS* 7 (1962) 339–51.

Vargon, S. *Sefer Mikha: ʿIyyunim ve-Perushim.* Ramat-Gan: Bar-Ilan University Press, 1994.

Wagner, M. *Die lexikalischen und grammatikalischen Aramaismen im alttestamentlichen Hebräisch.* BZAW 96. Berlin: Alfred Töpelmann, 1966.

Waltke, B. K., and M. O'Connor. *An Introduction to Biblical Hebrew Syntax.* Winona Lake, Ind.: Eisenbrauns, 1990.

Wehr H., and J. M. Cowan. *A Dictionary of Modern Written Arabic.* Wiesbaden: Otto Harrassowitz, 1979.

Weinfeld, M. *Deuteronomy 1–11.* AB 5. New York: Doubleday, 1991.

Weiss, R. "On Ligatures in the Hebrew Bible (*nw* = -*m*)," *JBL* 82 (1963) 188–94.

Wolff, H. W. *Hosea.* Hermenia. Philadelphia: Fortress Press, 1974.

Wright, R. M. *Linguistic Evidence for the Pre-Exilic Date of the Yahwist Source of the Pentateuch.* Ph.D. Dissertation. Ithaca: Cornell University, 1998.

Yoo, Y. J. *Israelian Hebrew in the Book of Hosea.* Ph.D. dissertation. Ithaca: Cornell University, 1999.

Young, I. "The 'Northernisms' of the Israelite Narratives in Kings," *ZAH* 8 (1995) 63–70.

Zevit, Z. "The So-Called Interchangeability of the Prepositions *b*, *l*, and *m(n)* in Northwest Semitic," *JANES* 7 (1975) 103–11.

Index of Sources Cited

Biblical Passages

RABBINIC TEXTS

TARGUMIM

UGARITIC TEXTS

Miscellaneous

Index of Scholars Cited

Abrahams, I., 95n

Academy of the Hebrew Language (including references to *HDHL* and *HLHDP*), 27n, 29n, 49n, 52n, 54n, 59n, 60n, 61n, 68n, 72n, 75n, 82n, 83n, 84n, 93n, 94n, 98n, 99n, 104n, 106n, 114n, 121n, 123n, 129n

Andersen, F. I., and D. N. Freedman, 50n

Andersen, T. D., 67n, 68n

Baltzer, D., 47n

Barth, L. M., see Ratner, R. J., L. M. Barth, M. L. Gevirtz, and B. Zuckerman

Bauer, H., and P. Leander, 40n, 62

Baumgartner, W., see Koehler, L., and W. Baumgartner

BDB, see Brown, F., S. R. Driver, and C. A. Briggs

Ben-Hayyim, Z., 38n, 53n

Beyer, K., 32n, 72n, 98n, 112n

Bin-Nun, S. R., 24, 149

Blau, J. (Y.), 60n, 65n, 101n, 102n, 114n

Boadt, L., 38n

Briggs, C. A., see Brown, F., S. R. Driver, and C. A. Briggs

Brinkman, J. A., 43n

Brockelmann, C., 53n, 82n, 87n, 89n, 93n

Brown, F., S. R. Driver, and C. A. Briggs (including references to BDB), 29, 32n, 33, 34, 35, 36, 44, 52n, 54n, 60n, 65n, 66n, 70n, 72n, 74n, 76n, 84n, 85n, 91, 92n, 94n, 104, 111n, 116n, 117n, 126, 136n

Burkitt, F. C., 80n

Burney, C. F., 18, 22, 30, 31n, 37, 52n, 55n, 56–57, 60, 61n, 64n, 69, 71, 72, 75n, 80, 85, 86n, 91, 92n, 96n, 99, 101n, 103n, 104, 105n, 107n, 115n, 116n, 125, 126n, 133, 136n, 141

Cassuto, U., 94, 95n

Chen, Y., 19n, 58n, 106n, 136n

Chomsky, W., 102n

Clarke, E. G., 50n

Clines, D. J. A. (including references to *DCH*), 88n, 92n

Cogan, M., and H. Tadmor, 18, 22, 86n, 88n, 91, 92n, 98, 104n, 111n, 112n, 114n, 123n, 128n, 129n, 133, 135n, 136n, 137n, 138, 141n

Cohen, A., 87n

Cohen, H. R. (C.), 34n, 95n

Cook, E. M., 48n

Cowan, J. M., see Wehr, H., and J. M. Cowan

Cowley, A. E., 27n, 53n, 86n; see also Gesenius, W., E. Kautzsch, and A. E. Cowley

Cryer, F., 149n

Cussini, E., see Hillers, D. R., and E. Cussini

Dahood, M., 30, 48n, 106n

Dalman, G., 89, 96n

Davila, J., 48

DCH, see Clines, D. J. A.

Degen, R., 118n

DeVries, S. J., 47

DLU, see del Olmo Lete, G., and J. Sanmartín

DNWSI, see Hoftijzer, J., and K. Jongeling

Index of Subjects

General terms (Canaanite, Hebrew, Northwest Semitic, etc.) and commonly occurring terms (Aramaic, Judahite Hebrew, Israelian Hebrew, etc.) are not indexed.

The Appendix to this volume on pp. 151–54 contains a catalog of Israelian Hebrew features isolated in this study, including references to the discussion of these features in the body of the study.